From —

Barb and Arnold.

July 87.

GUIDE to the coast of QUEENSLAND

Reader's Digest Guide to the coast of Queensland was edited and designed by Reader's Digest Services Pty Limited, Sydney

Contributing editor: Robert Pullan

Contributors
Elizabeth Denley, PhD, Hopkins Marine Station, California
Robert Duffield
Jenny Flute
Edgar Frankel, PhD, Lecturer in Sedimentology, Department of Geology
    and Mineralogy, University of Queensland
Carol Frith, BSc(Hons), Coastal Studies Unit, University of Sydney
Pat Hutchings, PhD, Curator of Marine Invertebrates, The Australian Museum, Sydney
Brian Lees, BA(Hons), Coastal Studies Unit, University of Sydney
Dick Lewers
Dr Ian Mackie, Honorary Education Officer, The Surf Life Saving Association of Australia
Gia Metherell
Jo Moss, BSc
David Pollard, PhD, Senior Research Scientist, New South Wales State Fisheries
Jeff Toghill
Lyle Vail, Technical Officer, The Australian Museum, Sydney
Alan Yuille, BArch

Aerial Photography
Qasco Pty Limited, Sydney
Additional aerial photography by Stereometric
Services, Melbourne

Illustrators
Sheila Hadley
David Horne
Sue Oakes
Margaret Senior
Robyn Single

Maps by Reader's Digest

First edition
Published by Reader's Digest Services Pty Limited (Inc. in NSW)
26-32 Waterloo Street, Surry Hills NSW 2010
Part of the material in this book first appeared in Reader's Digest
Guide to the Australian Coast, first published by Reader's Digest in 1983.

© 1986 Reader's Digest Services Pty Ltd
© 1986 Reader's Digest Association Far East Limited
Philippines copyright 1986 Reader's Digest Association Far East Limited

National Library of Australia cataloguing-in-publication data:
Reader's Digest Guide to the coast of Queensland.
  Includes index.
  ISBN 0 86438 011 9.
  1. Coasts – Queensland – Guide-books.
  2. Queensland – Description and travel – 1976 –
  Guide-books. I. Reader's Digest Services
  II. Title: Guide to the coast of Queensland.
919.43'0463

Typeset by Adtype Photocomposition, Sydney
Printed and bound by Dai Nippon Printing Co. Ltd., Hong Kong

Reader's Digest

GUIDE to the coast of QUEENSLAND

Contents

Introduction

QUEENSLAND could arguably award itself pride of place among Australia's coastal areas as it boasts not only the commercial wonderland of Surfers Paradise, capital of the Gold Coast, but the globally unique phenomenon of the Great Barrier Reef—both of them magnets for domestic and international travellers alike. In addition to these fabled and sharply contrasting destinations, there are endless dreamy expanses of uncrowded sandy shore. Queensland has by far the longest stretch of coastline suited to recreational purposes of any state in Australia.

It is a testimony to the attractions of the Queensland coast that despite its distance from the main centres of population, this is the nation's holiday state. Its geographic location gives it year-round warmth conducive to the enjoyment of all water sports, making it a popular alternative for residents of the winterbound south. When summer comes, however, Queensland's allure is partially compromised by the presence of the deadliest menace to swimmers in Australian waters—not sharks, but box jellyfish.

From the urban sands of Coolangatta to the wild, tropical tip of Cape York to the scattering of sublime islands in the shelter of the Great Barrier Reef, the coast of Queensland has something for every traveller.

Here, as elsewhere around Australia's shores, all water sports are enthusiastically pursued, with particular bonuses for snorkellers and divers in reef areas. Almost all Australians can swim; they surf in their hundreds of thousands and boat in their millions. But by far the most dominant water activity is fishing. An estimated 30 per cent of all Australians go fishing, and this proportion rises to 60 per cent among boys aged between 13 and 17.

Guide to the Coast of Queensland is for all those who visit the seashore—whatever their special interests. The core of the book, Discovering the Coast, is a guide for travellers and coast users. Scores of aerial photographs, many of them joined together into a unique series of panoramas, show the most attractive and easily accessible parts of the coast in unsurpassed detail. The photographs are supported by a thorough and up-to-date description of the places depicted and their attractions. We have divided coastal Queensland into three regions, each of which is introduced with notes on its general nature and climate, and a map.

Three additional parts of the book provide important information for those who visit the coast. Part one—Understanding the Coast—describes the range of plants and animals that live around the shore. The aim is to help visitors identify some of the things they see, and also to understand how plants and animals interact with one another in a range of habitats. Drawings of birds, shells and marine creatures make identification of common species easy.

Part two—The Ocean and the Weather—will be particularly useful for swimmers, surfers and boat owners. A basic understanding of winds, tides, waves and currents will help readers to avoid some of the dangers of nearshore waters, and also to make the best use of conditions they encounter.

Part three—Advice for Holidaymakers—is addressed to particular groups of coast users. There is information for fishermen, boat owners, swimmers and surfers as well as general advice on first aid, access and hazards.

Two indexes, one listing all the places mentioned in the book and the other the subjects, make it easy to find any information quickly.

THE EDITORS

PART 1

Understanding the coast

Nature's ingenuity meets no sterner test than on the seashore. Life forms have to contend with changeable environments— neither wholly marine nor wholly terrestrial —and on much of the coast they must withstand the violent assault of waves.

In the face of such adversity, shore zones could be assumed to be biologically impoverished.

On the contrary, they are the special domains of a diverse range of animals and plants, intriguing in their ways of adaptation and often astonishing in their profusion.

Many of the most interesting creatures go unnoticed. And such is their degree of specialisation that they are restricted to particular habitats.

The curious need to know not only what to look for, but also where to look.

A grasp of geological and geographical factors brings a fuller appreciation of the richness of coastal life.

With it comes awareness of how delicately this life is balanced—and of the dangers posed by unwise human pressure.

A group of sea lions basking among seaweed on a Kangaroo Island beach

What makes a coast Natural forms that change with time

A coast is a battlefront—a line where land, sea and air meet that changes from second to second, season to season, decade to decade and millennium to millennium. Short term changes, over a range of metres, occur as waves break and move sediments on or off shore and as tide-waves cause the local sea level to rise and fall. In the longer term erosion and accretion change the coastline, sometimes on a scale of kilometres a century. Over tens of thousands of years sea levels rise and fall by hundreds of metres as ice ages come and go. Coasts are always changing—they can never be regarded as permanent. It is only because the large scale changes seem to occur so slowly, in terms of human lifetimes, that people come to regard the shoreline as fixed.

Ancient coastlines can be found scores of kilometres inland. Others are far out to sea. The earliest fluctuations were associated with the evolution of land masses over hundreds of millions of years: their emergence and erosion, their repeated submergences and reappearances, the transformation of their material under pressure, their distortion by twisting, folding and fracturing, and their disruption by volcanic activity. The coast near Mount Gambier in South Australia has risen in the last few thousand years, while the Murray River mouth region has subsided; Melbourne's shores on Port Phillip Bay surround an area of recent sinking. Nevertheless the Australian land mass is now relatively stable. Unlike New Zealand or New Guinea, it is far from any point where the earth's mobile crustal plates collide. So throughout the time of human occupation, the most striking shifts of the Australian coastline have been caused by changes in the sea level.

The planet's total store of moisture has probably remained much the same since its crust solidified. But the distribution of that moisture—in the oceans, on or under the land, in the atmosphere or locked in ice—has varied vastly. Even a small change in temperature affects the density of water, causing it to expand or contract signifi-

cantly. A fall of just 1°C in the overall average temperature of the oceans would lower sea levels by about 2 metres. And that is only a minor effect of climatic change. Prolonged reduction of average atmospheric temperatures actually robs the oceans of water. Evaporated moisture, instead or returning in the usual cycle of conden-

sation, precipitation and run-off, stays frozen on the land. During the most recent ice age, which had its maximum effect between 50 000 and 10 000 years ago, so much moisture accumulated in icecaps that the sea level receded more than 100 metres. Its ascent when melting set in was an uneven process over thousands of years,

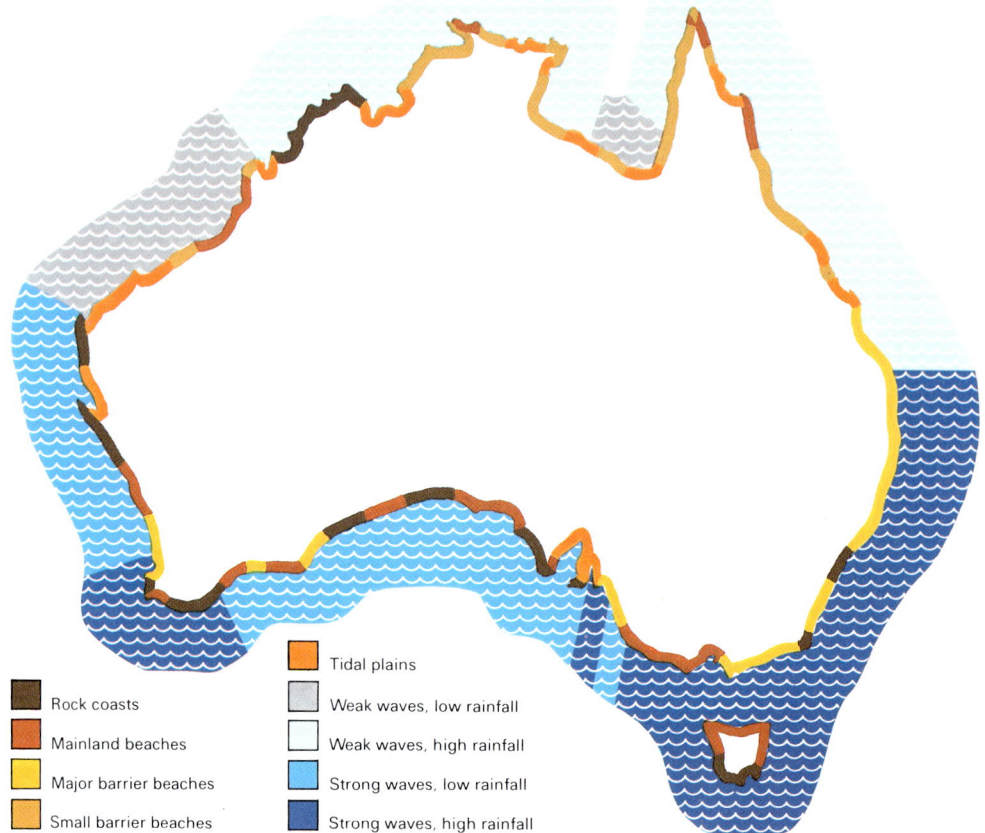

■ Rock coasts	■ Tidal plains
■ Mainland beaches	■ Weak waves, low rainfall
■ Major barrier beaches	□ Weak waves, high rainfall
■ Small barrier beaches	■ Strong waves, low rainfall
	■ Strong waves, high rainfall

Differences between coasts at various places around the continent are the result of a combination of factors, such as rock type, the power of local waves, the width of the continental shelf, rainfall and wind direction. Four broad structural categories describe the physical appearance of any particular coast, and four climatic categories encompass the important forces that helped to shape the shoreline

The evolution of Botany Bay

ANCIENT estuaries all around the coast were 'drowned' when the sea returned to its present level after the last ice age. It was a gradual process, with marine sand being pushed up to form barriers in places where there was a large enough supply of sand, and then driven ashore to form beach ridges and dunes, and also into estuaries. Here is a geologist's reconstruction of what happened in Botany Bay, Sydney.

■	Vegetated land
■	Cliffs, rock platforms
■	Mobile sand
■	Water
■	Vegetated sand

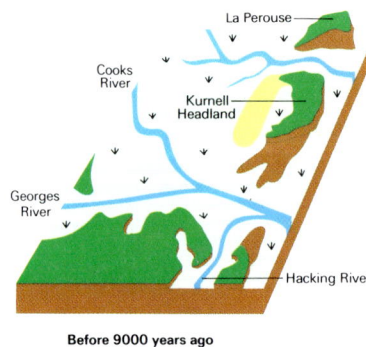

Before 9000 years ago

With the sea more than 20 metres below today's level, Botany Bay was a swampy plain, interrupted by occasional rocky outcrops. Many of the sediments were left over from the last period of high sea levels

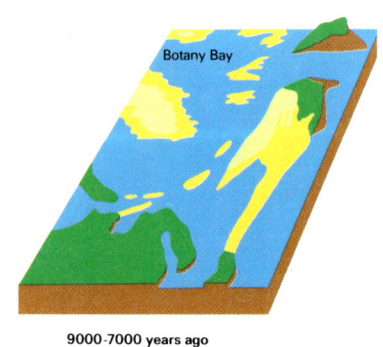

9000-7000 years ago

Seas rising to 9 metres below their present level moved a sand barrier onshore to enclose a shallow estuary: longshore drift swept sand north past the headland and around into the newly formed bay

interrupted by spells of renewed glaciation.

Sea levels regarded as normal today were attained about 6000 years ago. There are signs, however, that the oceans came even higher during some more recent periods. At no time may constancy be taken for granted.

Scientists may classify coasts of various kinds in a dozen or more categories, related mainly to their origins. In terms of natural life and the human use of Australia's shores, climatic conditions are more important and only four broad structural distinctions are needed: rock, mainland beach, barrier beach and tidal plain. **Rock coasts,** all cliffed to some degree, occur largely in the south and the north-west. If beaches occur at all, they are pockets of minor significance. **Mainland beach coasts** (the term applies also to Tasmania and other major islands) may have some rocky sections, accompanied by shore platforms, but extensive open beaches are predominant. On **barrier beach coasts,** beaches have formed offshore in the vicinity of rocky promontories, enclosing or nearly enclosing lagoons and estuaries between themselves and the old shore. Where wave action is consistently powerful the barrier is the dominant feature, containing a massive accumulation of sand. Otherwise it is the lagoon or estuary margins that give the coast its character. Major barriers are commonest on the east coast between the Tropic of Capricorn and Bass Strait, and in eastern South Australia and south of Perth. Small barriers are mostly found on the tropical Queensland and Northern Territory coasts. **Tidal plain coasts** are usually marked by the growth of salt-marsh plants or mangroves, and sometimes in the tropical zone by fringing coral. They are extensive between North-West Cape and Port Hedland, and occur elsewhere in gulfs.

On a coastline as extensive as Australia's, location and climate play significant roles in determining what kind of structure evolves. Deep ocean waves are generally bigger and more powerful in the southern latitudes, and day-to-day local winds are usually stronger. The offshore slope of the sea floor is also steeper towards

Measuring Australia's shores

THE MORE precisely a coast is measured, the longer it becomes. Tracing a simplified outline of Australia, for example, makes the mainland coast seem to be about 15 000 km long. Measurements from detailed sectional maps would produce a total twice as great. And taking the argument to absurdity, it is estimated that if the slighter twists and turns of the coast were charted millimetre by millimetre, the length would be more than 130 000 km. Precision is a matter of what is practical. Geographers have a choice of measuring methods, and a choice of rules as to what should be included—literally, where to draw the line.

Australia's officially recognised measurement was made by government cartographers in 1973. High-water lines were chosen, so mangrove flats and coral reefs were excluded. Open estuaries were cut off where they appeared to take the shape of rivers. On maps of 1:250 000 scale, points about 500 metres apart were plotted. Then it became a theoretical exercise: the straight-line distances between those points were computed and totalled. By that method, the shores of the mainland, Tasmania and the continental shelf islands were taken to be about 36 735 km long.

In 1980, a CSIRO geographer, Dr Robert Galloway, directed a manual measurement of greater precision. Maps of the same scale were used, but this time the entire line of coasts was followed with fine wire. A mid-tide level was taken; mangroves were included but coral reefs were still left out. Islands less than 12 hectares in area were ignored, as were straits less than 1 km wide. Estuaries were cut off where they narrowed to less than 1 km. The total length of the mainland and Tasmanian coasts came to about 30 270 km. Coastline lengths of islands, computed from their areas after one-sixth of them had been measured in detail, came to a further 16 800 km. So by Dr Galloway's method the total is 47 070 km—rather more than the circumference of the earth.

the south and the continental shelf is narrower, permitting more wave energy to be transmitted ashore. This north-south difference in wave energy levels is accentuated by the shape of the continent: its bulges at each side mean that the sections running south from North-West Cape and Fraser Island tend to confront the normal approach of waves, while the receding northern sections do not. Much of the Queensland east coast is further shielded from the full impact of waves by the Great Barrier Reef system.

Another major geographical distinction, in this case roughly between east and west, is created by unevenness of rainfall. Where there is a substantial run-off of rain, at least seasonally, material washed from inland formations contributes to the building of beaches, river mouth bars and nearshore barriers. It also hastens the infilling of enclosed waters, producing new land. But its long-term effects are not so constructive. Sand from inland rocks is rich in silica, which keeps it loose. Water soaks through easily, leaching out minerals that are redeposited on the grain surfaces of underlying material as a skin—this red skin gives silica sand its typical colour, as silica sand without such a skin is white. The layers of heavy 'black sand' sought by mining companies are a result of the different densities of mineral sand and silica sand, and the sorting effect of waves and swash. The sorting effect is similar to that used by prospectors in separating gold from gravel in a pan. Meanwhile the loose, light material above, whether in beaches or dunes, remains prone to destruction by high winds and storm waves.

On arid coasts, however, the major chemical component of beach material is often calcium. Where winds drive the sand inland, piling it up in dune ridges out of the reach of sea water, it is eventually calcified and forms a solid mass of new rock. Many of today's limestone cliffs, islands, offshore stacks and reefs originated as high dune ridges, formed when the sea level was lower and the climate of their hinterland was arid. In the scale of coastal evolution, eons long, such a transformation is merely a passing phase.

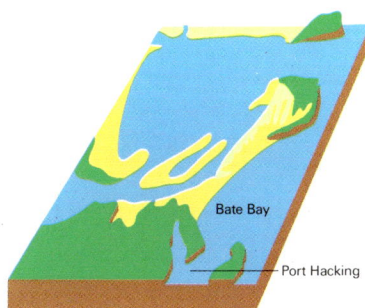

7000-4000 years ago

Seas reaching today's levels pushed barrier sand shoreward to form beach ridges along Bate Bay. Wind-waves transported sand from the bed of Botany Bay north and west to the shores of the bay

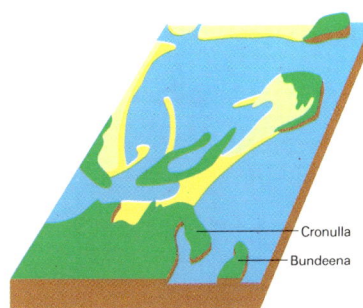

4000-1000 years ago

With the sea close to its present level, there were two phases of parabolic dune emplacement and stabilisation by plants; a long period of coastal stability seems to have followed

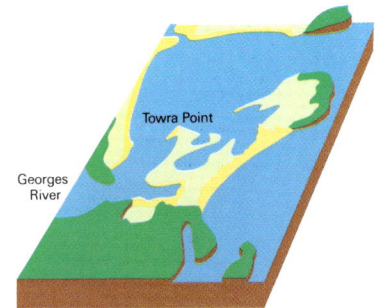

Last 1000 years

The tidal delta of the Georges River took shape, forming Towra Point from a complex of levees, spits and bars; renewed erosion of the barrier beach fed a dune sheet that continues to move today

Offshore
Region of deeper water, part of the sublittoral zone, which extends out to the edge of the continental shelf, down the continental slope and on to the ocean floor. The edge of the continental shelf, where the sea floor starts to slope down at a steeper angle, occurs at a depth of about 180 metres. Rises and falls in sea level during past ages have covered and uncovered parts of the continental shelf many times

Inshore
The area still shallow enough to be disturbed by incoming waves, but below the influence of daily tides. Part of the sublittoral zone. The sea floor is never uncovered, even at the time of the lowest spring tides. Plants and animals from this region are usually seen only after storms—when they may be washed up on a beach. Most frequently found are algae, or seaweeds

Foreshore
The zone covered and uncovered by the normal ebb and flow of the tides. Also known as the intertidal or littoral zone. Different proportions of the foreshore are exposed daily according to the height of the tide. Most of the small number of species of plants and animals that live on open sandy beaches are to be found there

Backshore
Land extending from the normal limits of the tide zone to the back of the beach. The sea may cover parts of the area during storms. Berms—flat-topped terraces—are sometimes formed during periods of little wave activity. Ridges, with an accompanying hollow on the landward side, can also run along the backshore

Sand dunes
Wind-blown sand from the beach may be formed into dunes many metres high

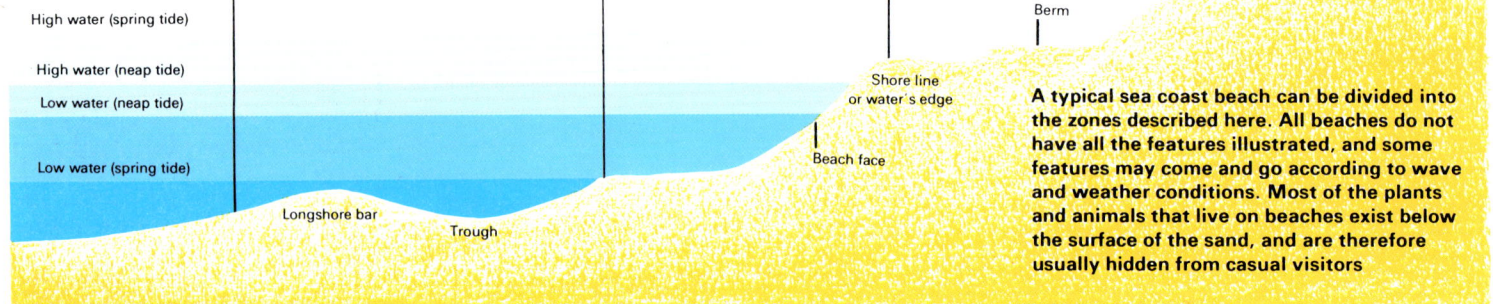

High water (spring tide)

High water (neap tide)

Low water (neap tide)

Low water (spring tide)

Longshore bar

Trough

Berm

Shore line or water's edge

Beach face

A typical sea coast beach can be divided into the zones described here. All beaches do not have all the features illustrated, and some features may come and go according to wave and weather conditions. Most of the plants and animals that live on beaches exist below the surface of the sand, and are therefore usually hidden from casual visitors

Sandy shores Beaches and the life they support

What lives on and under beaches, between the high and low tide limits, depends on how the beaches are composed. Beaches of coarse sand usually slope more sharply than those of fine sand, and are more exposed to wave action. They support the lowest number of organisms. Protected beaches with fine sand have many more creatures—provided that the sand is of the right consistency for them to burrow. Plenty of water must be held between the particles. Few animals will be found in the sort of sand that whitens around an area that is trodden. Such sand gives up its moisture too readily under pressure: deeper down, it is too tightly packed to allow much movement. Some fine sands, however, react to pressure in the opposite way. They become softer and easier to penetrate, and remain moist below the surface.

Sands behave differently because they are made differently—from rocks of varying structure and mineral content. That affects the size, smoothness and slipperiness of particles, as well as the colour of beaches. By no means all beach sand comes from coastal rock in the immediate vicinity. Much may be carried from inland by rivers, by rain run-off or by wind. In some places sand from other coasts is pushed onshore from the sea floor by waves. Tropical mainland beaches are often composed mostly of coral fragments from reefs. And sands nearly always contain worn-down shell from a multitude of marine organisms, in concentrations that vary locally. On Australia's most frequented non-tropical coasts, however, the mixture is usually dominated by silica in the form of quartz. Its glassy quality keeps the sand loose. Bigger particles and heavier minerals slip down easily, leaving the sands near the surface fine and light. They are prone to erosion and other damage, but in protected conditions they support a fairly large range of animals. Plants in the tide zone are almost non-existent, except for microscopic algae. Bigger seaweeds may inhabit the nearshore if they find purchase on pebbles or heavy shell fragments, and stable backshore and foredune areas are frequently vegetated by banksias, casuarinas and acacias among spinifex grasses and a few flowering plants.

Tiny organisms abound in the spaces between particles of subsurface sand, but special laboratory procedures are required to isolate and study them. In Australia almost nothing is known about such creatures. Only animals more than 3 mm long have been the subject of detailed study, and that has been concentrated on New South Wales beaches. The most obvious of beach-dwellers are ghost crabs, *Ocypode*, distinguished by their paleness and long eye-stalks. Their burrows are well above high water but they forage in the tide zone at night, scampering ahead of human intruders. Also common high on the shore are various species of isopods—little crustaceans that are sometimes called sea-slaters or marine lice. Nearer the water are their

When sand turns back into rock

SAND collecting at great depths in the ocean is converted by pressure into sandstone rock. On arid coasts, dunes rich in calcium solidify as limestone if left undisturbed. Both processes are very slow. But beach sands sometimes cement themselves together as if of their own accord, and with surprising speed. Recent artefacts such as coins and war relics are found in shelves of Australian beach rock.

Scientists are unable to agree on the binding agent in beach rock. Some believe it is calcium carbonate, precipitated during the repeated risings and fallings of the water table under the sand. Others think it is salts deposited when sea water evaporates. Micro-organisms deep in the sand and warm temperatures may aid the process.

The rock is tough enough to resist erosion, so that sheets of it are sometimes left jutting out as the only evidence of a vanished beach.

Beach rock with aircraft wreckage from 1945

Giant beach worms can exceed 2 metres in length. Fishermen use the worms for bait and lure them from their holes with rotten fish. Once the worm's head (below) emerges it can be grasped and the worm pulled from the sand

relatives the amphipods, often known as sand-hoppers or sea-fleas. Sand bubbler crabs, *Scopimera*, are prominent in the intertidal zone. They burrow to the water table, leaving blobs of sand in radiating lines on the surface. Battalions of little pink-and-blue soldier crabs, *Mictyris longicarpus*, frequently emerge from sandy tidal flats, but seldom from beaches where waves break. Of bivalve molluscs buried in the sand, by far the most common is the pipi, *Plebidonax deltoides*. Wedge pipis, cockles and dog cockles are found in deeper water. Smaller bivalves are the principal prey of the giant beach-worm, *Onuphis teres*, which grows to more than 2 metres in length. It is prolific, but seldom seen unless a lure of smelly fish is trailed in the backwash of waves. A smaller worm, *Diopatra dentata*, is best known by the tube that it builds to live in, consisting of shell fragments, small stones and other debris embedded in a fibrous substance. The worm can move freely in and out, so if a tube is pulled from the sand there is rarely an animal inside it.

Small holes seen in a beach surface behind a retreating wave are often assumed to be signs of animals below. If the wave was unusually strong, a few holes or depressions may have been left by pipis or crabs which were uncovered by it and had to burrow deeper. But most holes are formed by the escape of air bubbles, trapped among sediments washed onto the beach. Another false indicator of animal movement is a sharply etched, branched mark at the flattened 'toe' of a sloping beach. Such patterns, called rill marks, are made by runnels of water escaping from higher sand after the tide has ebbed. Other marks, more regularly formed, are clearly the result of water action. Swash marks—sand ridges about 1 mm high, overlapping like curved roof tiles—indicate the farthest points reached by waves. Sand ripples—ridges and troughs in roughly parallel rows—are formed by the churning action of waves running up a beach. If wave motion alone was responsible, the ridges are evenly curved. But if a current was present as well, each ridge is steeper on the side towards which the current was running.

An isopod or sea-slater

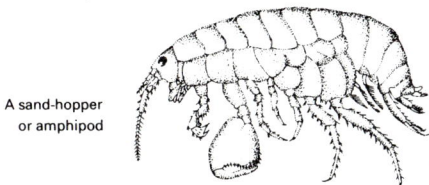

A sand-hopper or amphipod

Amphipods and isopods are common on beaches

What the colour of a beach reveals

ALL BEACH sands are mixtures. They include shell and other marine material as well as grains from various types of rock. Nearly all Australian beaches are essentially light-coloured, being dominated either by silica from quartz and feldspar rock or by calcium carbonate of marine origin. Other minerals can produce different hues—some by coating the sands. Colour can be an indicator of many of the principal materials:

Sparkling white	Quartz grains coated with extra silica deposit
Dull white (non-tropical)	Worn quartz on rainy coasts; limestone on arid coasts
Dull white (tropical)	Coral, perhaps with pumice
Creamy / pinkish white	More than 90 per cent quartz
Yellow / gold / light brown	Impure quartz, feldspar, coloured shell
Darker brown	Compounds of iron, etc., coating sand grains
Silver / gold sheen when wet	Surface mica
Grey	Higher concentrations of volcanic or darker sedimentary rock—e.g., basalt or shale
Dark olive	Iron-magnesium-silica compound (eastern Torres Strait)
Black	Basalt dominant; surface iron ore
Dark flecks on pale beach	Fragments of compound granitic rock
Red flecks on tropical beach	'Organ pipe' coral debris
Brown / black lower band	Rutile, ilmenite, iron
Red / brown lower band	Garnet, rutile
Brown / black beach streaks	Organic acid staining
Red / brown / green dune layers	Oxides, etc., of iron or other minerals coating quartz (Queensland 'coloured sands')
Brown / black 'coffee rock'	Sand coated and cemented by iron or manganese compounds

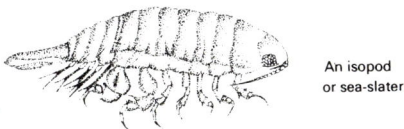

Elusive inhabitants of sandy beaches

The most obvious things on sandy beaches are usually dead plants and animals washed up by the waves. But there are also many things that live in the sand, although they are often difficult to find because they spend most of their lives below the surface, or are too small to see. Many migrate vertically underneath the sand—such as the tiny, shrimp-like amphipods and isopods—while others migrate up and down the beach, towards and away from the water. Very little plant life is found on beaches because there is nothing for the plants to hold on to. There is a greater variety of creatures to be found in fine sand than there is in coarse sand— not so much because of the size of the particles, but rather because fine sand is found where the beach is not being churned up. In particularly calm areas there are lugworms—burrowing worms that leave a coiled cast. Giant beach worms, some longer than 2 metres, abound in some places, but nearly all the bubbling that you see and hear at the water's edge is caused not by worms but by air.

Soldier crabs can sometimes be seen moving along the shore in huge numbers. They burrow with a sideways somersaulting action, using one side to dig, then the other

Brown seaweed, a relative of kelp, has bladders that allow it to float when the tide is in—the plant needs sunlight to live

Cuttlefish skeletons hold gas by which the animals rise in the water to feed at night, and descend to the bottom in the day. Cuttlefish have eight arms and two large grabbing tentacles—each tentacle is about three times as long as the skeleton

Bluebottles' bladders enable them to swim on the surface. Some sea slugs eat bluebottles without digesting the stinging cells, which are on the tentacles, and then use the toxin as their own defence mechanism

Sea urchins' shells have little bubbles which are the attachment points for the spines. The fine rays are the holes for the tube feet by which they move

Egg cases of the cartrut shell are moulded by the foot of the female as she lays. The first juveniles to hatch eat the remaining eggs

Coralline seaweed has segmented branches. Each time this sort divides, it divides in two

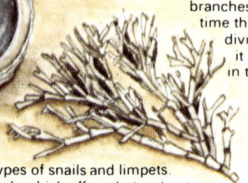

Abalone are types of snails and limpets. They eat seaweeds which affect their colouring. Farming of abalone is becoming successful in the United States

Coastal vegetation of this kind, including she-oaks (casuarinas) and banksias, grows best in estuaries and sheltered bays where there is some relief from salt spray and the pruning action of the wind. Since these areas are dry, the plant communities are particularly subject to fire

Sedges have narrow leaves and stiff stems to reduce moisture loss

Hairy spinifex has long runners which grow on bare sand so that it makes an excellent dune stabiliser. The male and female parts of this grass are on separate plants

Crabs often have elaborate mating rituals. It is invariably the male that has one colourful claw which it waves in a sort of dance

Pipis, of which this is an empty half-shell, are often killed by a whelk that drills into their shell with an action like a diamond cutting glass. You can often see the hole with its neatly chamfered edge

Kelp, a seaweed, has a holdfast to attach it to rock or the sea floor. Many creatures live in and around and on the holdfast—particularly worms, and sometimes mussels

Pigface or noonflower has an unusual method of photosynthesis, allowing it in particularly dry periods to absorb carbon dioxide at night and reduce moisture loss

Bubbler crabs roll the sand they excavate into tiny balls. They use the hole as a burrow during low tide, and come out at night to feed on algae during high tide

Sponges are very primitive animals. They feed off the planktonic animals and bacteria that enter the passages of the sponge. The part we use is their skeleton

Goose barnacles are ocean-dwellers, settling on anything that floats—bottles, lumps of oil, the bottom of ships. In medieval times they were thought to be the young of migrating geese

Common Australian sea shells

The tightly packed shelves and display boards in seaside museums exhibit the shells of only some of over 10 000 species of molluscs so far discovered in Australia. An estimated 80 000 species exist in the world, and new ones are constantly being found. Some large, brightly coloured and intricately patterned shells are much sought after by collectors and command high prices because of their rarity. The shells illustrated here are those commonly seen on beaches or in rock pools by casual visitors to the coast. Do not collect shells containing live animals. Sizes of average specimens are given.

Orange cockle
Acrosterigma reeveanum
Length 60 mm

Combed auger
Hastula strigilata
Length 30 mm

Orange jingle shell
Anomia descripta
Diameter 55 mm

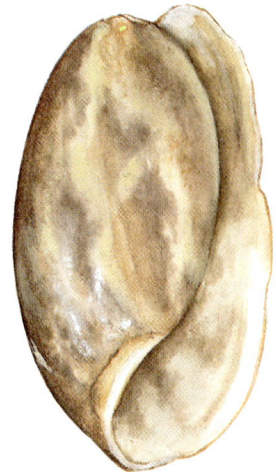

Bubble shell
Bulla quoyii
Length 50 mm

Venus shell
Katelysia rhytiphora
Width 45 mm

Common southern bean cowrie
Trivia merces
Length 10 mm

Banded or silver kelp shell
Bankivia fasciata
Length 15 mm

Arrowed sand snail
Tanea sagittata
Diameter 10 mm

Leafy chama
Chama pulchella
Diameter 40 mm

Erroneous cowrie
Cypraea errones
Length 30 mm

Pretty trough shell
Mactra eximia
Width 60 mm

Dog whelk
Nassarius pyrrhus
Length 15 mm

Melon or baler shell
Melo amphora
Length 70-220 mm

Doughboy scallop
Mimachlamys asperrimus
Width 65 mm

Sand snail
Natica gualtieriana
Length 30 mm

Orange sand snail
Polinices tumidus
Length 35 mm

Southern olive shell
Oliva australis
Length 30 mm

Olive shell
Oliva oliva
Length 30 mm

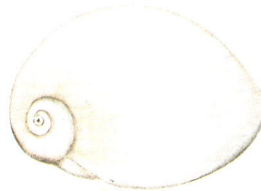

Dove shell
Pyrene scripta
Length 10 mm

Angas's murex
Pterynotus angasi
Length 20 mm

Pipi
Plebidonax deltoides
Width 60 mm

Creeper shell
Rhinoclavis sinensis
Length 50 mm

Dog winkle
Thais orbita
Length 70 mm

Pheasant shell
Phasianella australis
Length 55 mm

Turban shell
Turbo undulata
Length 65 mm

Long-spined thorny oyster
Spondylus wrightianus
Width 80 mm

Littoral fringe

Different communities live below the tide zones. Algae—usually known as seaweeds—become increasingly common

The low-shore, or sublittoral zone, is only uncovered when the tide is very low, and this may not occur every day. A dense covering of plants and animals leave almost no rock uncovered

The mid-tidal, or littoral zone, is covered and uncovered by the normal daily tides. Plants and animals that live there must be able to survive in air for at least part of their lives

Rocks in the littoral fringe are only covered by water at very high tides, although they may be splashed by waves and spray occasionally. Only very hardy plants and animals can survive in this harsh environment

Upper mid-tidal

Lower mid-tidal

Low-shore

The parts of rocky coasts between high and low tides can be divided into broad zones according to the amount of time they spend exposed to the air. These zones are a useful rough guide to the sorts of plants and animals that may be found at different parts of the shore, but other factors such as exposure to waves, or to fresh water in estuaries, also have a great influence on the life to be found in any particular place

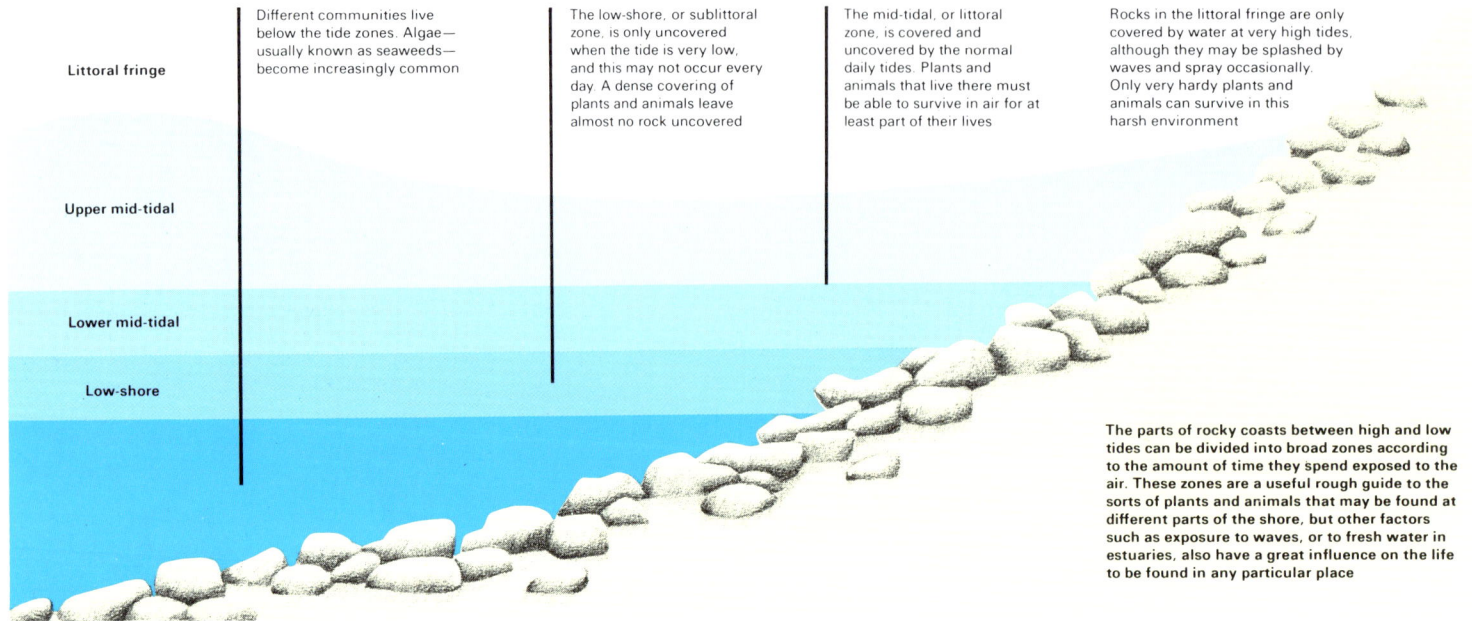

Rocky shores Where marine life takes a hold on the land

Shore platforms of rock, accommodating a rich diversity of marine animals and plants, are common in eastern and south-eastern Australia. They are formed by waves and rain eating at outcrops at and above the intertidal level. So they occur where wave energy is high and where the rock is only moderately durable. The sandstones of New South Wales, exposed to strong ocean swells and high rainfall, are ideal. Nearly every headland has its platform, to the delight of amateur fishermen. Platforms differ widely in character, however. Some are submerged at all but the lowest tides, while others are formed at or above the mean high tide level, and exposed to the air nearly all the time. Most are more or less flat but many have a slope, usually because a tilted block of more resistant rock has been uncovered. Some platforms have smooth surfaces; others are deeply fissured, pitted with pools, studded with pinnacles, raised with tiered benches, or strewn with boulders.

All those local differences have some bearing on the distribution of marine life. The degree of protection from heavy breakers is also important. So is the range between low and high tides: where it is greatest, marine communities are spread over the widest area. On many coasts the rock platforms are made up of discernible bands of height inhabited by different species. Many are fixed to the rock—for example, barnacles, oysters, tubeworms, sea-squirts, sponges and seaweeds. Some can move, but spend most of their time in one spot—anemones and mussels, for instance. Even the most mobile animals, such as gastropod shellfish, crabs and starfish, have habitual feeding areas. People who have learnt to distinguish a dozen or so dominant species of

animals, and a few seaweeds and grasses, can identify tide zones on different platforms. And they can tell where the tide is at a glance.

Many areas in the highest tide zone, the littoral fringe, are under water for only a tiny part of the tidal cycle. Some receive only the twice-monthly spring tides and a varying amount of spray. Marine organisms living here have to be hardy, and adaptable not only to fluctuating air temperatures but also to drastic changes in salinity—from salt water at high tide to fresh water if it rains while the tide is out. Littorinid snails of several species cope well with such conditions. The most common, throughout Australia

except in northern Queensland, is the periwinkle, Littorina unifasciata.

The mid-tidal area is often called the barnacle zone. At its higher levels barnacles are common except in Western Australia and so are gastropods such as sea snails and limpets. New South Wales has the six-plated grey barnacle, Chthamalus antennatus, and the small honeycomb barnacle, Chamaesipho columna. A limpet, Notoacmea petterdi, is widespread on vertical surfaces, and other gastropods occurring in some upper mid-tidal areas include a bigger limpet, Cellana tramoserica, and the black snail, Nerita atramentosa. Lower in the mid-tidal area,

Tools of the waves

CIRCULAR pools with smooth, vertical walls, often seen on wave-washed shore platforms, seem too perfectly formed to be natural. But at the bottom will be found at least one stray stone. It is these stones, of harder material than the platform rock, that make the pools. Lodging at first in shallow depressions, they are repeatedly spun about in swirling water. They become the tools of the waves, scouring the platform until they have drilled it to such a depth—sometimes more than 1 metre—that they are out of reach of disturbance by water movements and no longer move.

Pools still being scoured hold little marine life, though small fish are occasionally trapped in them. But when the drilling stones cease to move, the pools are soon colonised by seaweeds, anemones, gastropods and sometimes starfish—content to live in a sheltered environment.

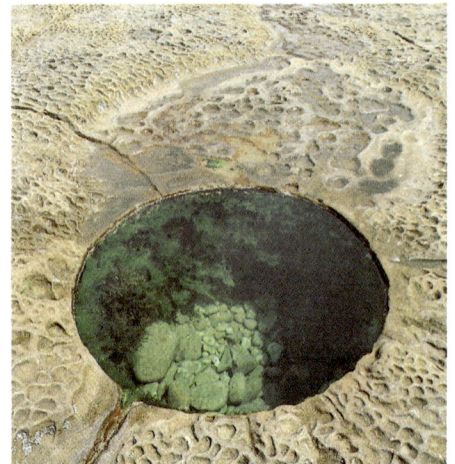

A circular pool on a Sydney rock platform

barnacles continue in company with mussels, gastropods and sometimes oysters. On the most protected NSW shores, gastropods such as the mulberry whelk, *Morula*, limpets and three common grazing snails are dominant along with starfish, chitons, often called coat-of-mail shells because of their eight armour-like plates, and anemones. In slightly less protected areas, dense beds of honeycomb barnacles are often found with the limpet *Cellana* grazing over them. Plants are seldom obvious. An encrusting alga on many Sydney shores blends with the colour of sandstone and is only noticeable at close quarters. Pools often contain the brown seaweed *Hormosira banksii*, commonly called Neptune's beads, along with gastropods, anemones, starfish and sometimes the hairy mussel, *Trichomya hirsuta*. Areas exposed to stronger waves are usually dominated by one or both species of surf barnacles, *Catomerus polymerus* and the pink *Tesseropora rosea*. In South Australia, Victoria and Tasmania, mussels occupy a lot of space in many mid-tidal areas, while in parts of northern Queensland oysters are much more common.

Moving into low-shore areas, the covering of plants and animals becomes so dense that often no bare rock can be seen. Organisms may be exposed to the air only at low tide, or in some places not at all. Algae, particularly brown seaweeds, increase markedly. A fixed tube-worm, *Galeolaria caespitosa*, is found just above the seaweed or on patches among it. In Victoria, NSW and southern Queensland the sea-squirt or cunjevoi is so prolific on some platforms that the low-shore area is often referred to as the cunjevoi zone. Many other organisms live where they can find room among the dominant groups. Along with some that are more characteristic of higher shore levels, such as barnacles and whelks, are found turban shells, starfish, sea-urchins, sponges, octopuses and crabs.

Marine life distribution is consistent in its general patterns, but from time to time and place to place there can be significant changes. The most obvious causes of such changes are storm damage, human interference and water pollution. Shore communities are variable anyway, because of breeding and feeding behaviour. Most species spend a juvenile stage at sea. Larvae or spores drift for days, weeks or months at the whim of ocean currents. Many may be eaten by predators, or die before reaching a platform. Those that survive the seaborne phase do not necessarily find the same area or even the same shore as their parent colonies, and new-found homes may be less suitable. Barnacle larvae, for example, can fix themselves only to bare rock or to the hard shells of older barnacles and other gastropods. If other species already cover the rock, there will be no barnacles. Among the adult animals, many species prey on others, compete with each other for food or space, or interfere with the settlement of the tiny larvae. Some are even more variable because they are short-lived and seasonal, or because their young do not settle every year. The distribution of species on a rocky shore is continually changing.

Getting to grips with the cunjevoi

CRUSTY yet spongy, like a vegetable outside yet meaty inside, the sea-squirt or cunjevoi is a puzzle even to the rock fishermen who cut it up for bait. Just for fun a leading marine biologist, the late William Dakin, wrote to the Sydney *Sun* in 1945 inviting theories about the nature of this organism. A Dr Archibald Grubb replied:

'My observations of and on cunjevoi have been frequent, long, and even lurid, and its facility in depriving me of hooks and sinkers has always suggested that it is an animal, and a very low and objectionable animal at that. And when you walk over it gingerly to recover your hook, it looks up malignantly and spits sea-water into your eye; and when, in rage, you slash off the top of its crust, withdraw the animal or vegetable and place it upon a hook, all the other lowest animals in the water rush to the feast—woorrahs, or old boots, fortescues, weedies, muddies, sweep, toebiters, crabs, onkterspronks, mugfrubs, etc, and so forth, and you lose the an. or veg. off the hook and get snagged on its contemporaries and lose half your line. Yes, if the cungevoi isn't a lower form of animal life, the barnacle is a melon-plant, or I'm an onion.'

Dr Grubb was right. The cunjevoi is an animal. It belongs to the same division of the animal kingdom as some free-swimming, sac-bodied creatures, some beach worms and all the vertebrates.

Hundreds of cunjevoi form a lumpy brown covering over rocks exposed only at very low tide

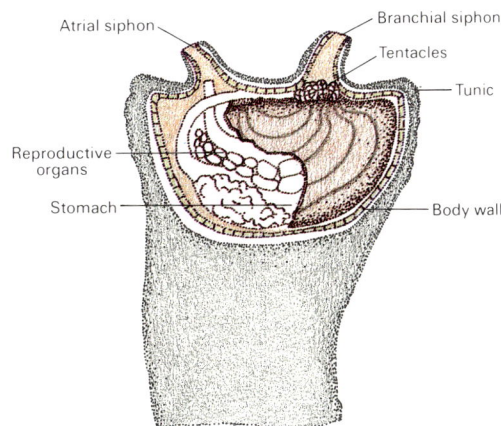

The most commonly encountered cunjevoi on Australia's rocky shores, *Pyura praeputialis*, is only one of some 250 known species. Inside the animal's leathery outer coat is the tough, muscular tissue sought after by anglers as bait. The tissue forms a body wall to protect the branchial sac, the main food collecting and respiratory organ. Food-laden water is sucked down the branchial siphon, filtered by the tentacles and trapped in the sac. Waste water is released in a stream through the atrial siphon. The cunjevoi is hermaphroditic, with both male and female cells

Miniature worlds along rocky shores

Rocky shores, and the pools along them, accommodate myriad fascinating animals and plants. Explore them in the early morning at low tide, before the animals have sheltered from the heat and glare. Cause as little interference as possible—even apparently bare rocks may be covered with microscopic life. If you turn over any rocks, replace them exactly as they were, otherwise you will kill the plants and animals living on both sides.

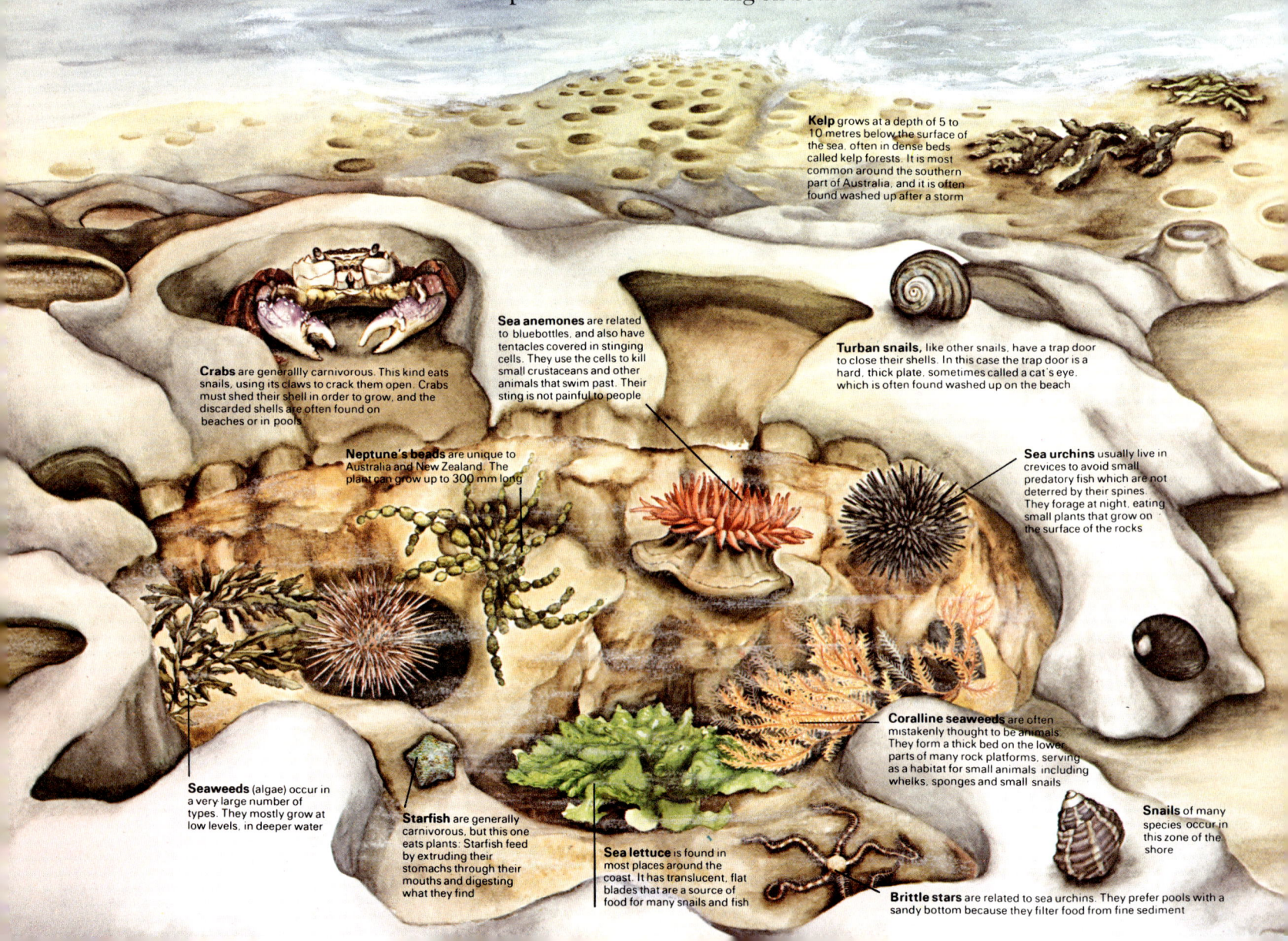

Kelp grows at a depth of 5 to 10 metres below the surface of the sea, often in dense beds called kelp forests. It is most common around the southern part of Australia, and it is often found washed up after a storm

Crabs are generally carnivorous. This kind eats snails, using its claws to crack them open. Crabs must shed their shell in order to grow, and the discarded shells are often found on beaches or in pools

Sea anemones are related to bluebottles, and also have tentacles covered in stinging cells. They use the cells to kill small crustaceans and other animals that swim past. Their sting is not painful to people

Turban snails, like other snails, have a trap door to close their shells. In this case the trap door is a hard, thick plate, sometimes called a cat's eye, which is often found washed up on the beach

Neptune's beads are unique to Australia and New Zealand. The plant can grow up to 300 mm long

Sea urchins usually live in crevices to avoid small predatory fish which are not deterred by their spines. They forage at night, eating small plants that grow on the surface of the rocks

Coralline seaweeds are often mistakenly thought to be animals. They form a thick bed on the lower parts of many rock platforms, serving as a habitat for small animals including whelks, sponges and small snails

Seaweeds (algae) occur in a very large number of types. They mostly grow at low levels, in deeper water

Starfish are generally carnivorous, but this one eats plants. Starfish feed by extruding their stomachs through their mouths and digesting what they find

Sea lettuce is found in most places around the coast. It has translucent, flat blades that are a source of food for many snails and fish

Snails of many species occur in this zone of the shore

Brittle stars are related to sea urchins. They prefer pools with a sandy bottom because they filter food from fine sediment

Do not take anything home. Even empty shells are used by
creatures such as hermit crabs. Never reach into a crevice—there is
the risk of encountering a blue-ringed octopus, a dangerous species
of cone shell or a moray eel that could crush a finger badly.

Alga found at high
levels usually occurs
where it receives some
rainwater. Lower down it
is eaten by grazing
animals

Mussels are nearly always
found in clumps. They are
filter feeders and pump
seawater through their
bodies, extracting all the
minute animals from it

Lichens are a mixture of a
fungus and an alga

**Chiton or coat-of-
mail shells** live on
algae. Some grow to
130 mm long

Barnacles are cemented to the rock
and do not move. They often form
dense clumps. There are very many
species of these animals, which are
related to shrimps

Mulberry whelks eat shelled
animals, particularly
barnacles, by softening the
shell with a secretion and then
drilling a hole in it with their
proboscis. The process can
take four days

Erosion holes in soft
rocks often contain patches
of salt formed when
seawater has evaporated in
the sun

Hermit crabs have soft shells so
they have to live in the shells of
other, dead, animals. They try to
dislodge other hermit crabs from
larger shells as they grow

Limpets are usually
slightly raised from
the rock, but they
clamp themselves
down if threatened

Estuarine waters Fish habitats under human threat

Estuaries are principally the tidal parts of river mouths. Biologists also class some bay areas and lagoons as estuarine because they support similar marine life and fringing vegetation. Australia has few estuaries, considering the extent of its coastline. Where their shores were firm they made ideal Aboriginal campsites, offering fresh water close to an abundance of seafood and waterfowl. European explorers made for the same spots, not only for sustenance but also for protected anchorages. With colonisation the landing places became ports for access to the hinterlands, and many grew to be cities and sites of industry. Estuary beds have been raised for reclamations, or dredged to provide land-fill elsewhere. Other estuarine waters serve as fishing grounds and ever-busier holiday playgrounds—and some even as waste dumps.

These relatively rare waters are crucial to the existence of many fish, including some that are normally associated with deeper seas offshore. Snapper, for example, spend a juvenile stage in estuaries, where they may be known as cockney or red bream. In New South Wales, 31 of the 43 most important commercial species are caught in estuaries. Half of the total inshore and offshore catch, in tonnage and value, comprises species that depend on estuaries for at least a part of their lives. Including other seafoods such as prawns and oysters, the NSW fishing industry is about 70 per cent reliant on estuaries. The availability of smaller organisms for these fish to eat varies greatly in nature. Now it is increasingly threatened by human activities.

Seagrasses probably hold the key to marine animal life in estuaries. They are not important as a direct source of food for commercial fish species, but they shield the youngest fish from predators and they generate the organic material on which a whole web of food supply is based. Dead or broken parts of eelgrass, *Zostera*, strapweed, *Posidonia*, or some other flowering plants and associated algae are grazed and further broken down by crustaceans and worms. The smaller particles are attacked by bacteria and fungi and eaten by other tiny organisms, which are in turn eaten. Reduced to its finest form—detritus—after repeated digestions and excretions, the organic matter readily yields up its mineral components to nourish more seagrass. Fringing mangroves and swamp plants contribute detritus in a similar way.

While the cycle continues, all marine animals have food—plant matter, micro-organisms, or

Protecting a complex environment

Careel Bay, north of Sydney, is a good example of a delicate estuarine environment threatened by residential and commercial development. The bay is rich in the number of species of plants and animals that live in and on its waters and surrounding mangrove forests, salt marshes and sandy beaches. Each of these areas plays a part in maintaining its neighbours, so the disturbance of one habitat could destroy others. Because the sheltered shores of estuaries offer so many possibilities for leisure activities, they will always be under threat until their importance in the life cycle of many creatures is properly understood and appreciated.

Grey mangroves, *Avicennia marina*, and river mangroves, *Aegicerus corniculatum*, grow here. Both need oxygen, which they obtain by their aerial roots or pneumatophores. The trees die if these are covered by even a shallow layer of silt or sand. Many species of crabs and snails live among the mangroves which are an important link in the food chain by which nutrients eventually enter estuarine waters. Mangroves also play an important part in stabilising mud so that surrounding water remains clear and seagrasses can grow

These brown areas are salt marsh. They are flooded with seawater only when the tide is particularly high, and they are an important part of the estuarine ecosystem, bridging the gap between mangroves and dry land, and producing much organic matter. Here there are sedges; the succulent, beaded glasswort, *Sarcocornia quinqueflora*; streaked arrowgrass, *Triglochin striata*; and she-oaks, *Casuarina*. The salt marsh is an important habitat for birds, and this one is the home of the bush stone-curlew, *Burhinus magnirostris*, which is rare in urban areas. Salt marshes are often misused because they seem to have little value—people dump rubbish in them and children enjoy riding bikes around in the mud. Because they border dry land and housing developments, residents are tempted to increase the extent of uninundated land by filling adjoining soft areas

Proposals have been put forward to enlarge boating facilities on the southern shore of the bay and to dredge a deep-water access channel. Scientists fear that such a development would increase the amount of pollution and would also stir up sediments to cloud what is at present clear water

This strip of land beside the road was once covered by wetland salt marsh and mangroves. It was used for many years as a garbage tip, and the reclaimed land has now been turned into playing fields. Around Australia many similar areas have been reclaimed in this way. In some instances industrial waste was dumped, and there is a possibility that harmful chemicals may be leached from these tips into surrounding waters

Owners of waterfront houses sometimes pull out mangrove seedlings to keep their beaches clear

Houses mean human waste. In unsewered suburbs septic tanks can leak or overflow, or effluent is released on purpose, into creeks and bays. Human waste is harmful because the bacteria that decompose it need a lot of oxygen, thus depriving the water of oxygen used by plants and animals

In this shallow water grow dense beds of seagrasses. Eelgrass, *Zostera*, grows on the flats uncovered at low tide, and strapweed, *Posidonia*, grows in the areas always submerged. Careel Bay favours seagrasses because it is well-flushed by tides and the water is quite clear, enabling light to filter through strongly. Fish and shellfish find this an ideal environment so the area is particularly rich in species and numbers. Unlike mangroves, with their ability to take oxygen directly from the air, seagrasses and the animals they shelter take oxygen from the water, so they are greatly affected by suspended sediment and pollution

one another. But entire meadows of seagrass can be destroyed by massive movements of silt or sand, especially in floods or after storms. Even a milder disturbance making the water murky can stop their growth by cutting out sunlight. And human interference is not limited to the obvious effects of large-scale engineering. Seagrass beds are frequently damaged by water pollution, by high-speed boating over shallows, by bottom-trawling and by the dumping of junk.

Estuary beds are the world's most productive areas. Seagrasses alone generate as much as 4 kg of organic matter per square metre per year. The average is 2 kg in dry weight—equalled only by tropical forests. Temperate grasslands yield only 0.5 kg on average, and total land areas 0.75 kg. Ocean beds produce a mere 0.15 kg.

In addition, staggering quantities of animal tissue are produced in estuaries. Sampling of seagrass meadows in the United States indicated that every square kilometre harboured 90 million prawns, including larvae, and 36 000 million molluscs. And cultivated mussel beds in Lancashire, England, were found to produce 80 times more weight of flesh than cattle could gain by grazing on an equivalent area of pasture.

Sea water is heavier than fresh water, so an estuary fed by a big river—the Derwent passing through Hobart, for example—may be split into two levels with a wedge of sea water flowing upstream under river water flowing downstream. But Australia's generally low rainfall means that many estuaries are totally marine environments for most of the time. Their salt content is not much lower than the ocean's, except after heavy rain. Periods of reduced salinity are spasmodic and seldom long-lasting. In the far north, however, where rainfall is extremely seasonal, estuaries are virtually fresh for months during the 'Wet'. And over-saltiness, through evaporation, can occur in a lagoon when drought cuts its freshwater flow and waves build a sand bar blocking the entrance. That is common in the south-east and in parts of South Australia, and leads to the death of many animals and plants.

Most estuarine animals are sea creatures: their body fluids are in balance with sea water because the salt concentrations are similar. If floods overwhelm their habitat and drastically lower its salinity, they start absorbing extra water. For some species this is fatal. Fish can quickly retreat to more suitable waters. Molluscs and crustaceans have shells and regulatory mechanisms to delay water absorption. They may also be able to close their shells or burrow into the estuary bed—at the risk of starvation—until the crisis is over. The chief sufferers are soft-bodied animals such as worms. Some can stand a limited intake of water, slightly inflating their bodies, for a short time. But if low salinity continues, they die. After heavy floods, entire populations are wiped out. Other worms, especially those adapted to upstream areas, have organs that act like primitive kidneys and pump out water. But their young lack these organs, so reproduction has to be geared to periods of higher salinity.

Fish and other marine animals are renewable

Seagrass meadows, found in many bays and estuaries around the Australian coast, are among the most productive areas in the world

resources, provided that their habitats are preserved. But the estuarine plant life on which they depend can be destroyed forever by human actions, whether deliberate or unthinking. Not only are many uses of estuaries in conflict with nature—they are also often in conflict with one another. Port development, commercial fishing, sand mining, sewage disposal, oyster cultivation and recreation, for example, simply do not mix. Scientists are urging governments to consider all estuaries that are subject to human pressure and to allocate specific uses to each of them, taking into account their different physical characteristics, their type of vegetation, and their nearness to population centres. A major problem in planning their conservation, however, is the multiplicity of authorities in control of the wetland fringes (see overleaf).

The saving of Jervis Bay

SEAGRASS meadows in the sheltered northern reaches of Jervis Bay are probably the most extensive in NSW, reaching to depths of more than 10 metres. As well as being nurseries for commercially valuable fish and crustaceans, they are important feeding grounds for vast flocks of black swans. Yet in 1972 the shores behind were proposed as the site of a gigantic industrial complex. The north-western corner was earmarked for a steelworks bigger than Port Kembla's. To its east were to be engineering plants, metal refineries, a woodchip mill, a petrochemical plant, an oil refinery and a power station. Separate port facilities for the steelworks, for bulk products, for general cargo and for oil products were to be strung along Callala Beach. Urban zones, at first on the coast to the north but later on the western shore of the bay, were to house 300 000 people. But evidence of the ecological impact was so damning that a government inquiry threw out the whole scheme, recommending that the bay shores be preserved for nature conservation and recreation.

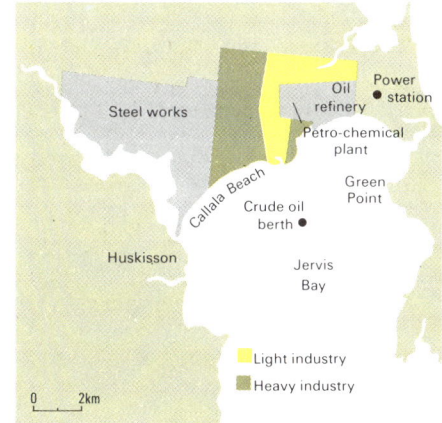

The plan of the 1972 development proposal gives some idea of the scope of the scheme

The shores of Jervis Bay remain unspoiled, despite attempts to establish heavy industry in the area

Wetland margins Where plants belong to both worlds

Mangrove swamps and salt marshes are customarily seen as nuisances. They are foul-smelling breeding grounds of mosquitoes and midges. They clog boating and fishing waters and impede land access to them. They collect floating rubbish. In the tropics, they harbour dangerous crocodiles. The eagerness of property developers to dredge out mangroves and wall the shoreline, or to refashion marshlands as canal estates, is understandable. But mangroves and marsh plants are vital, along with seagrasses, to estuary life. Where water, sunlight and nutrients are plentiful, each square metre of mangrove forest contributes an average 1 kg a year of organic matter to the food chain that supports most of the species sought-after by commercial fishermen.

The biological importance of mangroves was recognised only in the late 1960s, after pioneering research in southern Florida, USA. Only four species grow there, but Australia has more than 30, related to at least 15 different families of land-based trees. Mangroves were just as varied in South-east Asia, but their habitats are in heavily populated, underdeveloped tropical regions. Asian mangroves have been traditionally cut for firewood and for building jetties and fish traps. Now international companies in some places are mowing them down for woodchip production. They are being depleted so rapidly that by the

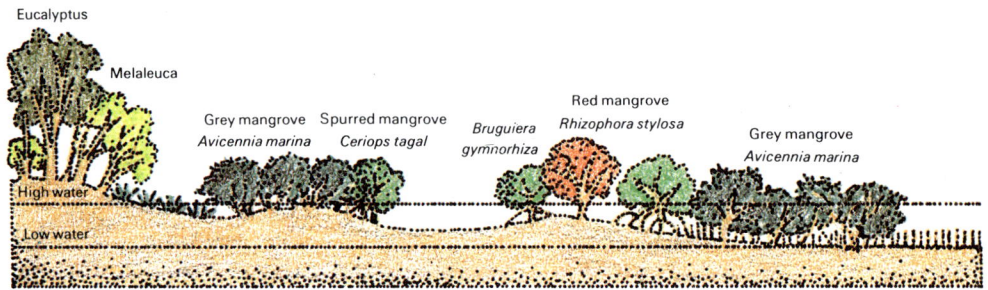

Different species of mangroves form distinct zones in tropical estuaries, partly as a result of the amount of time that the land spends under water. The landward zone is generally the richest in species

1990s Australia may have the world's last mature stands of highly diverse mangrove forest.

Mangroves are trees and shrubs with many different and unrelated characteristics. What they have in common is a unique tolerance of high concentrations of salt in their soil moisture. Some species discharge salt through glands on their leaves; others are able to restrict its entry through their roots. They have various ways of drawing air into oxygen-starved soil. All have adapted to daily flooding by sea water—in fact they rely on it. They use the tides to disperse their seeds, so that new areas can be colonised away from the shade of older trees.

Australia has the southernmost distribution of mangroves in the world. The common grey mangrove, *Avicennia marina*, is found in Corner Inlet, just north of Wilsons Promontory, and in other shallow, protected Victorian bays such as Western Port. Isolated *Avicennia* swamps also occur in the gulfs of South Australia and on the west coast, south of Perth. Mangroves are widespread in estuaries and sheltered bays on the east coast, with the number of species increasing northward. Two occur at Merimbula, NSW, and seven near Brisbane, while communities of more than 20 species are found in northern Queensland and north-western Australia. The breadth of swamps increases with the number of species, as does the height of plants. Southern mangroves are stunted and sparse; around Sydney they form open parklands and grow 10-20 metres tall; mangroves in the far north comprise broad,

Red mangroves, Rhyzophora stylosa, *with their tangled roots are the classic mangroves of tropical shores*

Fish that climb trees

MUDSKIPPERS, the oddest creatures in tropical mangrove swamps, are fish that prefer the open air and hot sun, as long as their skins are moist. They emerge from the water at low tide and walk over the mud on fins that are modified for use as limbs. Through stalked, swivelling eyes on top of their heads, these fish of the *Periophthalmus* genus watch for the small crabs and insects on which they feed. If alarmed they do not retreat into the water but skip across it to a safer mudbank. And if still hungry when the tide is rising, many species use their fins to elbow their way up mangrove trees. Queensland's commonest species grow to 100 mm in length, but others reach 250 mm.

A mudskipper, Periophthalmus koelreuteri

Altogether, over 30 species of mangroves live around the Australian coast, but all are only found north of 12°S. Only one species—the grey mangrove, Avicennia marina *(far left)*—grows in Victoria, South Australia and south-western Western Australia. Spurred mangroves, Ceriops tagal *(left)*, and milky mangroves, Exoecaria agallocha *(above)*, illustrate the diverse forms that these plants take

dense forest climbing to a height of 30 metres.

Because they grow in tidal mud, mangroves need extensive root systems to hold them in place. As well as subterranean systems, many species have branching aerial roots. The prop-roots of *Rhizophora* descend from higher on the trunk as the tree grows. *Bruguiera*, the tallest mangroves, send out low-level roots that travel horizontally and bend upwards before anchoring in the mud. Some other species have wide, flat aerial roots resembling planks wandering far from the tree. The tangle of roots put out by a community of mangroves traps fine silt carried down by any creeks draining into the swamp. Sediments brought in on the high tide also tend to settle out and remain among the mangroves. In this way the trees stabilise shorelines, and in the absence of floods or storm waves they can add to the land area.

Avicennia, *Bruguiera* and some other mangrove species send pegs into the air for metres around each tree. Called pneumatophores, these are root extensions with lip-like cracks through which the tree can draw oxygen while its lower levels are in poorly aerated mud. Other species have similar breathing openings in their aerial roots. Another peculiarity of many mangroves is that their seeds germinate before they leave the tree. In *Rhizophora* species, the seedling may protrude more than 300 mm from the fruit. When it falls into the water the fruit floats with the seedling shoot pointing down, ready to catch in shallows and quickly take root. *Avicennia* seeds, however, need long soaking in sea water before they will germinate.

Most land animals found in mangroves are casual visitors such as mice, canefield rats, flying foxes, snakes, goannas, crocodiles and many species of birds. Some come seasonally for protection while breeding, or because the trees are flowering or fruiting. A diverse community of insects includes some species found only in mangroves. Fish and prawns come in with the tide to feed. Mud crabs breed among the mangroves, but spend most of their lives in deeper water.

The permanent marine population is dominated by worms, molluscs and crustaceans. Some—especially molluscs with shells that resist dehydration—live on the surface. Fiddler and semaphore crabs, needing constant access to water, live in burrows, but feed on the surface and sometimes in the trees. Oysters encrust the tree bases on the seaward margins, along with limpets, small shrimps and worms. Other worms inhabit tubes in the mud or in pockets of water under fallen logs. Small crabs and snails also live under dead wood, while other creatures bore into it and gradually break it down. The 'ship worm', *Teredo*—really a tiny bivalve mollusc—is the dominant borer, though louse-like isopods such as the gribble may be locally common. Once such animals have made holes, other small creatures may move in.

Salt marshes, often found on the landward margins of mangrove swamps, present conditions so variable that few kinds of animals or plants can survive. Inundation by the sea normally occurs only during fortnightly spring tides. At other times, especially in dry summer weather, evaporation causes a build-up of salt concentrations. In the tropics and in arid regions there may by salt pans—areas where the soil is covered in salt crystals and devoid of vegetation. On the other hand fresh water may flood a salt marsh during heavy rain. Burrowing crabs and some small snails can cope with this range of conditions. Of the shrubby succulent plants that may grow, the dominant species is marsh samphire or glasswort, *Salicornia*. The shores of a marsh are often marked by a band of rushes and casuarinas.

How the law sees mangroves

Laws protecting mangroves were passed in all mainland states in the 1970s, after the importance of the trees was recognised. But biologists are far from satisfied with the effectiveness of such measures. In NSW, for example, the Fisheries Act was amended in 1979 so that any cutting of mangroves without a permit could incur a $500 fine. But three years later the amendent was still not in force: there was no machinery for apprehending and prosecuting offenders.

The effects of proposed coastal developments on mangroves can now be taken into account if environmental impact assessments are called for. The authority controlling a particular area of wetlands, however, need not call for such a study unless it already believes that the impact is likely to be significant. And that authority may have little ecological interest; its official concern could be port administration or shipping, or public works. Control of wetlands may be in the hands of as many as seven or eight different state government departments or statutory authorities, or it may be vested in local government councils.

Singling out certain mangrove areas for complete protection offers no permanent solution because they are changing environments. Through the gain or loss of soil, mangroves create their own fluctuations in sea levels and growth limits. And wildlife, especially migratory birdlife, is unpredictable. A mangrove swamp of no apparent interest in one season may become all-important breeding ground the following year.

Mangroves, an unattractive but vital nursery

Mangrove swamps have clearly zoned regions. In the waterfront mudflats exposed at low tide, the air-breathing roots of some mangrove species and sapling trees sprout through the oozing surface. Adult trees from over 30 kinds of mangroves found around the Australian coast form dense thickets of branches and ground and aerial roots further inland, but still on the tidal mudflats. As the swamp merges into firm land, mangroves intermingle with land plants.

Mud is trapped by the mangrove's tangled roots and, because the waters are unusually calm, algae, bacteria and fungi are held there. These organisms are what makes the swamps such smelly places, but they are also the basis of a food chain which supports a great diversity of molluscs, crustaceans and fish that are sought

Pulmonate slugs—like all slugs—are shell-less snails. They are air-breathers and feed on algae. The most common in mangrove swamps grow to about 70 mm long. They are very hard to see as they are usually covered in mud, but they can be traced by the trail they leave

Shipworms are misleadingly named—they are actually bivalves, relatives of oysters, mussels and cockles. They have a long siphon that they extend to the surface to breathe and eat. There are several species of shipworm; they used to be relished as food by Aborigines, but now they are only considered as pests, being responsible for much of the destruction of wooden pilings and other timber in water

Oysters occur in huge numbers around mangrove pneumatophores—many mangrove swamps in New South Wales are leased as nursery areas for the spats (young oysters). Sydney rock oysters change sex during their lifetime—they spawn as males but become females later. The females produce about

1 500 000 eggs every few weeks in the breeding season (mostly in summer); the eggs develop into larvae that can swim in a few hours. After two or three weeks they settle, and are collected from their first sites to be farmed in batteries. They take about three and a half years to grow to table size

Oysters are stationary, with one side of their shell cemented to a surface. They are filter feeders, using their gills—the gill forms a sieve and when taking in oxygen the creature also collects food particles

Snapping shrimps can often be heard in mangrove swamps, making a crack like glass breaking—it is not known why. Saltwater yabbies (which can be eaten but are generally used for bait) look somewhat similar, but snapping shrimps are quickly recognised by their single large-clawed leg—this has a peg on one finger which fits into a socket on the other. The feathered end sections are used as rudders

Hermit crabs are soft-bodied, with an abdomen that can be coiled to fit into their borrowed homes. As they grow they need to move into larger shells

after by commercial and amateur fishermen. Waterfowl find the swamps ideal feeding grounds. Worms live in both the mud and the tree roots, and the air is often thick with insects and the webs of spiders which prey on them.

Mangroves are not all coastal—grey mangroves occur in the Great Sandy Desert, about 40 km from the coast. There are about 30 kinds of mangroves in Australia, but they have different ways of dealing with the salt in their environment. One is to prevent salt from entering in the first place, by chemical activity in the root system. Mangroves in tropical areas store salt in succulent leaves, and when they are too full they become fleshy and drop off. The third method is to excrete salt through the leaves

Pneumatophores are parts of the root of certain kinds of mangroves, including two of the most common ones—*Avicennia* and *Brughuiera*. They function as gas exhangers, taking in oxygen at high tide and giving out carbon dioxide at low tide. They provide the tree with an increased surface over which to gather oxygen, and they also help to cement together the mud in which the tree grows

Grey mangroves (*Avicennia*) and the **short black mangroves** (*Aegiceras*) are the most common kinds in the south-eastern corner of Australia. At this stage of their development they can only be distinguished from one another by tasting the surface of a leaf—*Avicennia* excretes salt from the back of its leaf; *Aegiceras* does not. *Aegiceras* sometimes grows in very dense thickets

Small mangrove crabs have eyes on stalks which can fold down sideways into the small cavities visible in their shells. This one is a male with a highly coloured claw. These crabs feed by shovelling through the mud and extracting organisms—the shells outside the hole were probably cracked up by blue swimmer crabs that are also mangrove swamp dwellers, and were merely dug up by this crab when it excavated its burrow

Burrows of the small mangrove crab extend for several metres under the layer of mangrove tree roots, dug out sideways and downwards, housing several crabs. Sometimes they contain more than one nesting centre

Barnacles of this kind are more common low down on the sides of trees facing the water, since they depend on the tidal rise of the water to find their sites. Although at first glance barnacles may resemble shellfish such as mussels, they differ greatly, having many feathery limbs with which they sweep for food

Snails can have lungs and breathe air, like this kind and most others found in mangrove swamps, or have gills and breathe underwater, like the majority found on rocky shores

Snails of this sort generally live and graze on mangrove leaves. They retain their larvae, numbered in scores of eggs and developing young, inside the shell until they are strong enough to descend into the water

Rough periwinkles have a feather-like gill to increase the surface over which they draw in water for oxygen. They feed on the green algae which live on the mud and tree trunks

Coral reefs
Marine builders reaching for the light

Coral reefs are complex associations of marine animals and plants, living on and in a framework built primarily of the skeletons of corals. When coral polyps die their cups of calcium carbonate fill with the skeletal debris of other creatures such as molluscs and sea-urchins, and with limy material from seaweed. The skeletons and their contents are bound by encrusting red algae and cemented by carbonic acid salts to form reef rock. It is porous, but rigid and tough enough to resist waves and provide a platform on which more corals can build.

Water warmth is the paramount factor in reef-building. Average minimum temperatures must not be less than 18°C. Reefs are largely confined to the tropics, but consistent warm currents foster their growth far to the south at Lord Howe Island, off NSW, and at the Houtman Abrolhos Islands, opposite Geraldton, WA. Great Barrier Reef formations could perhaps have extended much farther, well to the south-east of Fraser Island, but for the masses of shifting sand north of the island. Loose sediments smother corals, or prevent them from gaining a hold on the rock. And they cloud the water, cutting out sunlight—the other major factor in reef-building. Plant organisms that stimulate coral tissue growth and bind the coral together are so restricted by poor light that reef corals do not flourish below about 50 metres. Drilling has shown that reef structures go much deeper under the sea

Limpid water covers Wistari Reef—a reef flat near Heron Island, which can be seen on the horizon

than that—they are many hundreds of metres thick—but the lower levels were built when the sea itself was lower, during the last ice age, or even earlier when the continental shelf stood higher. Reefs as they are known today are veneers, no more than about 8000 years old, overlaying the earlier structures.

When a reef reaches sea level, exposing its top surface at low tide, upward growth stops. Corals reaching any higher would be starved of their plankton food and dehydrated. But sideways growth takes over, principally in the direction from which ocean swells normally come. Incoming waves have more plankton, and the sluggish waters on the sheltered side of a reef may be muddy. The further development of

reef surfaces, once they are at sea level, is largely a matter of wave and wind action.

A *barrier* reef in the strict sense is a long, almost continuous chain of ribbon reefs roughly parallel to a mainland shore, at a considerable distance from it. It screens the coast from ocean movement and creates an offshore lagoon. The Great Barrier Reef is not one in that sense, though it contains some barriers among its complex mixture of formations. Matthew Flinders named it simply because of the difficulties it presented for sailing ships. Scientists prefer to call the Great Barrier region a 'reef province'.

Platform reefs rise from the shallower parts of continental shelves in the shelter of barrier reefs. They are flat-topped and commonly oval in

The animals that start it all

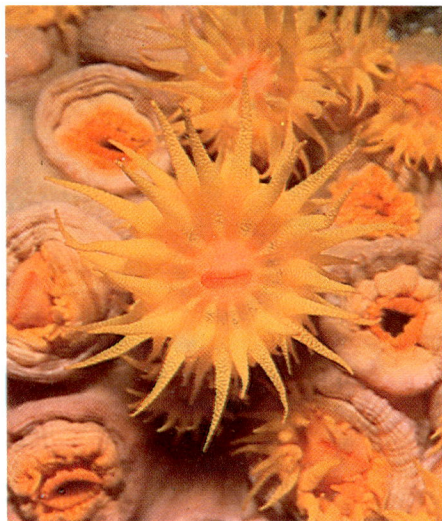
Coral polyps, some with their tentacles extended

CORALS are closely related to sea anemones. They can reproduce sexually, in which case the young have a free-swimming larval stage. Once a coral polyp has developed its tentacle-fringed mouth and gut, to catch and digest its diet of floating plankton, it settles on a firm support and secretes a limestone base. Then it starts building up a skeleton. In soft corals this is a set of splinters or ridges embedded in the body, or a horny or chalky central rod. But in true corals the skeleton forms a stone casing around the polyp, which can draw itself inside for protection. Corals of many kinds may be found on submerged rocks in most parts of the world—sometimes solitary, sometimes in clusters. But only in warm waters will they be reef-builders.

Reef corals, whose vast communities could in theory have been founded by just one polyp of each species, reproduce asexually by budding. They keep on building upwards, then outwards, basing themselves on the skeletons of their dead predecessors. They are linked with membranes of living tissue overlapping their inorganic casings. Each species has its own colour and each is genetically programmed to follow a particular growth pattern. Some are branch-like, others form clumps, layers, fans and so on, giving a diverse reef its extraordinary variety of hues and shapes.

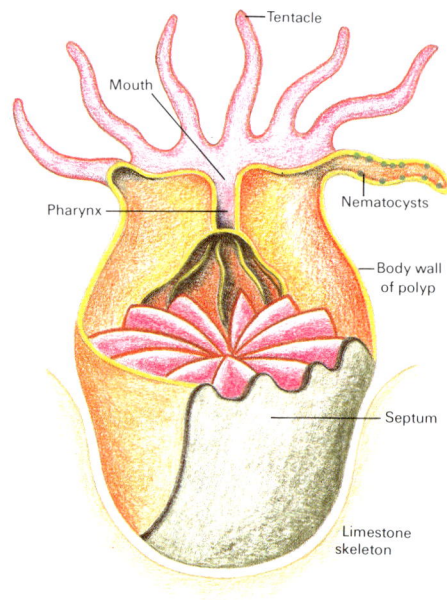
Cross-section through a polyp and its skeleton

Tentacle
Mouth
Pharynx
Nematocysts
Body wall of polyp
Septum
Limestone skeleton

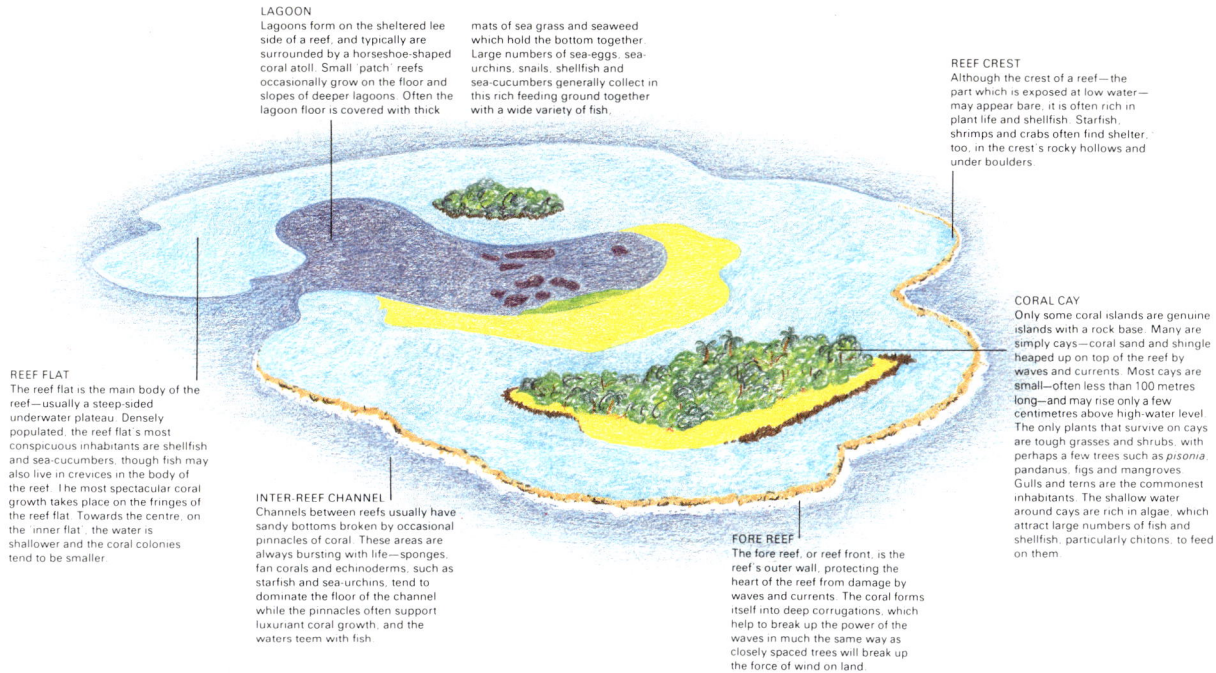

LAGOON
Lagoons form on the sheltered lee side of a reef, and typically are surrounded by a horseshoe-shaped coral atoll. Small 'patch' reefs occasionally grow on the floor and slopes of deeper lagoons. Often the lagoon floor is covered with thick mats of sea grass and seaweed which hold the bottom together. Large numbers of sea-eggs, sea-urchins, snails, shellfish and sea-cucumbers generally collect in this rich feeding ground together with a wide variety of fish.

REEF CREST
Although the crest of a reef—the part which is exposed at low water—may appear bare, it is often rich in plant life and shellfish. Starfish, shrimps and crabs often find shelter, too, in the crest's rocky hollows and under boulders.

REEF FLAT
The reef flat is the main body of the reef—usually a steep-sided underwater plateau. Densely populated, the reef flat's most conspicuous inhabitants are shellfish and sea-cucumbers, though fish may also live in crevices in the body of the reef. The most spectacular coral growth takes place on the fringes of the reef flat. Towards the centre, on the 'inner flat', the water is shallower and the coral colonies tend to be smaller.

CORAL CAY
Only some coral islands are genuine islands with a rock base. Many are simply cays—coral sand and shingle heaped up on top of the reef by waves and currents. Most cays are small—often less than 100 metres long—and may rise only a few centimetres above high-water level. The only plants that survive on cays are tough grasses and shrubs, with perhaps a few trees such as *pisonia*, pandanus, figs and mangroves. Gulls and terns are the commonest inhabitants. The shallow water around cays are rich in algae, which attract large numbers of fish and shellfish, particularly chitons, to feed on them.

INTER-REEF CHANNEL
Channels between reefs usually have sandy bottoms broken by occasional pinnacles of coral. These areas are always bursting with life—sponges, fan corals and echinoderms, such as starfish and sea-urchins, tend to dominate the floor of the channel while the pinnacles often support luxuriant coral growth, and the waters teem with fish.

FORE REEF
The fore reef, or reef front, is the reef's outer wall, protecting the heart of the reef from damage by waves and currents. The coral forms itself into deep corrugations, which help to break up the power of the waves in much the same way as closely spaced trees will break up the force of wind on land.

---

shape, with their longer axis aligned parallel to the prevailing wind direction. Smaller platform reefs may be called patch, shelf, bank, table or hummock reefs.

Fringing reefs grow outwards from continental or rocky island coasts. Because sedimentation and freshwater run-off are more pronounced on mainland shores, these reefs are more richly developed in the clear waters round islands.

An *atoll* is a ring of reefs, some surmounted by low cays of sand or shingle, enclosing a lagoon. Australia has none of the atolls common in the central Pacific—they usually occur in open oceanic waters, and are associated with volcanic activity. But some *lagoonal reefs* in Queensland waters, rising above the lagoon floors of bigger structures, may be ring-shaped.

All types of coral reefs have similar zones, running in bands that usually parallel their outer edges. Each zone is a distinct environment for characteristic forms of natural life. The *fore reef* extends from the lower limit of coral growth, up through the tide zone to the windward crest of the reef. The top edge often has closely spaced grooves running between ridges of coral. The grooves are pathways for tidal waves moving on to the reef, and for sediments to be removed. The *reef flat* extends to the back slope of the reef, or to a lagoon if there is one. The inner flats of some reefs may collect so much sediment that they are termed sand flats. Occasionally waves and currents push sand or shingle to a point towards the back of the reef where it forms a *cay*, permanently above the high-water mark. Cays, generally low-lying but up to 1 km long, are often colonised by vegetation and stabilised by the formation of beach rock around their rims. Green Island and Heron Island, well known to holiday-makers, are cays based on much more extensive reef platforms.

Subtidal fore reefs, with their profusion of

Enemies of coral

STARFISH are the leading predators of living corals, but few species do much harm. Since the 1960s, however, swarms of the huge, fast-breeding crown-of-thorns starfish, *Acanthaster planci*, have done immense damage to Great Barrier Reef structures. Adults may measure more than 500 mm across, and each may be capable of eating the polyps from a square metre of coral every week. In one survey at Green Island, off Cairns, nearly 6000 of them were found in 100 minutes. The crown-of-thorns seems to thrive on pollution that kills its own natural predators, such as the big triton shellfish. That may be the reason for the present population explosion, although there appear to have been others in the past.

Some coral is killed accidentally during the attacks of big marauding fish on other species. The swallowing of smaller invertebrates by predators such as crabs and octopuses depletes the supply of skeletal material that goes into reef rock. Burrowers and borers, including sponges, molluscs, algae and bacteria, penetrate the rock at all levels. Algae-grazing fish, sea-urchins and molluscs further erode the rock in their quest for food. Browsing animals break down the sediment to extract nutrients.

A crown-of-thorns starfish eating polyps

living corals, seaweeds and colourful fish, can be adequately examined only by snorkelling or scuba diving. The outer reef flat, also with living corals as well as an abundance of sea-urchins, starfish and molluscs, can be viewed in a glass-bottom boat or on foot at the lowest tide. Walkers must exercise great caution, however, to avoid unintentional damage to reef life. The reef crest is usually swept clear by waves, and supports only an algal mat. But big blocks of reef rock, broken from the mass below and cast up in storms, are often found just inside the crest. Many small animals shelter beneath them.

Sandy inner zones of reef flats have occasional clumps of living corals interspersed with patches of dead coral supporting heavy algal growths. Sausage-like sea-cucumbers are the most obvious animal inhabitants, but the sands hide a variety of burrowing molluscs. Some reef flats have mangrove swamps, with features generally similar to those of coastal wetlands. Reef lagoons, if they have internal reefs of their own reaching to low-water level, may provide the best viewing of all with a variety of true corals and soft corals and a multitude of small mobile fauna. The sheets of fine sediment of lagoon floors are constantly reworked by molluscs, shrimps and worms.

Vegetated cays are commonly dominated by dense stands of *Pisonia grandis*—sometimes called 'the bird killing tree'. Its seeds have a sticky coating which can trap nesting sea birds. The central forest is surrounded by a bank of small salt-tolerant trees and shrubs, with grasses on the seaward side. Along with a wide variety of birds, the inner parts of cays are inhabited by reptiles—mainly lizards—and numerous insects. Ghost crabs are the most prominent occupants of cay beaches, although big turtles are nocturnal visitors during their breeding season. If beach rock has formed, it will be encrusted with limpets and 'coat-of-mail' chitons.

Builders and inhabitants of coral reefs

The Great Barrier Reef's massive coral ramparts and maze of island-fringing reefs stretch for 2000 km along the Queensland coast and support an amazing range of marine plants and animals. The reefs, and especially the 1400 species of fish that live around them, are best seen with the help of a mask and snorkel. But even walkers on the upper surface, when it is exposed or awash at low tide, can discover the great variety of coral shapes and the brilliant colours of the reef's other inhabitants, just some of which are illustrated here.

Tiger cowrie
Cypraea tigris
Length up to 125 mm
The body of a cowrie is often as vividly coloured as its shell, and completely covers it when the animal is active

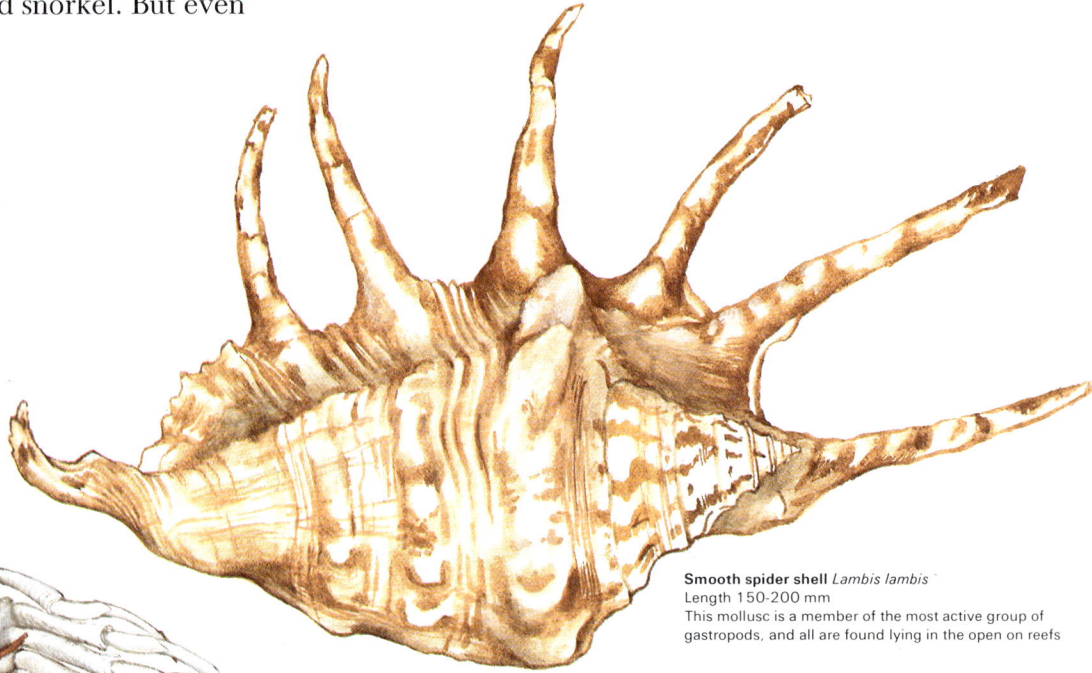

Smooth spider shell *Lambis lambis*
Length 150-200 mm
This mollusc is a member of the most active group of gastropods, and all are found lying in the open on reefs

Horny-eyed ghost crab
Ocypode ceratophthalma
Width, 50 mm across carapace.
On sandy beaches above the waterline, conical piles of sand beside a small hole betray the ghost crab's spiral burrow

Spotted peddle crab
Carpilius maculatus
Very heavy shell on both body and legs, and 11 large round spots, distinguish this slow-moving crab which is found from the shallows down to a depth of over 30 metres

Crenate swimming crab
Thalamita crenata
Width 100 mm across carapace
Five sharp spines behind the eyes on each side clearly identify this crab. It is caught in large numbers for commercial markets

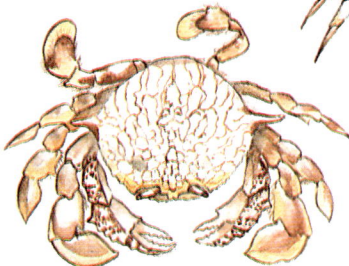

Double-lined sand crab
Matuta planipes
Width, 40 mm across carapace
This crab has wide, flattened claws, well adapted for digging and swimming. *Matuta* are common all around the continent

Leopard-spotted sea-cucumber
Bohadschia argus Length 250 mm
Sea cucumbers are animals, related to starfish and sea urchins. They live among coral debris on reef flats

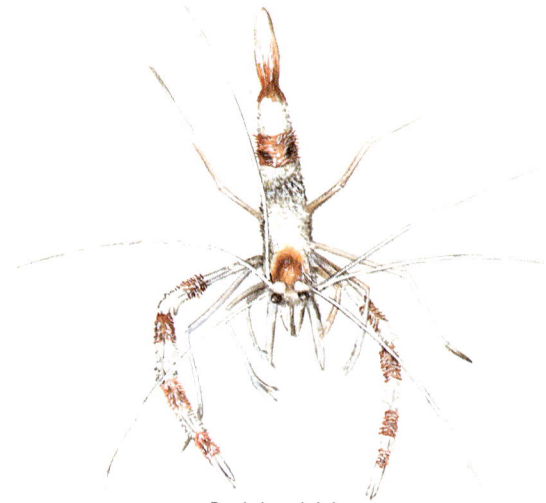

Banded coral shrimp
Stenopus hispidus
Length 50 mm. From crevices in coral, *Stenopus* picks parasites and fungus growths from reef fish which remain still while being cleaned

Staghorn coral *Acropora*
Forests of staghorn can
be up to 1.5 metres high and often cover
75 per cent of the reef area

Turban shell
Turbo perspeciosus
Length 50 mm
A hard, round plate on the
foot of the animal that inhabits
this shell allows it to withdraw
into complete protection

Orange-spotted mitre *Mitra mitra*
Length up to 150 mm
Also known as the giant mitre.
When alive, the shell of this
mollusc is covered with a thin skin
which partly hides the pattern

Cloth-of-gold cone shell
Conus textile
Length up to 100 mm. The timid *Conus* will
shrink into its shell at the least disturbance, but
it has a deadly venom, and a live one
should never be handled

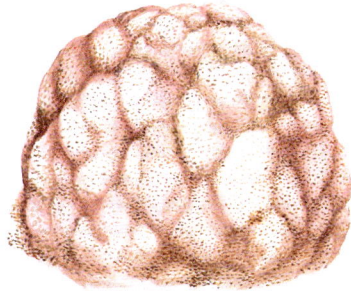

Round-head coral *Porites*
Some species of *Porites* form micro-atolls,
over 2 metres in diameter, which are
common on many reef flats

Soft coral *Xenia*
Soft corals do not make hard skeletons, and are
therefore not reef builders. When exposed at low tide
they look tough and leathery

Brittle star
Ophiocoma scolopendrina
Diameter 200 mm
Brittle stars move much faster than starfish and have a more
clearly defined central disc. They inhabit rubble areas of
coral reefs and lie with only part of their bodies exposed

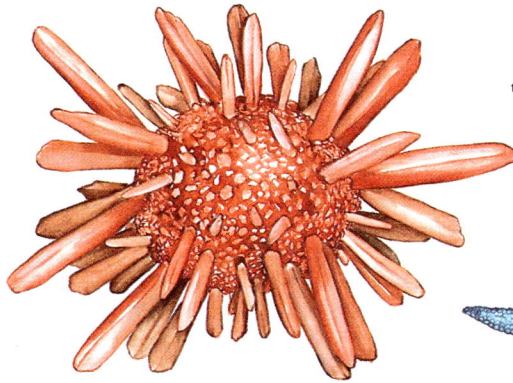

Sea slug *Halgerda aurantiomaculata*
Length ♂0-50 mm
Colourful sea slugs carry their gills
on the outside of their bodies

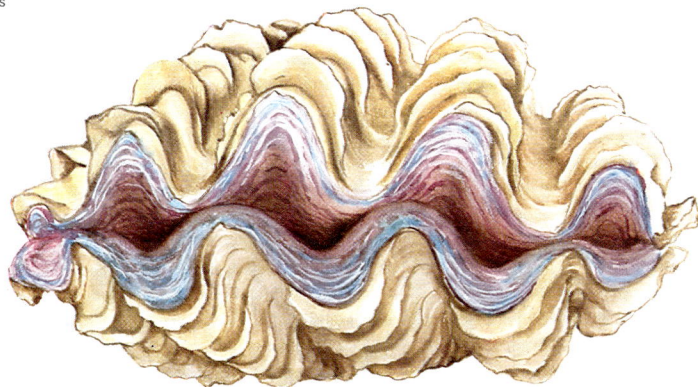

Slate-pencil urchin
Heterocentrotus mammillatus
Diameter 250 mm
The heavy, blunt spines of this sea
urchin may be up to 10 mm thick and
125 mm in length

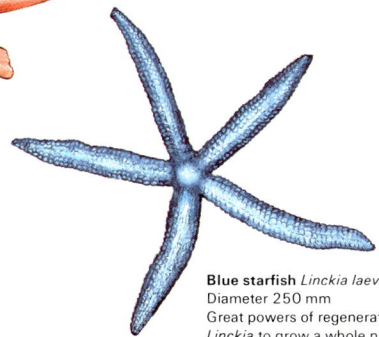

Blue starfish *Linckia laevigata*
Diameter 250 mm
Great powers of regeneration allow
Linckia to grow a whole new disc and set
of arms on any severed arm

Giant clam *Tridacna*
Width up to 350 mm. A pair of shells from
the largest of all giant clams, *Tridacna gigas*,
exhibited at the Australian Museum
in Sydney, weighs over 220 kg

Honeycomb coral *Favites*
Colonies of honeycomb coral, up to 300 mm across,
grow on reef fronts and flats. Individual corallites
are about 15 mm wide

Birds of ocean and shore

Australia's extensive coastline is made up of many natural habitats—from rocky cliffs to tropical forests. Each habitat is the home of a great variety of birds. The 75 species illustrated on the following pages are the ones most commonly seen near the coast, although there are also occasional casual visitors and rarer species. The birds are all illustrated in their usual adult plumage, but there are sometimes slight differences between the sexes, and between adult and immature birds. The drawings are not all in proportion to one another, but an average length is given for each bird.

Sooty tern
Sterna fuscata
Length 460 mm,
wing-span 920 mm

Common tern
Sterna hirundo
Length 305-380 mm

Crested tern
Sterna bergii
Length 460 mm,
wing-span 1020 mm

Caspian tern
Hydroprogne caspia
Length 560 mm,
wing-span 1400 mm

Fairy tern
Sterna nereis
Length 215-265 mm,
wing-span 455-510 mm

Little tern
Sterna albifrons
Length 205-255 mm,
wing-span 445-495 mm

Roseate tern
Sterna dougallii
Length 360 mm,
wing-span 630 mm

White-fronted tern
Sterna striata
Length 420 mm,
wing-span 760 mm

Gull-billed tern
Gelochelidon nilotica
Length 355-430 mm

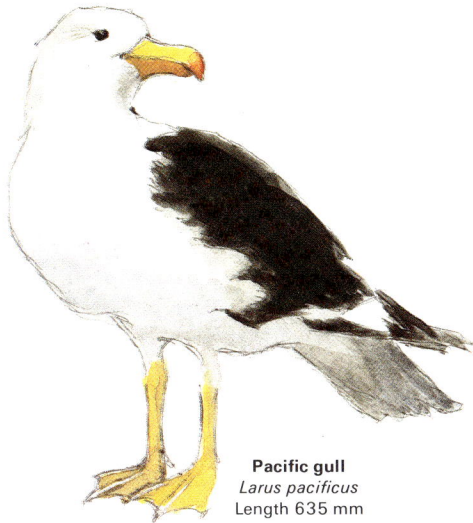

Pacific gull
Larus pacificus
Length 635 mm

Silver gull
Larus novaehollandiae
Length 400 425 mm

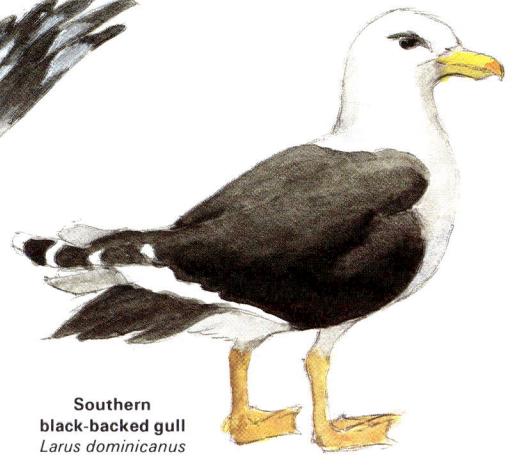

**Southern
black-backed gull**
Larus dominicanus
Length 570 mm

Sacred kingfisher
Halcyon sancta
Length 190-230 mm

Grey-tailed tattler
Tringa brevipes
Length 270 mm

Ruddy turnstone
Arenaria interpres
Length 230 mm

White-capped noddy
Anous minutus
Length 360 mm,
wing-span 650 mm

Mangrove kingfisher
Halcyon chloris
Length 250 280 mm

Banded stilt
Cladorhynchus leucocephalus
Length 380-410 mm

Common noddy
Anous stolidus
Length 400 mm,
wing-span 800 mm

Pied stilt
Himantopus himantopus
Length 385 mm

Beach stone curlew
Burhinus neglectus
Length 530-570 mm

Whimbrel
Numenius phaeopus
Length 400-460 mm

White-necked heron
Ardea pacifica
Length 910 mm

White-faced heron
Ardea novaehollandiae
Length 670 mm

Royal spoonbill
Platalea regia
Length 750 mm

White ibis
Threskiornis molucca
Length 700 mm

Little black cormorant
Phalacrocorax sulcirostris
Length 610 mm

Black cormorant
Phalacrocorax carbo
Length 800 mm

Mangrove heron
Butorides striatus
Length 480 mm

Pied cormorant
Phalacrocorax varius
Length 760 mm

Little pied cormorant
Phalacrocorax melanoleucos
Length 610 mm

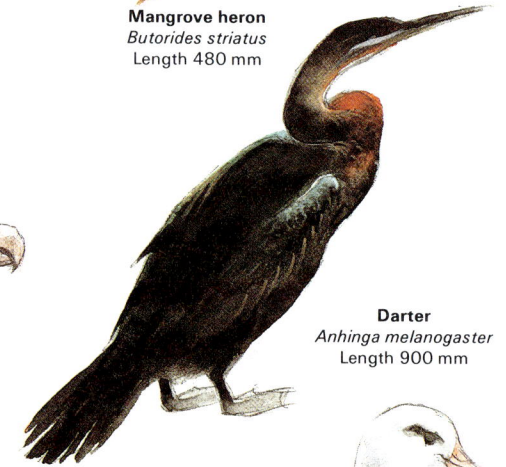

Darter
Anhinga melanogaster
Length 900 mm

Black-faced cormorant
Phalacrocorax fuscescens
Length 650 mm

Wandering albatross
Diomedea exulans
Length up to 1350 mm,
wing-span to 3250 mm

Black-browed albatross
Diomedea melanophrys
Length 880 mm,
wing-span 2200 mm

Little egret
Egretta garzetta
Length 560 mm

Brown booby
Sula leucogaster
Length 740 mm

Large egret
Egretta alba
Length 830 mm

Sooty oystercatcher
Haematopus fuliginosus
Length 480 mm,
female usually larger
than male

Australian pelican
Pelecanus conspicillatus
Length 1600-1800 mm

Pied oystercatcher
Haematopus ostralegus
Length 480 mm,
female usually
larger than male

Swamp hen
Porphyrio porphyrio
Length 440-480 mm

Southern giant petrel
Macronectes giganteus
Length 900 mm, male
larger than female

Great skua
Stercorarius skua
Length up to 630 mm,
wing-span up to 900 mm.
Female larger than male

Australasian gannet
Morus serrator
Length 875 mm

Northern giant petrel
Macronectes halli
Length 900 mm,
male larger than female

Black swan
Cygnus atratus
Length 1200-1300 mm,
male larger than female

Bar-tailed godwit
Limosa lapponica
Length 380-430 mm,
female larger than male

Eastern curlew
Numenius madagascariensis
Length 650 mm

Reef heron
Egretta sacra
Length 600-750 mm

Black-tailed godwit
Limosa limosa
Length 380 mm,
female larger than male

Red-necked avocet
*Recurvirostra
novaehollandiae*
Length 440 mm

Greenshank
Tringa nebularia
Length 340-360 mm

Knot
Calidris canutus
Length 250 mm

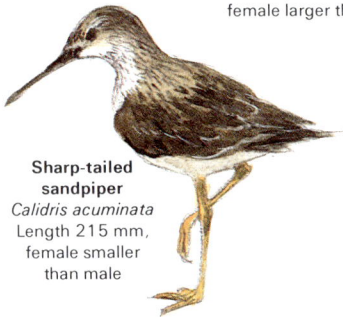

**Sharp-tailed
sandpiper**
Calidris acuminata
Length 215 mm,
female smaller
than male

Curlew sandpiper
Calidris ferruginea
Length 210 mm

Large-billed dotterel
Charadrius leschenaultii
Length 225 mm

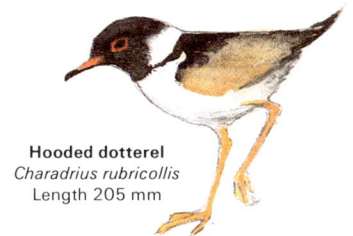

Hooded dotterel
Charadrius rubricollis
Length 205 mm

Terek sandpiper
Tringa terek
Length 240-290 mm

Mongolian dotterel
Charadrius mongolus
Length 200 mm

Double-banded dotterel
Charadrius bicinctus
Length 180 mm

Red-capped dotterel
Charadrius ruficapillus
Length 150 mm

Brahminy kite
Haliastur indus
Length 450-510 mm

White-breasted sea eagle
Haliaeetus leucogaster
Length of female 840 mm,
male 760 mm

Osprey
Pandion haliaetus
Length 500-630 mm

Grey plover
Pluvialis squatarola
Length 290 mm

Little penguin
Eudyptula minor
Length 330 mm
standing

Red-necked stint
Calidris ruficollis
Length 150 mm

Eastern golden plover
Pluvialis dominica
Length 250 mm

Black duck
Anas superciliosa
Length 470-610 mm,
male larger than female

Fluttering shearwater
Puffinus gavia
Length 330 mm

Fairy prion
Pachyptila turtur
Length 230 mm

Short-tailed shearwater
Puffinus tenuirostris
Length 400 mm

Flesh-footed shearwater
Puffinus carneipes
Length 450 mm

Wedge-tailed shearwater
Puffinus pacificus
Length 430 mm

PART 2

The ocean and the weather

The sea, even at its most placid, is the ruler of coasts. It draws its own boundaries. It determines the nature and extent of shoreline life.

Often its action moulds land margins and nearshore contours, prescribing what human activities a coast will support. Yet the sea is never its own master.

Global forces direct its movements, and atmospheric conditions dictate its moods. The ocean must do the bidding of winds.

And it can be made an agent of awesome destructiveness.

Science has achieved a broad understanding of weather systems and the sea's responses to them.

Vast current circulations can be charted and surface disturbances tracked.

But the complexity of coastal effects, in fair weather or foul, remains endlessly fascinating. Waves and shore formations, interacting, give each locality its own rules of water and sand movement.

Those rules can change—sometimes forever. People are learning, usually from costly errors, that coasts are dynamic environments.

They cannot conform with human notions of stability.

Winter winds whip spray from the crests of a choppy sea

Ocean currents How warm water can flow on a cold coast

Gentle currents in the world's great oceans represent massive movements of water. They carry chilled polar seas towards the equator, and they shift warm water far from the tropics. Near a coast, they are more important than the local climate in determining water temperature and the range of marine life.

Major currents have their origins in the push of prevailing winds. The steadiest winds—from the east near the equator and from the west in high latitudes—are deflected by the earth's rotation so that they circulate. Currents follow the same pattern of circulation—counter-clockwise in the Southern Hemisphere and clockwise in the Northern Hemisphere. Incidental winds may produce surface flows in other directions, but the basic pattern is constant.

Only northern Australia, shielded by islands, is not subject to currents flowing on an oceanic scale. The rest of the coast lies between the vast circulation systems of the South Indian, Southern and South Pacific Oceans.

Australia differs from all other continents in having no cold surface current on its west coast. A cold current does run consistently northward in the depths, but the central-west coast has two warm currents on the surface at different times of the year. Between October and April, anti-cyclones passing to the south push warm surface water up the coast from the Great Australian Bight at 1-2 km/h. From May to September, when anti-cyclones cross farther to the north, they push warm water from the Timor Sea to the Bight, usually at less than 1 km/h.

In the Southern Ocean the currents, forced by westerly winds, move generally eastward along the South Australian and Tasmanian coasts, but they are not constant. The water at any point may flow in any direction, usually at less than 1 km/h but often more rapidly in Bass Strait.

The East Australian current is really a series of eddies from a westward tropical flow which

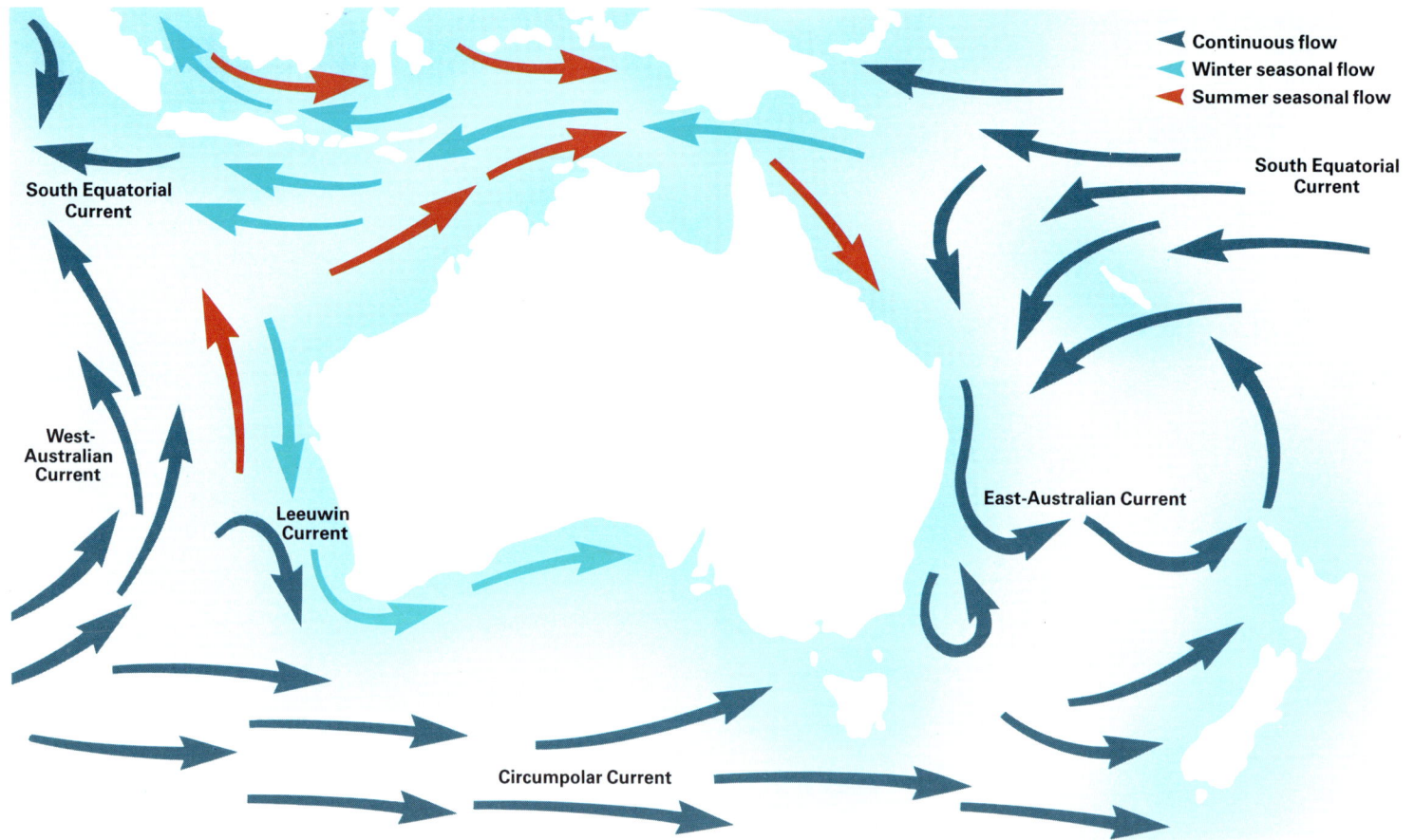

Legend:
- Continuous flow
- Winter seasonal flow
- Summer seasonal flow

South Equatorial Current

South Equatorial Current

West-Australian Current

Leeuwin Current

East-Australian Current

Circumpolar Current

Australia is bounded on three sides by large oceans; as a result much of the coast is affected by large, oceanic scale movements of water. In northern Australia, currents change direction in response to the annual monsoon winds.

Different fish for different water

FISH are called 'cold-blooded' but their body heat closely matches that of the surrounding water and varies with it. Each species has its own range of tolerance; at too high or too low a temperature, it may stop breeding or eating.

Fish and other creatures capable of moving can stay within their safe temperature range by travelling as seasons change. Many species, for example sharks and squid, migrate to warmer waters, and others simply change depth. Within the survival range of temperatures, fish have a narrower range at which they exhibit certain patterns of behaviour. Southern bluefin tuna, for example, feed alone in water below 16.7°C. Above 20° they move in schools but do not bite well. Only between these two temperatures are large quantities caught.

Under 16.7°C	16.7 to 20°C	Over 20°C

Exploring the currents from space

Buoys fitted with radio beacons have been set adrift off eastern Australia since the early 1970s. Their movements have been monitored by space satellites and charted by the Commonwealth Scientific and Industrial Research Organisation.

In 1979, as part of a much bigger international global atmosphere research programme, nearly 300 buoys carrying instrument packages were released in Southern Hemisphere oceans. Three satellites, Tiros-N and NOAA from the USA, and Argos from France, pick up transmissions. Their information, along with shipboard measurements, is expected to add much to the understanding of Australia's ocean currents, water temperatures and coastal weather. Other satellites, such as the US Seasat, continue and expand radar and microwave experiments that were begun with the Landsat and Skylab satellites. Seasat is presently testing an all-weather system of monitoring major currents, ice movements, sea conditions and fish productivity.

Satellite scanning of surface heat radiation can produce images, similar to photographs, known as thermal maps. Around the Australian coast they show the persistent but seasonally shifting fronts between bodies of water of different temperature, where fish congregate to feed.

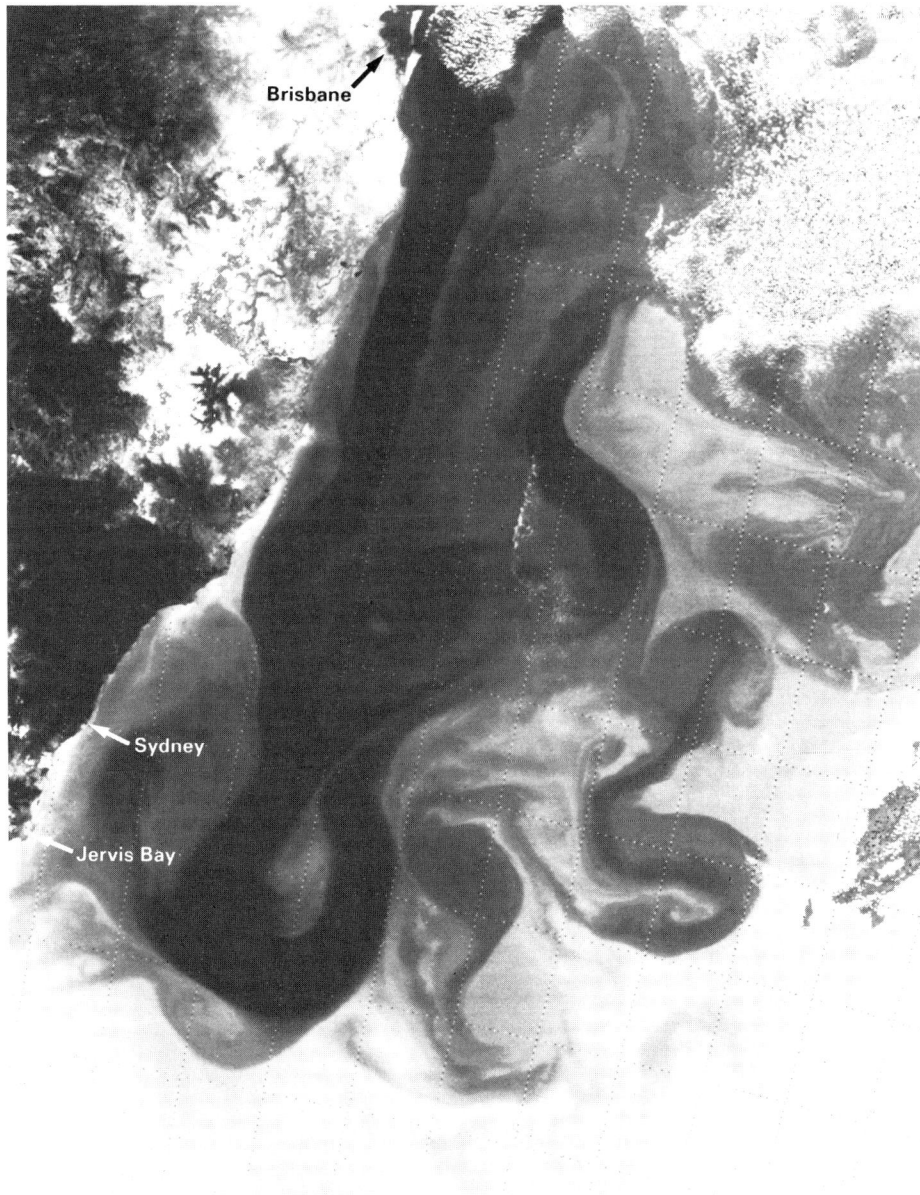

An infra-red satellite picture of the north Tasman and south Coral Seas in early December. Warm areas appear dark and cool areas light. The broad, warm East-Australian Current, flowing down the coast past Brisbane and Sydney and looping around off Jervis Bay, is very prominent

splits north-west towards Torres Strait and southward along the Great Barrier Reef. Inside the reef, circulation patterns are confused. The southward flow is strongest and most constant from outside the reef opposite Townsville, Qld, to Coffs Harbour, NSW. There it forms a belt 30-100 km wide and reaches speeds of 2-4 km/h in summer. Farther south the flow is less consistent and normal speeds are about 1.5 km/h in summer and 1 km/h in winter.

In northern Australia, currents are slow-moving and they change direction in response to the annual monsoon winds. Close to the north-west coast, the current flows predominantly north-east to east in winter, and north in summer. In Torres Strait the current flows eastward from December to March—when it is driven by the monsoons blowing from the north-west, and westward for the rest of the year.

The greatest temperature variation in Australian waters occurs off the mid-latitude Pacific coast, from central Queensland to central New South Wales. There the ocean currents shift most, and the origins of water masses change with the seasons. The temperature in a current can quite often vary as much as 3°C from that of the surrounding seas.

The surface of the sea also warms and cools with changes in air temperature, but not nearly as much as land surfaces. The sea is scarcely affected by day-and-night contrasts, and lags in its response to summer or winter extremes. It is usually warmest in February and coldest in August, with a year-round range in one place of only about 10°C.

Deeper in the ocean, temperatures vary little and the water is always cold. Shifts of current or strong winds blowing persistently from the shore can drive warm surface water out to sea, to be replaced by an upwelling of cold water. Upwelling from the continental shelf occurs within 15 km of the central east coast between July and December. It increases the concentration of dissolved nitrates and phosphates that nourish marine organisms. In extreme cases, the surface bloom of algae can be so profuse that the sea takes on a red tinge.

The richest concentrations of nutrients occur at the boundaries between bodies of water of different temperature. So fish—whether their diet is marine organisms or other species of fish—head for the margins of currents. They find them by aligning themselves to the flow of the current and adapting to its speed, or even by using visual markers such as the sun. Eggs and larvae drift passively with a current until they reach its edge.

Fishermen can sometimes spot a front of contrasting temperature as choppy water—caused by conflicting currents—or as a line of litter or scum. Often a change of colour can be seen. Another clue may be sea birds flocking to feed. But commercial fishing boats are increasingly equipped with instruments to detect changes in water temperature at a distance. Others follow courses plotted from thermal maps—aerial or satellite 'pictures' of the heat radiated from different bodies of water.

The tides Intricate rhythms of ocean advance and retreat

High tide comes twice a day to some parts of the Australian coast and only once to others. Even where two tides a day are usual, they may arrive at uneven intervals and reach markedly different levels. The height of the tide also differs widely on different parts of the coast. In the north-west the water level sometimes rises and falls by as much as 12 metres, changing the look of the coast beyond recognition in an hour or two. Yet along the coast south of Perth the tidal range is sometimes negligible.

The diversity of Australian tides is partly accounted for by the fact that each of the oceans and semi-enclosed seas around the continent has its own tidal system. Where systems meet, the tidal forces combine in some places and cancel each other out in others.

All the tidal systems have their origins in the gravitational pulls of the Moon and the Sun. The waters of the oceans are drawn towards the point of the Earth's surface nearest the Sun or the Moon so that they bulge outwards. This ocean bulging is slight, but if the world were a smooth sphere and covered to an even depth by water the bulges could be depicted as low waves, half as long as the world's circumference, moving continuously round the globe in company with the Moon and the Sun.

In practice, tides do not cross entire oceans but are trapped in ocean basins of irregular shape and depth, and they rock around one or more points in mid-ocean. Because the Earth is rotating beneath them, they take apparently curving courses, rebounding from coasts sideways so that they progress around the rims of ocean basins. They cannot match the speed at which the Moon orbits around the Earth. That is why the highest tides come just after new or full Moon.

Tidal waves rebounding from land masses run

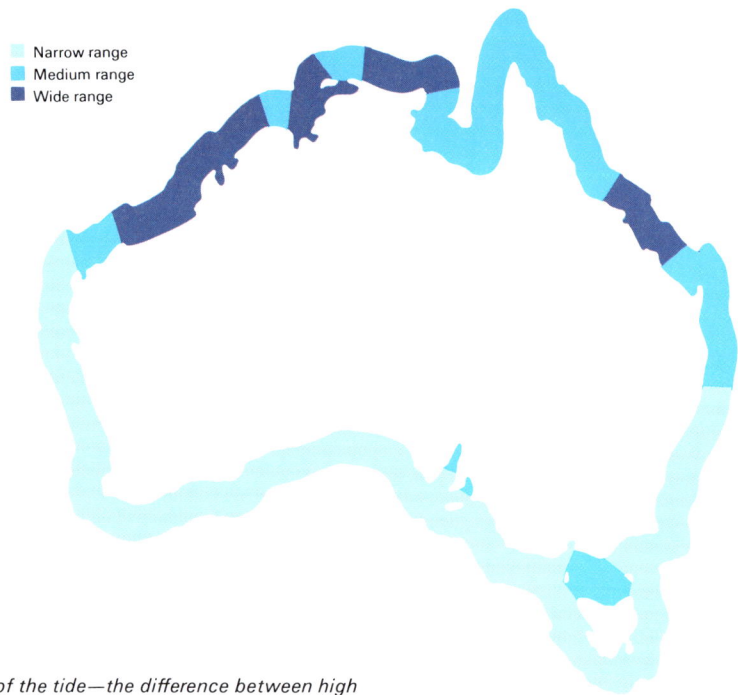

Narrow range
Medium range
Wide range

The range of the tide—the difference between high water and low water—around the Australian coast varies from 600 mm in the south-west to more than 12 metres in the north-west of the continent

into one another. If they meet head-on and their wave motions match, they form 'standing waves' of constantly high water. Those waves are extremely long and low compared with the waves kicked up by winds at sea.

When a tidal wave travels in over a continental shelf, it shoals—slows and steepens—in much the same way as an ordinary wind-wave reaching a beach. The more extensive the shelf, the

steeper the tidal wave when it reaches the coast. But even after steepening, tidal waves are low in relation to the slope of most beaches. So they usually rebound without breaking.

If a tidal wave carries on into an estuary or a river mouth, it continues to shoal. In extreme cases it may oversteepen and break, picking up speed and moving up the river as a wall of surf called a tidal bore. Bores have been reported

How the oceans are pulled out of shape

THE MOON's gravitational pull reduces the weight of anything on the part of the Earth's surface facing it by a mere 0.0000001 per cent, or 1 gram in 10 tonnes. The Sun, because it is so far away, exerts only about half that

pull. But each of these gravitational forces causes the oceans to bulge slightly towards it. The Earth's rotation produces a balancing force and on the opposite side of the planet the oceans bulge away from the direction of

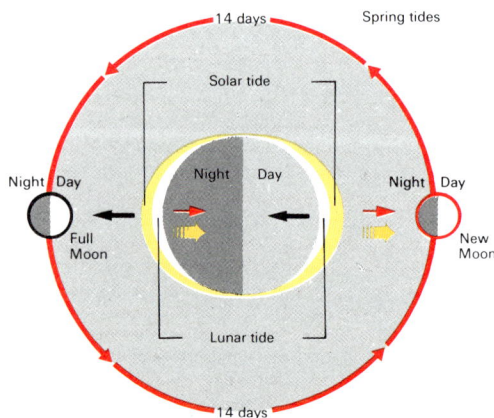

Spring tides

14 days
Solar tide
Night | Day
Night | Day
Full Moon
Night | Day
New Moon
Lunar tide
14 days

Tides are formed as ocean waters bulge towards the gravitational pulls of the Sun and the Moon. The Earth's rotation causes a balancing bulge on the opposite side. When Moon and Sun are in line their pulls combine to produce the greatest tidal bulge and spring tides result. The lowest tides, neap tides, occur when Moon and Sun are at right angles to each other

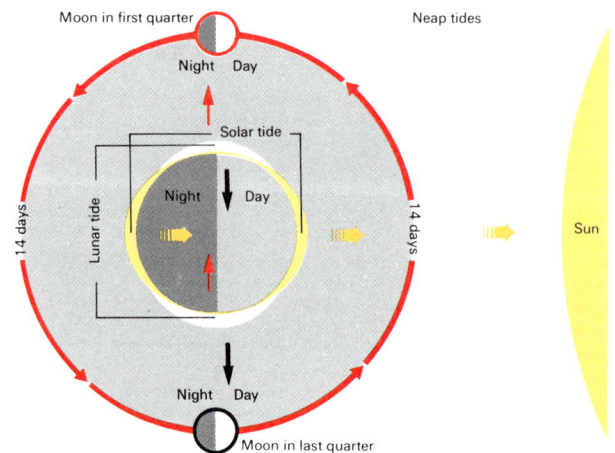

Moon in first quarter
Neap tides
Night | Day
Solar tide
Night | Day
Lunar tide
14 days
14 days
Night | Day
Moon in last quarter
Sun

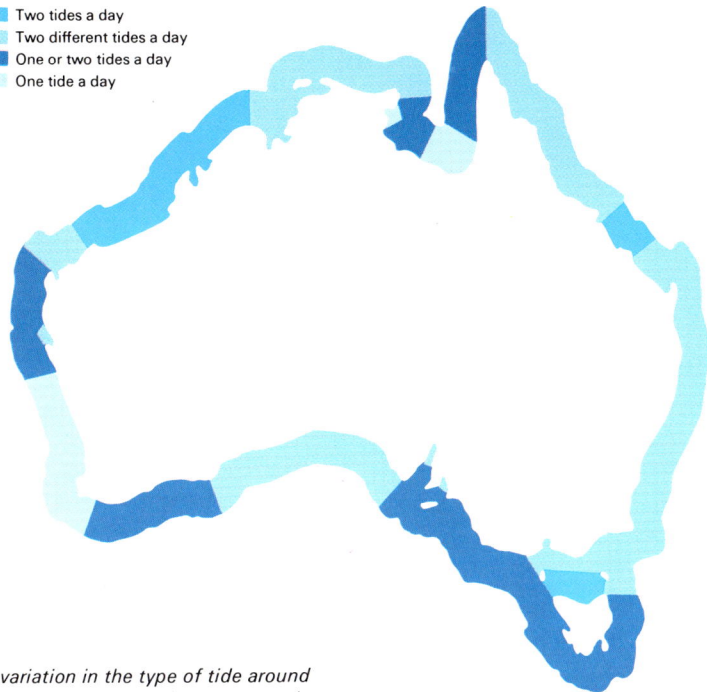

Key:
- Two tides a day
- Two different tides a day
- One or two tides a day
- One tide a day

There is wide variation in the type of tide around Australia. Little of the coast receives two equal tides daily. The part of the south-west that has only one tide a day is also a region of low tide range

more than 80 km upstream in the Victoria River, 300 km south of Darwin.

Shoaling over a broad continental shelf causes a tide to rise quickly but ebb more slowly. It also increases the difference between high and low water levels. This tidal range is generally greatest on a broad continental shelf or in a wide-mouthed bay or gulf where the inner shores confine the rising tide and amplify it. In a wide

bay with a narrow entrance, such as Port Phillip Bay in Victoria, the tidal range is reduced because the flow in and out is restricted.

Only one high tide a day reaches the shore on the Western Australian coast from Geraldton south, and in corners of the Gulf of Carpentaria. Many other parts of coastal Australia, including the stretch between Melbourne and Adelaide, receive a mixture of daily and twice-daily tides.

Why tides bend

ANYTHING moving on the Earth or in its atmosphere, except along the Equator, is subject to a constant force, called Coriolus deflection, which pulls the moving body off a straight path. Caused by the earth's spinning, the pull is always to the left in the Southern Hemisphere and to the right in the Northern Hemisphere.

Friction is usually too great for the deflection to have any effect on movement over land. But if there is little or no friction, as with air and water movements, the moving body goes on a curving course. Free of any interference, it will travel in circles. If there were no coast, tides would swing in the direction of Coriolus deflection, as do all winds, except cyclones. Southern Hemisphere tides, continually bent leftward, would circulate anticlockwise, like bath water spiralling toward a plug hole. But interference by the coast is great. The tide rebounds from a shore and the leftward deflection sends it farther along the same coast, so that its progress is to the right of its original direction—clockwise in the Southern Hemisphere.

The times and levels of tides are predicted in the national tide tables, which are drawn up by the Royal Australian Navy's hydrographic office. They predict low and high water for each day of the year at 66 primary ports.

The tables also list variations for 352 secondary ports which have tidal characteristics related to a primary port. There are additional data from which to calculate levels at times between high and low water, and information on tidal currents.

The tide at any particular time and place may, however, be markedly different from the prediction in the tables. The calculations cannot allow for short-term local weather forces such as wind or atmospheric pressure.

---

the gravitational force. The oceans bulge most when the Sun, Moon and Earth are in line, at new Moon and full Moon. Then the gravitational effects of Sun and Moon are combined in the same direction. Soon afterwards, coasts receive spring tides—so called not because of the time of year but because of the way they jump up. The range between low and high water levels is up to 20 per cent greater than average.

When the Moon and Sun are at right-angles in relation to the Earth, at the first and third quarters of the Moon, each counteracts the other's effect. Ocean bulging is spread around the globe instead of being concentrated on two sides. The tides that result have a range of about 20 per cent less than average. They are called neap tides, from an Old English word which probably meant 'weak'.

The Moon exerts its strongest pull at any point every 24 hours 50.5 minutes, and its tidal effects on the open ocean occur twice in this period—when the point is nearest the Moon, and when the two are on opposite sides of the Earth.

Meanwhile, the Sun exerts its pull every 24 hours at any point, and its tidal effects at sea occur every 12 hours. Therefore after the Moon's and Sun's effects have

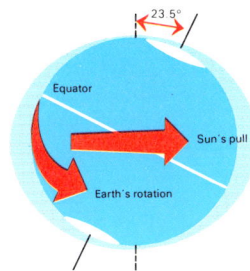

Tidal bulges of southern winter

The height of successive tides varies as the year progresses, because tidal bulges caused by the Sun's pull and the Earth's rotation change position on the Earth's surface. Like the seasons, the bulges move north and south, because the Earth's axis is tilted at 23.5° to its plane of orbit

coincided, at new and full Moon, there is a delay between solar and lunar influences, increasing by 25.25 minutes each time they occur.

The gap widens for seven days, with tides becoming correspondingly weaker, then starts to close again because the Moon's twice-daily effects catch up with those of the Sun. Tide heights go through a 14-day cycle of increase and decrease, twice every lunar month.

Heights of tides are further varied day by day because

the Moon's plane of orbit is tilted in relation to the Earth's axis of rotation, and because the Earth's axis is tilted in relation to the plane of its orbit around the Sun. A point on the Earth's surface passes through slightly different parts of the lunar and solar bulges in the oceans each time the Earth revolves. The Sun's maximum influence occurs when it is overhead at the Equator, so the highest tides of all come at the equinoxes, in late March and September.

Other slight variations in tide height occur because the Moon's orbit wavers, and because both it and the Earth's orbit are not circular but elliptical. The Moon repeats exactly the same orbit only every 18.6 years, although it swings in from farthest to its nearest point—a difference of 24 000 km—and out again every 27.55 days. The Sun is closest, exerting its greatest pull, in early January. Early in July it is about 5.5 million km farther away.

Friction is generated between the tides and the ocean beds and it is slowing the Earth's rotation by about a second every 120 000 years. Before land masses and oceans formed, the world probably rotated quickly so that days may have been less than 10 hours long and there may have been 1000 to the year.

Waves and their patterns
How the ocean carries wind energy to the coast

Ocean waves, arriving in never-ending procession, suggest to the eye that the sea is travelling with them. It seldom is. Apart from the slow movement of currents, the water beyond a coastal shelf virtually stays in the same place, rotating under the waves and rising and falling with them.

Some wave energy comes from tidal movement, and occasionally from disturbances such as coastal landslides or undersea earthquakes. But nearly all waves seen around the coast have been generated by winds transferring energy to the water surface.

The highest waves normally seen approaching a coast are driven by local storms. Sailors and weather forecasters call them 'seas'. Beneath them there is a smoother, more regular 'swell', born of faraway, long-ago gales. Their energy may have crossed an entire ocean.

Because winds seldom maintain exactly the same direction and strength for more than a few seconds, the waves they generate are confused and choppy at first. They have sharp individual peaks, and the intervals between successive peaks vary. Once waves move away from the influence of the wind, however, they settle into the regular patterns of ocean swell. They fan out about 35° on each side of the direction of the wind and take curving courses across the sea.

Eventually they form groups of long, low waves travelling at matching speeds. The group's width is that of the storm front generating the waves, and its length is determined by the location and duration of the storm.

Wave groups tend to generate long period waves. At the coast this long wave is often reflected seawards, and waves are higher or lower in relation to the shoreline depending on whether they arrive on the crest or in the trough of the long wave. Waves at the crest of groups are larger than those between groups, and the length of the group determines the number of waves between crests. The myth of the 7th or 9th wave being larger arises from local observation and may be correct for many days of the year—but it is only relevant to fully developed seas; developing seas are almost random.

Each wave in a swell pattern is evenly shaped. Smoothly curved crests are centred between troughs, with each crest as high above normal sea level as the following trough is below it. Water particles rotate under each wind-generated wave to a depth equal to about half the distance between successive crests. As the water shallows, the waves slow and bunch up. They steepen at the front and their crests mount to a peak.

Whether a wave breaks or not depends on its steepness in relation to the shore slope. Ocean swell waves and wind-driven local seas generally break if the slope is no steeper than 1:10. A gradual run-in gives them the distance needed to increase their height and angle of tilt. Where the sea meets a smooth cliff face, unstable local storm waves explode against it in showers of spray, but swell waves do not—unless they have already shoaled on a shelf at the cliff base.

The most consistent and easily observable result of wave action is beach drift. Waves rarely come in at right-angles to the shoreline: usually they carry sand, shingle and other debris obliquely up a beach. But when the water runs back, it takes the shortest way down. So successive waves shunt sand along in a series of zigzags.

More debris is drawn along, below the waterline, in a current set up by the thrust of the angled waves after they break. The combined effect is a gradual, massive shift of sediment. If, over the years, waves arrive predominantly from the same direction, sand accumulates at one end of the beach, and may form a spit jutting out into the sea, or a tombolo linking the mainland shore with a nearby island.

Waves generally break when their height is slightly less than the depth of water under them, and isolated early breakers indicate a submerged reef. A line of breakers curving in towards both ends of a beach shows that the sea bed is raised in the middle; if the breaker line fans the other way, there is shallower water at the ends. Interrupted lines indicate variations in depth.

In general, the greater the distance over which waves are affected by a shallowing sea bed, the more they slow and bunch up and the higher they

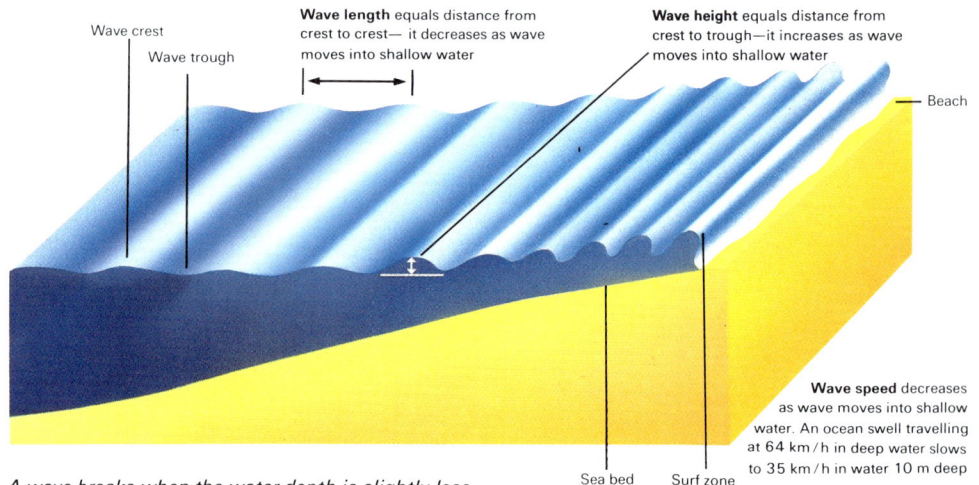

Wave crest

Wave trough

Wave length equals distance from crest to crest— it decreases as wave moves into shallow water

Wave height equals distance from crest to trough—it increases as wave moves into shallow water

Beach

Wave speed decreases as wave moves into shallow water. An ocean swell travelling at 64 km/h in deep water slows to 35 km/h in water 10 m deep

Sea bed

Surf zone

A wave breaks when the water depth is slightly less than its height. When waves enter shallow water successive crests catch up with one another, they slow down and grow taller until eventually they become unstable, topple over, and break

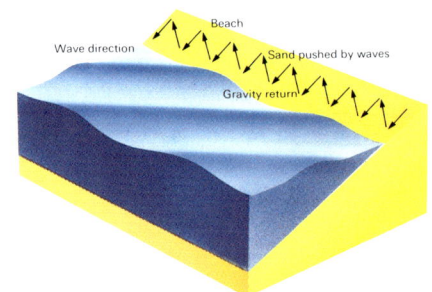

Beach

Wave direction

Sand pushed by waves

Gravity return

Incoming waves sweep water and sand up a beach at an oblique angle. Gravity pulls the same material down to the waterline again. In this fashion waves transport sand along beaches. This movement may be reversed when waves come from another direction, but over many years waves arriving from one principal direction can shift millions of tonnes of sand along an entire coast

Constant movement of sand in one direction can form a barrier that turns an inlet into a lagoon, or build a tombolo like that at Sydney's Palm Beach

How waves are bent

A WAVE slows only where the water particles rotating under it encounter friction with the sea floor. Elsewhere along the wave, in deeper water, its forward momentum is unchanged. So the wave bends around the point of interference—it is refracted. By the time all parts of a wave have reached shoaling depth, it may have been shaped into a curve almost matching that of the shoreline.

If a wave has no time to adapt fully and comes in at an angle, and if the beach is steep, it may rebound without breaking. Then it will be refracted further on its way out. It may even loop back, and in this fashion progress along the shore.

The refraction of waves around headlands into bays has a particularly noticeable effect on beaches. The bunching of waves just inside a headland concentrates their energy there. The surf is not high but the volume of water is. Farther up the bay, the waves are stretched—their energy and water volume are dispersed. The inequality creates a strong longshore flow, keeping sand out of the corner of the bay and depositing it in increasing amounts towards the other end.

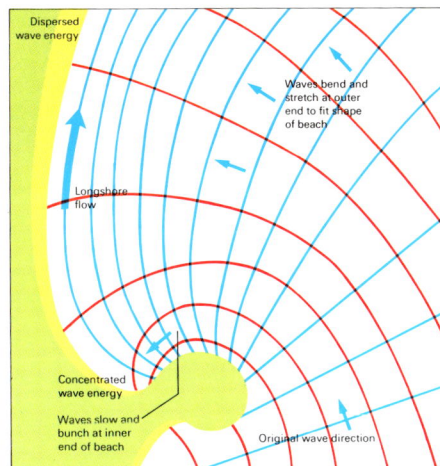

Above: A simplified headland refraction pattern, with red lines showing how wave energy is diverted to generate a longshore flow of water and sand. Left: Intricate refractions around a headland and islands at Batehaven, NSW

rise. Once this starts, all waves travel at the same speed over the same depth of water—regardless of their earlier velocity.

The tallest waves ordinarily seen on a coast, driven by gales in the immediate area, may break from heights of 20 metres or more. They may arrive twice as frequently as ocean swell waves, and be immensely destructive. But they travel no faster. And the harder a wind blows, the higher they mount. A wind averaging 37 km/h, blowing in a consistent direction for 10 hours, could be expected to produce waves about 2.44 metres high.

Even in violent and far-reaching gales, waves rarely exceed 25 metres on the deep ocean. If they are pushed to a height of more than one-seventh of their length, their surface tension is destroyed and they disintegrate in spray. There are exceptions, and the tallest ocean wave for which there is good evidence was observed from a US Navy tanker in the North Pacific in 1933, during a 125 km/h gale. It was judged to be 34 metres from trough to crest.

The length of a wave moving in a group does not have to be measured: it can be calculated from the time between the passage of one wave and the next. If a wave is followed 10 seconds later by another, it is about 157 metres long.

In ocean swell waves, the time interval can also be used to calculate velocity. So waves 10 seconds apart are travelling at about 16 metres per second, or 57 km/h. Wind-driven waves may hold together at more than 80 km/h, but do not normally exceed 60 km/h.

When any wave is crossing water of a depth less than half of the wave length, its speed is governed by water depth alone: a depth of 3 metres permits a speed of 20 km/h, but at six times the depth—18 metres—a wave cannot travel much more than twice as fast.

Mysterious patterns on the beach

No complete explanation for beach cusps has yet been found. They are probably the result of complex wave motions caused by the interaction of reflected and incoming waves. Cusp formations on surf beaches— such as these at Pearl Beach on the New South Wales central coast—are also often associated with the presence of rip currents. The effect is a scalloped waterline, with a series of crescent-shaped depressions regularly spaced along the beach face. The scooped-out areas may be only a few metres wide; or could reach for hundreds of metres.

Shock waves that cross the ocean

VIOLENT disturbances of ocean water occur with earthquakes and volcanic eruptions in or around an ocean basin. After such an event, waves hundreds of kilometres long and up to half an hour apart race from the shock zone at speeds approaching 800 km/h. Quite commonly but, in fact, wrongly called 'tidal waves', they are known to scientists as tsunami. The name comes from the Japanese words *tsu*, meaning port, and *nami*, meaning waves.

In mid-ocean, tsunami may be only a few centimetres high, and they are often so low away from the coast that their passing may not be noticed. But even over the deepest ocean they still slow and steepen—like all waves in shallowing water. They have time to build to terrifying heights—sometimes more than 30 metres—before running ashore for minutes on end with catastrophic effects. The highest recorded tsunami, which occurred off Alaska in 1964, measured 67 metres.

The coasts most menaced by tsunami are those facing and lying parallel to an earthquake fault line. The only area of Australia threatened this way is the east coast, which is aligned with major faults under the central South Pacific and on its eastern rim. But tsunami effects are largely buffered by the land mass of New Zealand and by the Great Barrier Reef.

Nearshore currents Powerful local water movements

No two parts of the coast are exactly the same. In places that look alike at first glance, shoreline features differ subtly—and swimming or boating conditions can vary drastically. In the interplay of waves and tides with the land and the sea bottom, each area has its own complex patterns.

The simplest local movement of water—and the one that most frequently surprises inexperienced swimmers—is the longshore current. This is the force that makes it difficult for a surf bather to stay between safety flags. It runs along any shore where waves break at an angle—and waves rarely come in exactly parallel to the beach.

When angled waves break they thrust water not only in a swash up the beach, but also in a persistent flow parallel to the shore. The current is spread right across the surf zone, but it is strongest about halfway between the breaker line and the beach. Its speed, which is related to the height and steepness of waves, may be as much as 1 metre a second. Longshore currents are not hazardous, however, unless they carry a swimmer into a deep channel or a rip.

Variations in the slope of the sea bed or the shape of a shore may cause unevenness in the height of a line of waves along a beach. When they break, the water level inside the surf zone is also uneven. That results in longshore currents of a different type: they run from high levels to low, and then they turn seawards to become feeders for rip currents.

Rips are strong, narrow currents running out through the surf zone to beyond the breakers. They flow at speeds up to 4 metres a second—a boon to board surfers seeking a free ride out, but a hazard for swimmers. People caught in rips exhaust themselves if they try to swim back to the shore against such a current. Confident swimmers are better off striking out sideways: rips are seldom more than 15 metres wide.

Weaker swimmers should conserve their energy and let a rip carry them out past the breakers. There, when the current slackens, it is easy to move to one side and make for a different point on the beach. Never rest for long on a sand bar—if the wave pattern changes even slightly the bar can collapse, with disastrous results.

Rip locations are not constant, however. They may come and go, or shift position, with changes in the direction of wave approach. And they do not always run straight out to sea: if the waves break at a considerable angle to the beach, rips are angled away in the opposite direction.

Tide movements are seldom of much significance in comparison with wave-induced currents near a mainland shore. In shallow estuaries and around islands and headlands, however, the effects of tidal currents are more pronounced, and sometimes startling.

Speeds of tidal currents fluctuate with the rise and fall of the tide, and there are usually two

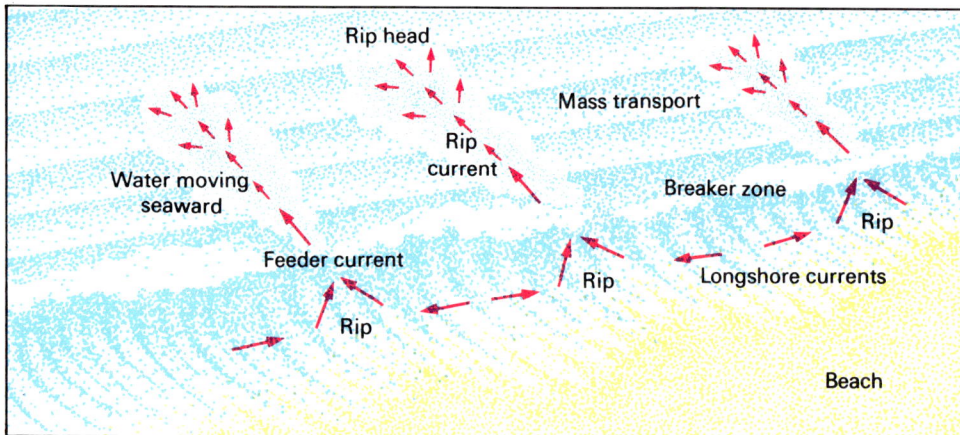

Rips are formed as the mass of water pushed up to a beach by breaking waves finds its path back to the sea in narrow, fast-flowing currents. Water runs down the beach, and sideways along the beach face, creating longshore currents which feed rips as they travel seaward through the surf zone, and between channels in any sand bars. The current dissipates beyond the breakers at the rip head

Twin, parallel rips push water seaward from Dee Why beach, north of Sydney. The two channels of deep, fast-moving water interrupt the lines of incoming waves. Plumes of sand, carried from the beach by the currents, spread out into the calm water beyond the breaker zone. Rips like these are usually less than 15 metres wide, and may be moving as fast as 4 metres per second

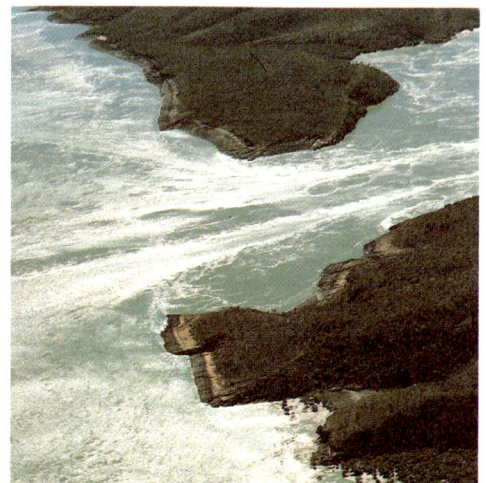

Channelled tidal races, such as this one at Walcott Inlet in the Kimberleys, WA, can reach 28 km/h

The empty threat of 'undertow'

STANDING in the shallows, you feel the seaward backwash of broken waves tugging at your feet. Just ahead of a sharply steepening wave, you may feel water being drawn backwards into it. And if a breaker dumps you, its churning motion pulls you down and away from the shore for a moment. But it is not undertow. No subsurface motion exists that can take people out to sea against the advance of waves on a beach. If the word undertow is used to describe a real danger, it is usually a mistaken reference to a localised rip, or to the existence of a channel with a strong ebb-tide current.

maximum and two minimum rates during each cycle. The currents reverse themselves so quickly that there is scarcely a moment when they are not running. In deep water their top speed is seldom more than about 1 km/h. Even in shallow water, as long as it is not confined, a tidal current rarely exceeds 7 km/h. But where tides are channelled, the currents can easily achieve twice that speed.

In areas of extreme tide range, such as north-western Australia, a channelled tidal race may reach 28 km/h. In the rocky estuaries of the Kimberleys district of Western Australia, water velocities on that scale produce tidal bores —steep-fronted, breaking waves that run far upriver. Dangerous bores, to be avoided by small boats, are usually noted in the official sailing directions for more frequented areas.

Fast tidal races also produce dangerous eddies and whirlpools. Vigorous eddies are encountered in Cambridge Gulf, the approach to the port of Wyndham, WA. There the tidal current reaches 17 km/h. Even in areas where the tide range is much less—in Sydney Harbour, for example—eddies frequently make boating tricky.

One area where tidal currents can be particularly surprising is around islands ringed by barrier reefs. However slowly the currents move in deep water at the edge of a reef, they may run over its shallow coral terraces at speeds as high as 7 km/h. When they are at their maximum speed, alternating eddies form and break away at the downstream margin of the reef.

Barrier reefs normally lie near mean sea level—the mid-tide height—and are uncovered at low tide. Often during high tide they are covered by less than 1 metre of water. For a major part of the tidal cycle, breakers carry water across the reef and keep the lagoon level above the sea level outside. So there may be a continuous flow of water out through channels in the reef, even when the tide is coming in.

Where a coral barrier is always above the water level, forming an atoll, there is no water inflow from breakers. Then the lagoon behaves like any bay with a restricted entrance: if the passage of a large lagoon is narrow, powerful tidal currents will flow through it.

Bars rebuild a beach

AFTER storm waves have left a beach, nearshore water circulation starts returning lost sand. Complex oscillations formed by rip currents and surface currents caused directly by winds blowing over the water, deposit sand in a series of half-loops, called crescentic bars, which are fully formed in about two days. They may remain static for weeks, but gradually they link up with beach cusps and the troughs between fill with sand. Eventually the bars are cut by channels. They decay, and all the sand is pushed on to the beach.

Crescentic bars about to decay and deposit their sand on to the beach at Redhead, near Newcastle, NSW

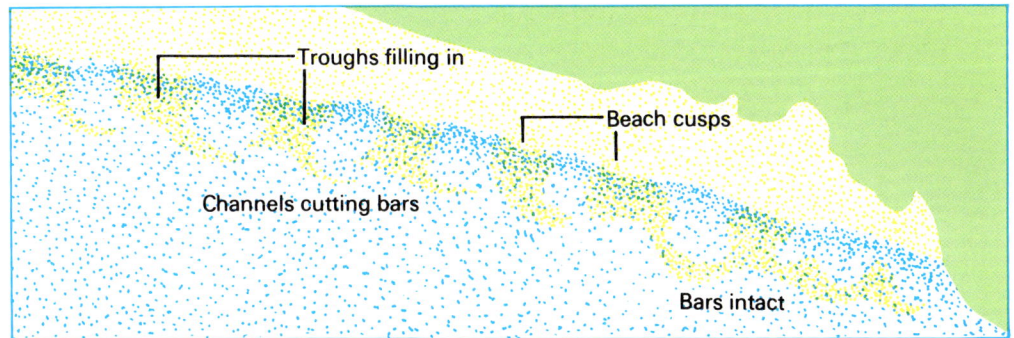

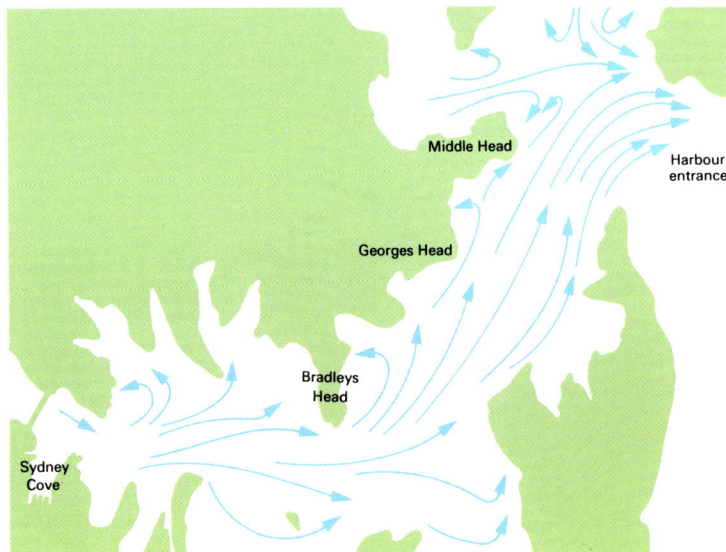

Wherever an estuary, bay or lagoon has its access to the open sea restricted by a narrow entrance channel, strong tidal currents can occur as the level within attempts to adjust to the level outside. This is most noticeable in the rocky estuaries of north-western Australia under extreme tidal ranges. But even in areas such as Sydney Harbour, where the tide range is much less, strong eddies can form, although they are much less dangerous. In this chart of the tidal pattern in Sydney Harbour at maximum ebb tide, eddies can be seen forming around Bradleys Head and Georges Head

Wind and weather patterns

The interaction of ocean and atmosphere

All weather stems from differences in air temperature and pressure. The earth's surface forms the bottom of an ocean of air, extending about 160 km above it. Although the gas molecules of the atmosphere are light, collectively they exert enormous pressure on the earth—about 10 tonnes per square metre at sea level. People are unaware of it because the pressure is not merely downwards: it is equal in all directions.

Air heated from the sun's radiation on the earth's surface expands and rises, carrying evaporated moisture if it is over an ocean. Expansion reduces its pressure, and this loss of pressure—not the height to which the air rises—causes it to cool and contract. Moisture condenses in clouds of water droplets. As contraction goes on the air sinks, and its increasing pressure raises its temperature again.

The sun's radiation promotes permanent convection systems which carry air from equatorial to subtropical regions at high level, and back to the equator at low level. This creates belts of sinking, high pressure air in both hemispheres, centred about latitude 30° but shifting with the seasonal track of the sun, and constant north-east or south-east 'trade' winds. There are further convection systems between the subtropical belt and the polar regions, causing strong airstreams from the west above latitude 40°.

Locally, however, the sun's effect is intermittent, especially over land. So the result is patchy: neighbouring bodies of air behave in contrasting ways. Sinking air creating a warm, calm, pressurised 'high' may be followed in a day or two by a cold, stormy, depressed 'low' of rising air. Moving pressure systems maintain their contrasts for days because of the time air takes to rise—to 15 000 metres above sea level—and sink again.

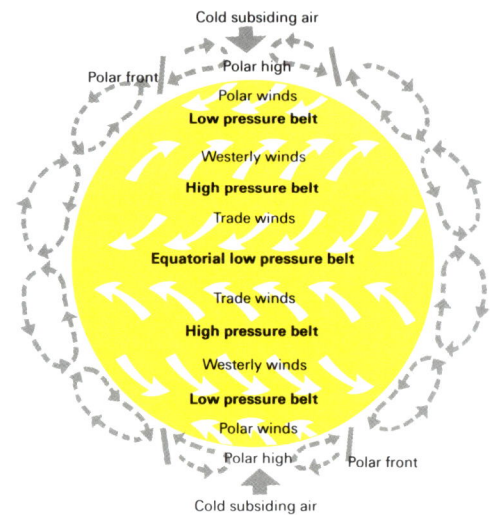

Surface winds and vertical convection systems create the basic pattern of global air movements

Prevailing winds are evidence of the movement of air of different origin, temperature and moisture in vast, consistent patterns. They play a big part in determining the basic climate of a coast. But its day-to-day weather is more noticeably affected by incidental, ever-changing winds created by a local unevenness of air pressure.

The air seeks to equalise pressure by flowing from a high to a low, but it cannot do so directly. The earth's rotation bends the airstream into an almost circular curve. Winds spiral gently out from a high until they are close to a low. Then they spiral in towards it much more rapidly.

At the same time, both the high and the low are moving. The distance between them may be changing, and each of them may also be changing in shape and intensity. So the direction and force of the winds they produce are highly variable in any one place. They can be forecast only by trying to predict exactly where the pressure systems will go and how they may by modified.

Winds around highs and lows spiral in opposite directions. In the Southern Hemisphere their motions are counter-clockwise around a high and clockwise around a low. High-pressure wind circulations are called anticyclones, and all low-pressure systems are technically cyclones. But those originating outside the tropics are normally termed depressions.

Subtropical anticyclones, separated by troughs of low pressure, move fairly regularly across Australia in a generally eastward direction. They are particularly well defined because they have formed from air sinking on to the flat surface of the Indian Ocean, and few mountains disturb them as they pass over the continent.

The anticyclone belt, shifting seasonally, is centred in late winter from around Geraldton, WA, to Cape Byron, NSW, and in late summer across northern Tasmania. On average, five individual highs occur every month, and each takes about five days to cross the continent. But at any particular time, a high may be almost stationary, or it may be travelling at more than 2000 km a day. The movement of one body of air is largely governed by the position of others.

Between highs and troughs there are frequently sharply defined boundaries—'cold

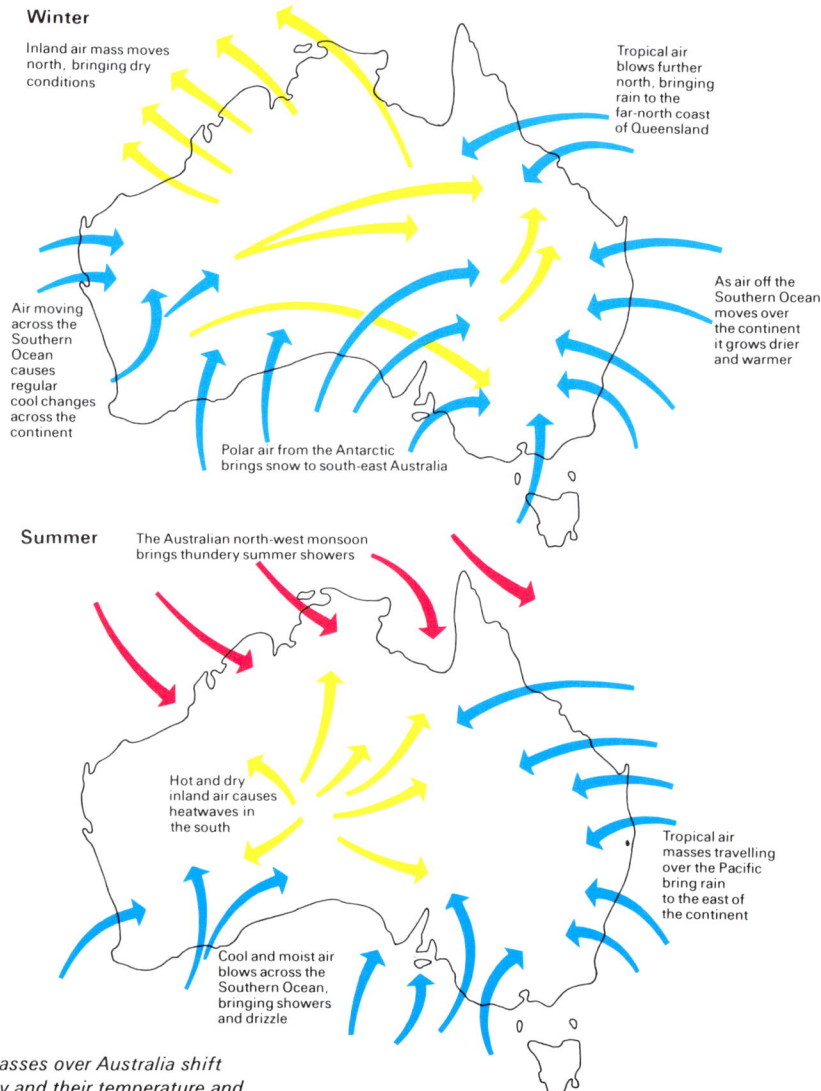

Winter

Inland air mass moves north, bringing dry conditions

Tropical air blows further north, bringing rain to the far-north coast of Queensland

Air moving across the Southern Ocean causes regular cool changes across the continent

As air off the Southern Ocean moves over the continent it grows drier and warmer

Polar air from the Antarctic brings snow to south-east Australia

Summer

The Australian north-west monsoon brings thundery summer showers

Hot and dry inland air causes heatwaves in the south

Tropical air masses travelling over the Pacific bring rain to the east of the continent

Cool and moist air blows across the Southern Ocean, bringing showers and drizzle

The air masses over Australia shift seasonally and their temperature and water content change as they move

fronts' marked in coastal regions by towering clouds, squalls, heavy rain and sometimes thunderstorms. Otherwise the weather in the anticyclone belt is dry and clear. Winds are light, and variable in direction.

South of the subtropical highs, and shifting seasonally in the same way, is an east-moving low-pressure system. Its major depressions are centred well towards Antarctica, but secondary lows and troughs bring disturbed winter weather to the south-western corner of Western Australia, to Victoria and Tasmania, and to New South Wales as far as its mid-north coast. Winter winds in these regions are mainly from the west, varying day by day from breezes to gales, and swinging from mild, drizzling north-westerlies to cold, showery south-westerlies.

North of the anticyclone belt, coastal regions are dominated except in summer by the strong, persistent flow of south-east 'trade' winds from the Pacific. Warm and moist when they cross the east coast, they are hot and parched by the time they reach the north-west. In Darwin they may blow at 50 km/h, and the accompanying dust haze may cut visibility to less than 2.5 km.

A third pressure belt rules summer conditions in northern Australia. The intertropical front—a 'weather equator' of rising air where the wind systems of the two hemispheres converge—starts to move south in October, carrying with it a string of highly unstable lows. The Asian north-east monsoon becomes the Australian north-west monsoon. From November to April, thundery showers saturate the far north. Winds are squally but light, except for stiff afternoon sea breezes—or unless a tropical cyclone develops.

Victoria and New South Wales, south of Port Macquarie, have Australia's most frequently changing coastal weather. Except in summer they lie just in the zone of disturbed westerlies, cold anticyclones and southern depressions. In summer a similar changeability comes from the troughs which separate warm anticyclones. Summer patterns may also be varied by the distant effects of tropical cyclones, bringing heavy rain and high seas.

Of all the coastal cities, Sydney is the most prone to sudden bouts of bad weather in summer. These spells come most commonly with south-easterlies after a cold front. Within about three hours, broken low cloud scuds in to the coast and showery squalls follow. Less commonly, a 'black nor-easter' with similar low cloud pattern may develop ahead of a trough.

A view from 1450 km above the South Pole shows the summer cloud patterns

Simple ways to measure the wind

SAILING ship crews judged surface wind force from the sea's appearance. In the Royal Navy, various observations were graded on the Beaufort scale—named after an admiral—as a quick indicator of how much sail a man-o'-war could safely carry. Early aviators revised and extended the scale to include land-based observations.

Signs at sea	Signs on land	Description	Beaufort number	Speed (km/h)
Surface like a mirror	Smoke rises vertically	Calm	0	0-1
Ripples look like scales	Smoke drifts	Light air	1	1-5
Wavelet crests look glassy and do not break	Leaves rustle, wind vanes move	Light breeze	2	6-10
Large but short wavelets; crests starting to break	Leaves and twigs move constantly, flags stand out	Gentle breeze	3	11-20
Small waves lengthening; some foam crests	Dust and loose paper are raised	Moderate breeze	4	21-30
Moderate waves obviously longer; many foam crests	Small trees sway	Fresh breeze	5	31-40
Large waves start to form; perhaps some spray	Power lines whistle	Strong breeze	6	41-50
Sea heaps up; foam starts to blow	Big trees sway	Moderate gale	7	51-60
Spindrift foam blown in well-defined streaks	Twigs break off; walking impeded	Fresh gale	8	61-75
Dense streaks of foam; sea starts to roll	Slight structural damage—roof tiles, etc.	Strong gale	9	76-87
Waves with long, overhanging crests; foam in sheets; heavy rolling	Trees uprooted	Whole gale	10	88-100
Waves high enough to hide medium-sized ships; all crests blown into froth; sea covered with foam patches	Widespread damage	Storm	11	101-120
Air filled with foam and spray, seriously impairing visibility; sea completely white	Severe damage—weaker structures demolished	Hurricane	12	over 120

Old sayings that foretell bad weather

BEFORE weather watchers could exchange information quickly and meteorology was developed as a science, farmers and fishing folk passed weather lore to new generations in little rhymes or sayings. Many have a scientific basis and apply in southern Australia—especially those which indicate rain:

'A red sun has water in his eye'
The probable cause of redness, apart from bushfire smoke, is water droplets screening out other light waves. Moist air is condensing, clouds will form and rain may follow.

'Red sky at night, Sailor's delight; Red sky in the morning, Sailor's warning'
At sunset, light reflecting from high clouds indicates that the western horizon—over which most weather approaches—is clear. The same occurrence at sunrise means the eastern horizon is clear but clouds are building up on the weather side.

'Take shelter when the sun (or moon) is in his (her) house'
The 'house' is the halo sometimes seen around the sun or moon. Invisible, high-altitude cirrostratus cloud is forming. Heavier cloud will build downwards and rain may follow.

'When the stars begin to huddle, The earth will soon become a puddle'
If cirrostratus cloud starts to form at night, it may blot out stars of lesser magnitude and blur the light from major ones. So familiar groups seem to move into clusters.

'Rainbow at morning, Shepherd's warning; Rainbow at night, Shepherd's delight'
Rainbows, the result of sunlight striking water droplets, are visible to people with the sun at their backs. So a rainbow in the morning means moisture in the west—the usual weather quarter. An evening rainbow is in the eastern sky and probably means the rain is going away.

'Sunshine and showers, Rain again tomorrow'
When rain is interspersed with sunny periods, especially near the coast, the moist airstream is unstable and cumulus clouds are being built up by surface heating. Such conditions often last for more than a day.

Thunderstorms, with high-piling cumulonimbus clouds, are the most common—and most consistently damaging—weather system over the Australian coastline

Storms and cyclones Threats to life, property and beaches

Coastal regions of Australia, so often the meeting ground of air masses of different moisture and temperature, are prone to some of the world's most violent weather. It can produce winds to rip apart houses, bolts of lightning that spark raging bushfires, hail to devastate crops, and rain torrents and floods that wash away buildings, livestock and roads. And it whips the ocean into storm surges and waves of enormous force, hastening the erosion of coasts and sometimes destroying beaches completely (*see* Beach Erosion, overleaf).

In terms of loss of life and property damage, the tropical cyclone is the most dangerous weather system on earth. But on average only five or six each summer have any marked effect on the Australian coast. Tornadoes rarely strike populated regions, and never attain the wind speeds that make them so terrifying in the United States. Gales and flooding from intense southern depressions affect only a limited area. In total

impact—high frequency, wide occurrence and damaging effect—Australia's worst weather system is the thunderstorm.

Thunderstorms begin as small clumps of fleecy cumulus cloud. Cumulus normally blows away or evaporates readily, but if there is a tall mass of unstable cold air above the warm, moist air that is forming the cumulus, and if something pushes from below—a mountain slope acting as a wedge, or a dense cold front moving in—a vigorous updraught starts. Cumulonimbus clouds pile higher, their moisture cooling and condensing beyond the point at which rain would normally be produced. Ice crystals form instead.

At the storm's mature stage, so much ice and water collect that the updraught can no longer support their weight. They sink, and forceful downdraughts start. These can produce surface winds of 110 km/h and more, with phenomenal rain and sometimes hail. Cold low-level air spreads for kilometres ahead of the storm.

Air turbulence and the freezing process break up water particles and regroup them so that some parts of the cloud system have a positive electrical charge and some are negative. Early in the storm's life, huge sparks flash from positive to negative zones. Their reflections are seen as 'sheet' lightning. When the storm is mature, directly visible 'fork' lightning flashes between the cloud and the gound. The electrical charge may be as much as 30 million volts. It heats the air along its path to about 10 000°C, causing instant expansion and pressure waves that are heard as thunder. The sound travels at about 0.3 km a second, and can sometimes be heard more than 40 km away.

In the storm's dying stages, rain gradually eases and the remaining ice crystals are blown out by high-level winds into a cloud of flat-topped, anvil shape. The usual duration of one system is about half an hour, but it may start a chain of storms lasting for hours.

Calm surface zone

Cooled and dried air spills out of storm centre

Air ascends wall of eye

Air descends

Limit of ascent: 15 km

Warm, moist air spirals into centre

Starting over warm water, the great majority of cyclones stay at sea until they weaken over cold water. The 'eye' of a tropical cyclone is a column of rising air, surrounded by a fast-spinning wall of cloud and bands of other cloud spiralling towards it

---

Warning signs of a tropical cyclone

UNEXPECTEDLY heavy swell in tropical waters may be the first visible sign of a distant cyclone. Any marked increase of wind should be taken as a reliable warning. The most dangerous winds—as well as the safe 'eye'—will be to the left of a person facing the wind. At close quarters, a cyclone system may be seen as bands of cloud arranged along the wind and spiralling in to a dark, unbroken mass. But the eye is seldom exactly in the middle, so barometric pressure readings are the surest indicators of an approaching or developing cyclone. It will cause an abrupt disturbance, followed by a general, continuing fall in pressure. Weather stations in Australia's north are constantly alert to the danger of cyclones during their summer season. Special radar allows the paths of approaching storms to be tracked, so that warnings can be broadcast well before the vicious winds strike.

As each new cyclone menace is reported, meteorologists allot it a name from the year's agreed alphabetical list. The practice of giving cyclones names began in Queensland in the 1890s and was followed by the Americans in World War II. In 1975 officials decided to alternate male and female names.

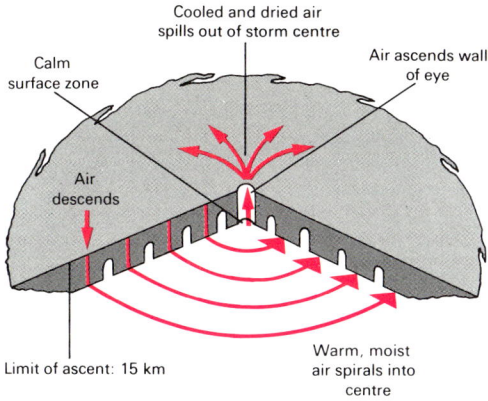

Tropical cyclone tracks, July 1979 to June 1980

Destructive tropical cyclones—also called hurricanes or typhoons in some parts of the world—start when existing depressions move over unusually warm patches of water. The normal process of rising air and falling pressure is intensified, and the heat of evaporated moisture is converted into wind energy that pulls the surrounding air into a tight, fast spiral.

A tropical cyclone's violence comes not from freakishly low pressure—some ordinary depressions are just as low—but from its compactness. Variation from highest to lowest pressure may be crammed into a diameter of less than 150 km in the early stages, resulting in winds so strong that they smash measuring instruments: their speed must be assumed from the impact of flying debris. Cyclone Althea recorded gusts of 194 km/h at Townsville in 1971.

Dangerous cyclone development requires open sea with a surface temperature of at least 27°C, high humidity, unstable air, and rotational wind deflection caused by the earth's movement. Only in two belts, between about 5° and 20° each side of the equator, do all those conditions coincide. Near Australia, the likeliest areas are to the north-east and north-west. Some cyclones originate to the north, in the Timor and Arafura Seas, and a few in the Gulf of Carpentaria, but they rarely occur before December or after March in any of these areas, and the great majority remain at sea until their force weakens over bodies of cold water.

Tropical cyclones never form over land even when conditions are very unstable. Surface friction slows the very low level air flows and too little water vapour is available to create a sufficiently high humidity. Water vapour is essential because cyclones derive much of their energy from the heat given off as the vapour condenses.

As a tropical cyclone develops, a spiralling mass of dense cloud forms, reaching from about 300 metres above sea level to 15 000 metres. The cloud base may descend to the sea with the rain torrent that soon sheets down, driven by violent winds. Lightning is frequent at first.

In a fully developed system there is an 'eye' of light winds or complete calm, more or less in the middle. It is a rainless area of fairly clear skies, averaging about 35 km in diameter in Australian waters, caused by condensed air sinking from the top of the cloud column. By this time the whole system is moving across the ocean, usually at less than 30 km/h.

The changing courses of tropical cyclones are determined by the locations of other pressure systems, which are themselves moving. A cyclone travels towards its side of steepest pressure gradient—where the rise to normal pressure occurs in the shortest distance. The general direction is easily seen on a weather map from the crowding of isobars, or lines of pressure.

When a cyclone moves outside the warm waters of the tropics, its width increases and its winds slacken. If it moves over land—even if still in the tropics—it is also quickly stretched and weakened. Its force is usually spent on the coastal region. There the destruction may be massive—because of the effect on the sea.

Storm surges of 5 metres above normal tide level, topped by waves 7 metres tall, are commonly reported. How disastrous such a surge may be depends on whether it coincides with high tide. The biggest surge reported in Australia, at Barrow Point, N. Qld, in 1899, was said to have swamped a policeman on a ridge more than 13 metres above normal sea level.

A tornado is most likely to form at the base of a high cumulonimbus thunderstorm system. Its fierce rotation results from a twisting of the updraught that feeds such a storm. A narrow funnel, widening towards the cloud, creates a small zone of such low pressure that movable objects —including people—can be sucked up in the spiralling column of air.

Tornadoes are so localised and destructive that central pressures and wind speeds cannot be measured. Pressure may fall below 800 millibars—compared with an average of 980 in tropical cyclones and 1013 in normal air. Their track of destruction may be only a few metres wide, and they usually occur in sparsely populated inland areas. Seen out to sea, they are often called waterspouts.

Willy-willies are small, short-lived eddies that can spin sand, dust and light debris up to about 2 metres from the ground. They are minicyclones created when air already of low pressure passes over a particularly hot patch of ground. Some people call them 'dust devils'.

Tornadoes can occur on coasts and inland

Beach erosion

When shifting sands are not replaced

Sand movement is as natural as the weather. Beaches are fluid zones that respond to wave and wind action, sometimes losing material and sometimes gaining it. Sediments added during calm weather are taken offshore in storms, to be replaced during the next quiet spell. In Australia this normal cycle of cut-and-fill is accompanied on the east and west coasts by an overall northward transport of sand. The majority of strong waves strike those coasts at a more or less southerly angle. Sand pulled from a beach is carried by longshore currents and most often returned to the shore at a point farther north. The loss is made good by other sand from the south—as long as the supply is adequate. If it is not, long-term erosion sets in and the shoreline recedes.

The past century has been a period of widespread erosion and coastal recession. Reports have come from areas representing virtually all the eastern coast south of the Great Barrier Reef, and from much of the west coast. Erosion arouses the greatest public concern in settled districts, when properties or holiday amenities are menaced. Aggravated storm damage and slower recovery are noted where human works and behaviour interfere with beach structure and vegetation. But shoreline recession is occurring widely in remote areas and in protected coastal reserves and national parks. Clearly, the supply of replacement beach materials from the south is not sufficient at present to compensate for the

A satellite view of the New South Wales central coast taken from a height of 920 km above the Earth. The photograph stretches from Newcastle Bight and Port Stephens in the south to Port Macquarie and the Hastings River in the north. The hook-shaped beaches, narrow at the southern end and broad at the north, are formed by waves that arrive consistently from the south

heavy and continuing northward loss of sand.

Urgent problems created by erosion are problems only because people, in committing capital resources to the seashore, have misunderstood the nature of beaches. They may recede—or advance—for centuries. The wave movements to which they respond are themselves subject to variations in world climate patterns. Predominant wave directions can change. So can the sea level, depending on how much water is held in glaciers and polar icecaps. The position and extent of a beach signify only the net effect of physical forces at one particular time—not something that people can indicate on a map or a property title and expect to stay put forever. The human sense of equilibrium may be static, but nature's is dynamic.

The sea off eastern Australia has been near its present level for only about 6000 years. During the most intensive phase of the last ice age, about 20 000 years ago, it was more than 100 metres lower. Rivers carved valleys across the land that was exposed. The return of the sea 'drowned' those extended river systems and made deep inlets where there had been shallow estuaries. For that reason, many rivers no longer carry material eroded from inland rock—a major contributor to beach supply—all the way to the coast. Instead they deposit rock debris and sediments in the upper parts of estuaries, where the water first deepens.

On many parts of the coast, from Gippsland in eastern Victoria to southern Queensland, there are dual barrier-beach formations. They consist of sand mostly of marine origin, including a sub-

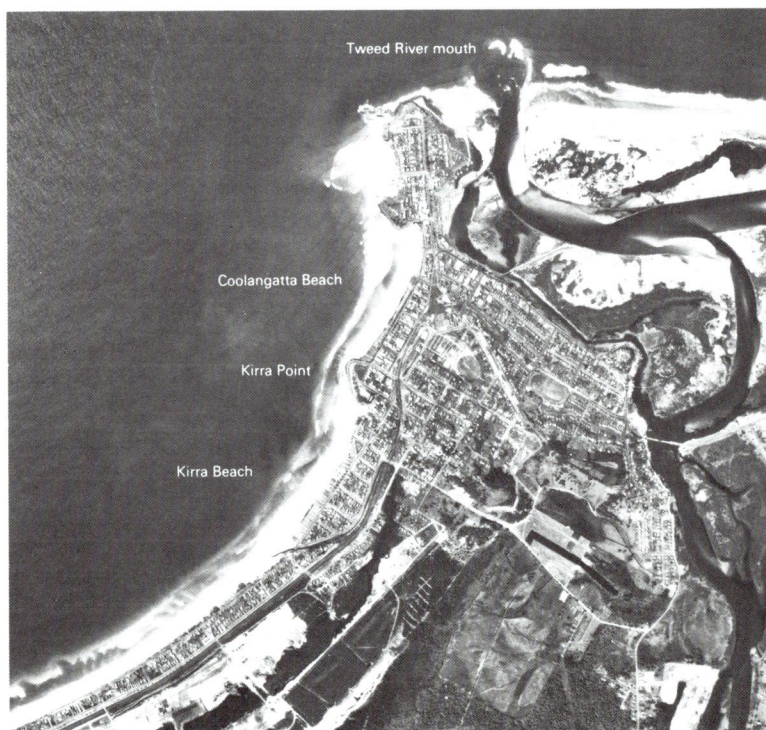

Sandy beaches around Tweed Heads and Coolangatta in 1962

Training walls impeding sand drift led to severe beach erosion by 1971

stantial input of material derived from the shells or skeletons of marine animals. Inner barriers were deposited about 125 000 years ago, when the sea was last near its present level. Modern barriers, established a little more than 6000 years ago, formed seaward of the ancient ones. Troughs of low-lying land were left in between. They became swamps and lagoons, typified by the Gippsland Lakes and the chains of waterways and wetlands on the NSW central coast. Such troughs act as traps for river-borne sediments that would otherwise have reached the coast. They also absorb wind-blown beach sand.

When the sea level was slightly lower than at present, Australia's eastern shores were probably one long barrier beach coast, with dunes stretching along the base of what are now the familiar cliff faces of central and southern New South Wales. As the sea level rose massive amounts of sand were lost when waves and tidal forces began to push barrier material into the deep inlets of newly drowned estuaries. The barrier system, with its easy northward flow of material, was broken at every such estuary—at Sydney's big sea inlets, for example. At the same time, rocky headlands began to interrupt the longshore drift pattern. More barrier material was pushed inshore between promontories, forming mainland beaches. Isolated longshore currents redistributed the material, scouring the southern ends of beaches and heaping sand to the north. Dunes and ramps of sand climbed cliff faces, spread over hilltops and spilled down the inland side. Sydney's eastern suburbs are founded on marine sand pushed up ramps that have long been stripped away.

Most of the conditions for large-scale beach depletion and shoreline recession are set by nature. There is nothing people can do about them. But the most active cause of further sand loss, contributed to by human activities, is the movement of destabilised dunes. Phases of dune migration seem to have been interspersed by periods of coastal stability for the past 4000 years. The changes were probably related to variations in the frequency of storms. If the cycle of storm-calm-storm cutting and filling is repeated too rapidly, plants may not have time to colonise regained sand and trap wind-blown sand at the back of the beach to rebuild foredunes. Without plant cover and foredune shelter, the inner dunes are mobile. Strong winds can drive them inland to swamp and kill any vegetation in their path. In that way formerly stable surfaces are also mobilised, and even more sand migrates. People destroying dune vegetation run the risk of triggering massive sand movements.

Man-made obstructions to normal longshore drift can cause dramatically sudden local erosion. A groyne built out from a beach, for example, traps sand on one side. But sand moving away from the other side cannot be replaced. The updrift beach, starved of materials, is progressively scoured by strong wave action. Such a situation has caused alarm on Queensland's lower Gold Coast since the 1960s. The region should not have much of a problem with erosion: its rivers supply plenty of sediments to the coast, and losses of sand into estuaries and inland-moving dunes are minor. But in 1964, to stabilise the Tweed River entrance for navigation, projecting training walls were built. The net quantity of sand supplied to beaches at Coolangatta and beyond decreased immediately. By 1967 they were unable to recover fully from storm effects. And the remedy, applied after severe storm damage in 1972, was worse than the ailment. A groyne built out to sea at Kirra Point trapped 300 000 cubic metres of sand on Coolangatta Beach within two years. But 500 000 cubic metres were lost from Kirra Beach, updrift of the groyne. The region's beaches, crucial to its tourist industry, are now maintained in their pre-1960s state by pumping enormous volumes of sand through a pipeline from the Tweed estuary, at heavy expense.

Dramatic changes to ocean beaches beside the mouth of the Tweed River, on the border between New South Wales and Queensland, demonstrate some of the problems caused by man-made alterations to the coast. In 1962 (far left) beaches to the north of the Tweed estuary had broad stretches of sand. In 1964 training walls were built at the mouth of the river to stabilise it for navigation. By 1971 (centre left) much of the sand had left Coolangatta Beach. A groyne built at Kirra Point in 1972, and another beside it (above), have solved Coolangatta's problem, but now the south end of Kirra Beach has all but disappeared

What can be done to save beaches

ANY approach to erosion that views the coastline as a fixed boundary is doomed to failure, or at best to be a never-ending drain on funds. But some steps can be taken to aid natural restoration fairly cheaply, and to reduce harmful human impact:

- Legal protection of foredune vegetation and the active encouragement of suitable plants on the upper parts of beaches, to reduce wind-blown sand losses.
- Measurement of a beach's sediment 'budget'—its income and outgoings of material—before positioning engineering works such as breakwaters and groynes.
- Zoning against future building in erosion-prone areas, to forestall community demands for costly and often fruitless protection measures.
- Educational emphasis on the dynamic nature of the shoreline, so that its change-ability is respected and normal processes need no longer be regarded as disasters.

PART 3

Advice for holidaymakers

Seaside recreation is easy for most Australians. Ample beaches, coastal parks and inshore waters are seen not merely as holiday playgrounds but as enhancements of daily life. It is doubtful, however, whether many people take advantage of all their opportunities.

Leaving aside the limitations of expense and physical disability, there are benefits in exploring the fullest range of leisure activities. But the sea is an alien medium: it can be hostile, and so can its shores.

The drawbacks and dangers of inexperience cannot be lightly dismissed.

Information in the following pages is aimed at helping readers make more of the coast, without placing them in jeopardy.

It is presumed that they will also seek the best local advice before venturing into the unfamiliar.

They are urged to acquaint themselves fully with their rights of access and use, and to respect the rights of others.

And it is hoped that they will treat a fragile environment with all the care that a national treasure deserves.

Late afternoon sunlight turns the sea to the colour of liquid gold

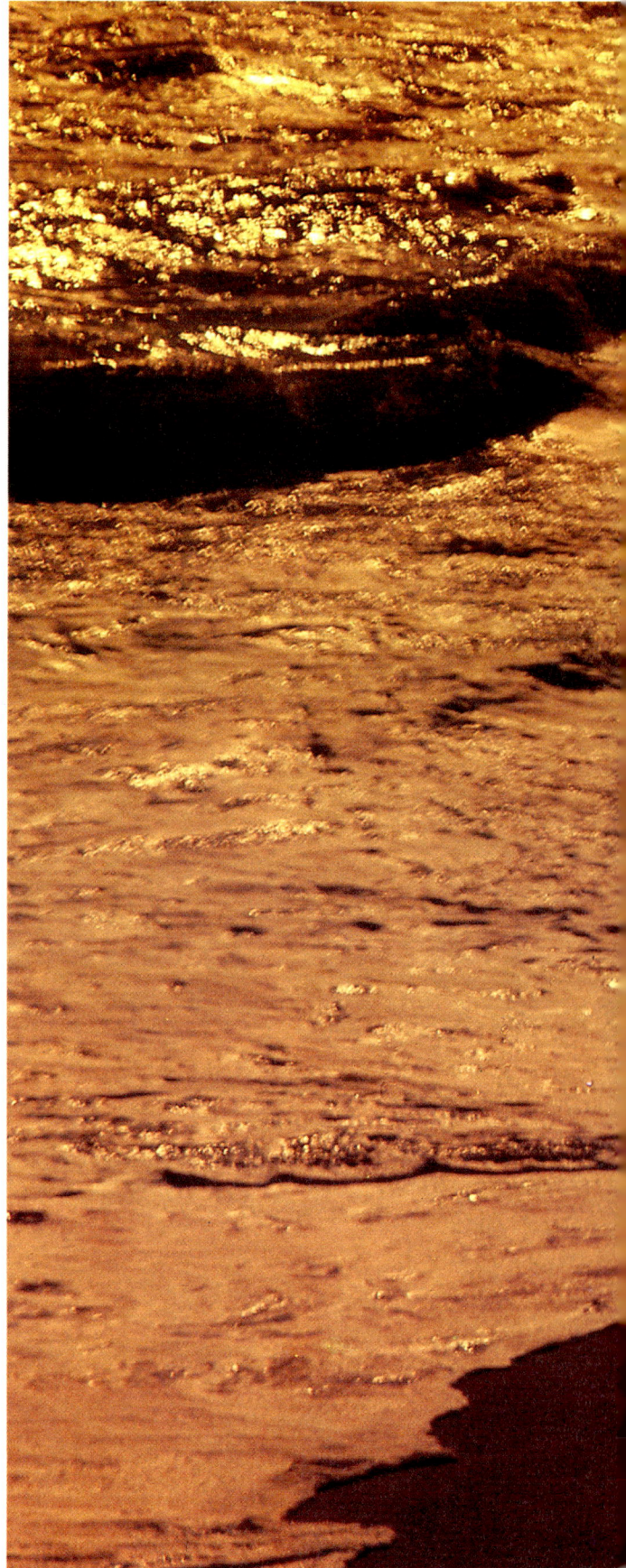

Who owns the coast? Answers to a complex question

The expanses of land around the Australian coast which have avoided the auctioneer's hammer and the developer's bulldozer remain unalienated public lands. They are necessary not only to preserve indigenous plants and animals, but also to provide valuable recreation space for an expanding human· population. Before governments were concerned with preserving the community's right of access to river banks, bay shores and ocean coasts, private ownership of waterfront property was not discouraged, and quite often only the narrow strip between low and high water marks remains public. Today, some coasts are not easily accessible because pasture lands back on to beachfronts, fences create barriers to public waterways, and industrial estates and port facilities create daunting obstructions.

Even the regulations governing public land form barriers of their own, with a maze of restrictions covering access, camping and caravanning, fire-lighting, vehicle entry and fishing. Consistent regulations face travellers all around the coast, but exceptions to the rule and temporary restrictions are frequent. When in doubt, always apply for information to regulating authorities, all of which have offices in the state capitals and branches in major towns. In some cases visitors may have to apply to a resident manager, ranger or forester for specific and seasonal restrictions.

Laws of trespass
It is generally not a crime simply to enter someone else's land whether it is privately owned or leased. The owner's only recourse is to sue for damages caused, though force in proportion to any danger or damage threatened may be used to eject a trespasser. Only if violence is threatened or appears to be threatened can injury to a trespasser be justified. Reasonable force may also be used to evict squatters, such as campers, who try to stay on a person's property without permission, and a caravan may be towed away if its owner refuses to leave. But no damage should be done to the trespasser's property. Laws relating to trespass on government installations such as port facilities, lighthouses, research stations and military reserves involve special offences and in some instances trespass on federal government property can incur a jail sentence of up to three months.

Crown land
Ocean beaches and the foreshores of tidal rivers and lakes are all part of Crown property. Like all unoccupied Crown land, they are generally accessible to the public, though entry may be restricted to paying users in places where commercial camping areas, boat ramps and other facilities have been established. Along popular city beaches, boating may be prohibited from nearshore waters during daylight hours to avoid danger to swimmers, but anglers are permitted inside the marker buoys after sunset. Beaching of boats is allowable in emergencies.

Where private property adjoins a tidal foreshore, public pedestrian access is preserved, although private ownership may extend to the high water mark. The point reached by water at a mean high tide can be accurately defined only by a surveyor, but can often be judged by the extent of land vegetation or marine growth on rocky foreshores.

Clubs or individuals may have permits or leases allowing jetties or club houses to be built over the foreshore for mooring and fishing. Permission to occupy this land must be obtained in the form of leases or licences which generally relate only to the structure itself. If public access to the foreshore is blocked, people have right of passage over the structure. In some regions, Port Phillip Bay for example, the public also has the right to embark and disembark from all private and public jetties. In many places there is a reserve 30 metres wide adjoining the mean high water mark. This may extend up to 150 metres or more inland and may be difficult to distinguish from the adjacent privately owned land. Where there is doubt about the status of foreshore land and the structures on it, a local government authority or lands department should be consulted.

Aboriginal lands
Most of the big sections of coast reserved for Aboriginal communities, or held freehold by them, are well out of populated areas. Some are only accessible by sea or air and there is little conflict with the routes taken by all but the best equipped and most adventurous travellers. Where the reserve lands are easy to get to, in areas of coastline attractive to tourists, they must be treated at all times as the property of their residents. The state offices of the Department of Aboriginal Affairs will direct people to the appropriate authority for the granting of entry permits, though few are issued for recreational purposes and the Aboriginal communities themselves review all applications. Transit permits are normally freely available and expeditions by scientific groups and wildlife clubs are given special consideration. Travellers to Cape York are provided with a camping ground within the Aboriginal township of Bamaga, but it is advisable to apply in writing to the community's council chairman giving comprehensive details of your proposed trips. On Bathurst Island the Tiwi people's community actively encourages visitors on scheduled air tours from Darwin and permission for entry is automatically included with tour bookings

---

Mining the rich 'black sands'

SAND mining leases are granted under the authority of state government mines departments, like any other mining right. Leases are held on extensive tracts of coastal Crown land, including some in national parks. Modern leases require mining companies to restore worked-over dunes as nearly as possible to their natural state. Since ecological objections aroused public protest in the 1970s, some leases have been terminated by agreement. In the case of Fraser Island (see page 331) the Federal Government halted mining by using its power to control exports. The unworked leases are still held, however. If profitable local markets could be found, a resumption of mining could be proposed and environmental arguments would start all over again.

Beach mining began in 1870, when gold was found in deposits of dark, heavy minerals at Ballina, NSW. 'Black sands' occurred then in surface outcrops called sniggers. Such easily found deposits were cleaned out by miners who extracted gold, tin and platinum. They dumped the major components—rutile (titanium dioxide), ilmenite (titanium iron oxide) and zircon (zirconium silicate). In roughly equal proportions, those three compounds comprise about 97 per cent of the heavy minerals that work their way to the bottom of Australian quartz sands. Their density is about twice that of quartz, and their grain size about half.

Soon after the turn of the century, titanium began to be sought after as the basis of white paint. Rutile and ilmenite were wanted as furnace linings, or as welding fluxes. Zircon became valuable as a lining material or a ceramics glaze. Rutile fetched high prices in the 1950s, with the use of titanium in jet engines.

Mining at Myall Lakes involved one of the largest dune systems in the Southern Hemisphere. The 110-metre high dunes were blown there only about 2000 years ago. It is hoped that replanted areas (right)—seen here after five years—will eventually return to their original condition (crest of dune, left)

Parks and reserves

Australia's first national park, Royal National Park near Sydney, was declared in 1879 with a Crown grant to the park's trustees exhorting them to use the land for the recreation of the inhabitants of the colony. Authority was given to establish lawns, ornamental gardens, a zoo, cricket pitch, racecourse and rifle range—which created a large bushland amusement park. The management of national parks has changed greatly over the past 100 years; interference with the natural environment to provide facilities for the community has been tempered by a greater appreciation of conservation requirements. Park administrations are now keenly aware that they hold the key to the survival of rare and vanishing wildlife species and the preservation of representative samples of all major habitats, as well as areas of geological and historic significance.

Many coastal reserves still principally aim to fulfil the recreational needs of the public—Victoria's Coastal Parks, Tasmania's State Recreation Areas and Coastal Reserves, State Recreation Areas in New South Wales and some of the Environmental Parks in Queensland. Such areas are normally narrow coastal strips with some land left in its natural state, but with picnic areas, walking tracks and camping grounds provided, and waterways where motorboating may be allowed. Some of the older national parks, such as the Royal in New South Wales, Victoria's Wilson's Promontory National Park, and Yanchep National Park in Western Australia, retain a legacy of facilities from days when their role was largely to cater for family holidays and recreational sportsmen. Newer national parks, with extensive areas of forest and heathland, are more firmly dedicated to the preservation of the natural environment—an important goal in Australia, where plants and animals are rapidly disappearing even in areas of little or no settlement.

Such conservation areas must be large enough to ensure that the environment is undisturbed by man's activities and that the ecological balance of plant and animal communities is maintained. Research has suggested that only areas of 20 250 hectares or more are likely to support the range of plants and animals that are representative of a particular Australian habitat. The largest proportion of all national park area is consequently left in its natural state. Vehicles are allowed only on existing tracks and roads provided for access to camp sites, picnic grounds and along scenic drives. Use of off-road vehicles, such as trail bikes, dune buggies and four-wheel drives, away from existing tracks, is expressly forbidden because of the threat to soil and vegetation.

Occasionally conservation requirements may lead to the closure of parts of a park. Overuse and damage by fire require long periods free of disturbance for plant regrowth and animal recolonisation. Areas of special conservation significance—the breeding site of a rare bird or the habitat of an endangered plant—may be permanently closed. Such areas include the wetlands of coastal lagoons and estuaries, which are a sanctuary for waterfowl during the interior's

A female noisy scrub bird and nest

Preserving endangered wildlife

As MORE and more of Australia's coastal fringe is developed for housing or industry, it becomes increasingly important that some areas of natural landscape are set aside to conserve the plants and animals that live there. Occasionally the demands of conservation may conflict with the wishes of holidaymakers. Access may have to be forbidden or restricted in areas where a delicate natural habitat may be destroyed or rare animals frightened away by the presence of people. In some cases, such as that of the noisy scrub bird in Western Australia, such action may be necessary to save a species from extinction.

In 1961 plans for a new township to be called Casuarina at Two Peoples Bay, just east of Albany, were abandoned after new sightings of a bird thought to be extinct since 1889. The 4639 hectares around the bay still carry the only known population of noisy scrub birds, *Atrichornis clamosus*, and were declared a nature reserve in 1966 to protect the species. Most of the population of about 72 breeding pairs and 20 non-breeding males lives in densely vegetated gullies in the Mount Gardner Peninsula, part of which has been declared a prohibited area to prevent interference with research programmes. No public entry is permitted into this part of the reserve and there are clearly marked signs on the access tracks. But about half the peninsula is a limited access area, and may be entered on foot by birdwatchers wishing to catch a glimpse of the shy and secretive bird. Its brown colouring and dark cross bars blend in with the vegetation and make it extremely difficult to see; it rarely flies, moving mainly in the thick, low scrub. But the loud song of the male bird is a strong and persistent reminder of its presence, and can be heard over a distance of nearly 1.5 km on calm days.

dry months, and many rugged and mostly inaccessible offshore islands where migratory birds and seal colonies breed for short seasons. Only people with genuine scientific interests are issued permits to enter these areas. Parks known as fauna sanctuaries, nature reserves, or conservation parks, unlike national parks, allow only limited public access, and camping is often prohibited or restricted to small areas and for short periods such as school holidays, when special consideration for camping permits is given to groups involved in educational wildlife projects.

Marine parks control activities below the waterline and aim to restrict spearfishing, specimen collecting and some surface fishing in favour of pastimes such as snorkelling and scuba diving. Australia's largest marine park, The Great Barrier Reef Marine Park, was empowered in 1976 to provide protection for the delicate coral formations by controlling tourist operations; some vulnerable areas have been made off-limits for boating and fishing.

Permits must generally be obtained for camping at organised camp sites in national parks and it may be necessary to make bookings well ahead, especially for holiday periods. For Wilson's Promontory National Park bookings for the busy Christmas season are open only during July, after which a ballot is held to allocate the camping and caravan sites. Even the traffic on walking trails in heavily used parks is strictly controlled.

State forests

In State Forests, multiple-use management ensures the country's timber industry a continuity of supply, while providing for recreation and education as well as the protection of wildlife habitats. The forests are most widespread in humid coastal regions; many adjoin national parks, where they act as conservation buffer zones. State Forests are normally open to the public and, with fire trails and former logger routes, are well served by tracks for vehicles. Many have recommended scenic drives, and developed areas for camping. Others permit hiking trips into remote regions where there are no facilities. Check with the local forestry office, where maps and information on the best routes to take, spots to see and locations of picnic grounds, as well as advice on logging and fire restrictions, may be readily obtained. Particular care in State Forests is recommended for drivers unused to rural roads which are often narrow and winding, offer poor visibility and are used by heavy trucks. Only firm gravel roads should be used during wet weather as many forest roads become slippery after even light rain.

Lighting campfires

Campfires are allowed in national parks, state forests and on Crown land for cooking and warmth, but should be kept small to conserve wood and, wherever possible, portable stoves should be used. Great care and attention should be given to the siting and extinguishing of fires and to the exact legal requirements in each state.

On days of total fire ban no fires are permitted in parks and forests. In campgrounds and picnic areas fires may be lit only in the fireplaces provided, or as directed by signs. Where there are no properly constructed fireplaces, fires should be contained in a trench at least 500 mm deep. All flammable material on the ground or overhanging the fire within a distance of 3 metres must be removed before the fire is lit. The fire must not be left unattended and must be completely extinguished, preferably with water, before leaving. Trenches must be filled in.

Water safety   Surviving in the surf and still water

It is safer to swim at a beach patrolled by members of the surf lifesaving association or professional lifeguards than it is to take a bath, according to statistics published on accidental drownings in Australia. More and more people, however, are venturing to unpatrolled and remote areas, where the surf may be better but the statistics are worse. In the decade of the 1970s there were no drownings on patrolled beaches, while an average of eight a year occurred at unsupervised surfing spots.

Groups who venture to isolated beaches must remember that they have the responsibility for their own safety. It is important to understand the sea, the surf and the formation of beaches, and to be able to recognize any danger signs that may be present. Anyone using the sea must also know their own swimming ability and level of fitness. Reasonable pool-swimmers may perform poorly in the surf, where there are no edges, the bottom is irregular, the water continually moving and the depth forever changing.

Swells erode the sandy face of a beach and carry a great deal of it seawards to deposit it as offshore bars or sandbanks. A sandbank absorbs the force of incoming waves so that the eroding action of storms is lessened. But even when a sandbank is present, turbulent waves are constantly moving masses of water towards the shore, all of which must return seawards. Much returns in the rip currents which form channels through the sandbanks. Where curved beaches end at rocky outcrops—either natural or man-made—corner rips sweep the water along its face. Most people have heard of rips, but will be unable to avoid their dangers unless they can recognise them.

Before entering the water always spend some time watching a beach and its near-shore waters to try and spot any rips. If you plan to surf at an unpatrolled spot, find an elevated place at the back of the beach, or on a headland, and study the water until the pattern of banks and rips becomes clear. Rips can usually be seen from the beach, but they may be obscured by heavy seas, onshore winds and high tide. At such times you cannot be confident of your safety in the water.

The waves and water over a rip are obviously different from those over adjoining sand banks. A headland view of a rip at the centre of Maroubra Beach, NSW (top) clearly shows a band of foam and churned-up sand moving seawards in the current. Foam towards the furthest line of breakers indicates the point at which the rip has reached its head and begun to dissipate after passing through a channel in the sand bank. Choppy water interrupts the pattern of the surf over the same rip seen from the beach (centre). Waves break irregularly over the channel, do not roll and are often out of line with those in surrounding water. On other beaches the colours of rips may be darker because the water is deeper. At times they may look clear and undisturbed, and thus attractive to swimmers. Do not fight against a rip, but allow it to carry you out until it weakens. Strong swimmers can move diagonally out of a rip, but weaker swimmers should swim parallel to the beach and then back to shore. Children must not leave their surfboards if carried out on a rip, but stay with them till help arrives as their support may be vital

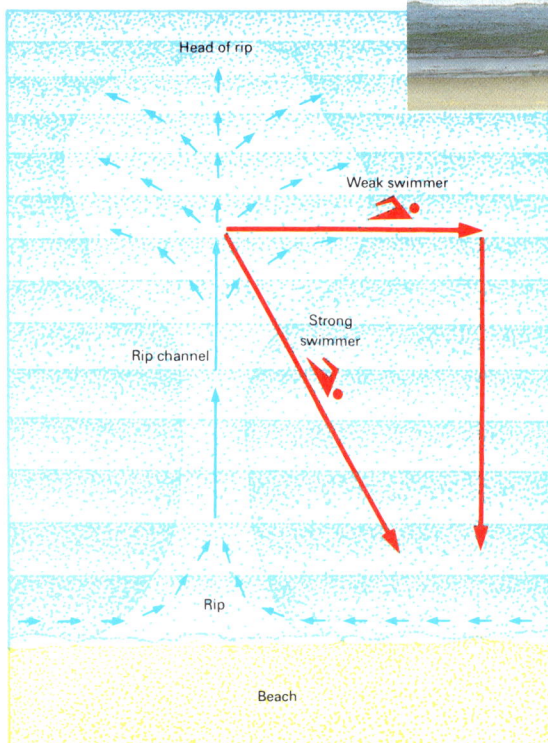

Head of rip
Weak swimmer
Strong swimmer
Rip channel
Rip
Beach

A corner rip at Avoca Beach, NSW, sweeps a deep channel of darker water along the face of a man-made rock pool. Large waves break regularly to the left of the rip which appears deceptively calm

What happened on Black Sunday

STABILITY of an offshore sandbar cannot be taken for granted, even in the best of weather. A bar modifies the interaction of incoming and reflected waves, but only up to a point that they can tolerate. If it is interfering too much with their movements, they may change their patterns and suddenly destroy it.

At Sydney's Bondi Beach on 'Black Sunday'— 6 Feb 1938—about 300 novice surfers using a bar had it dissolve beneath their feet after a spontaneous change of wave movement. They were left well out of their depth, and most were panic stricken. Surf club members, on the beach preparing for a race, went quickly to the rescue but five people drowned.

In a medium to heavy surf, rips can alter rapidly, creating very hazardous conditions. In a small surf, rips are fairly stable and predictable, but even so they should not be trusted.

If you are caught in a rip, calmly swim or scull sideways towards a sandbank. If possible, signal for help by raising one arm. There is little point in shouting for help because it causes fatigue and cannot be heard above the noise of waves. While waiting for help, lie face up in the water and float with your head partly submerged. A relaxed horizontal position aids flotation and the body's natural buoyancy will keep your face above water with a minimum of effort. Treading water—moving the legs as if walking upstairs and pressing outwards and down with the arms—gives a better view, but it is tiring.

On unpatrolled or deserted beaches, where there is no help available, you must be able to swim out of rips by yourself. Conserve strength as much as possible and do not fight against the current. As the rip reaches its head, on the seaward side of its path through the sandbar, the current will dissipate. Swim parallel to the shore for about 30 metres before turning back towards the beach. At low tide sandbars close to the edge of a rip may only be covered by shallow water and if you are in difficulty you can use them to rest on while making your way back to the beach.

The breast stroke is less fatiguing for the return swim than the crawl, and it will still enable you to maintain a reasonable speed. Use side stroke and back stroke for relief. Turn your head away from the wind and breathe in a regular rhythm. If possible swim out of a rip in the same direction as the longshore current is flowing. This is the current which is commonly noticed moving along a beach. It carries swimmers away from their point of entry and may sweep them into a rip or deep channel. When returning to the beach be careful not to swim back into a rip. Not all rips run at right angles to land. If waves strike the shorelines at an angle, the rip, too, will be angled away from the beach.

Children who are carried out of their depth by rips often jump off their surf craft and try to swim against the current. This is exactly the opposite to what should be done. Instead they should stay with their craft, paddle to calm water—even if it is beyond the breakers—raise an arm and wait for help. In such circumstances a surf mat is as important as a life jacket. A flexible strap attaching a surf craft to an ankle or wrist is a valuable additional safety device.

While the hazards of ocean swimming are usually obvious, rivers, bays and lagoons conceal their dangers beneath still waters. Most fatal drowning accidents occur in sheltered waterways—often in peaceful conditions. The misuse of power boats in swimming areas and the consumption of alcohol before swimming, particularly from houseboats, are major causes of accidents. The currents of fast-flowing rivers discourage most swimmers simply because they look dangerous. But slower streams and enclosed waters are often just as hazardous. The main problem is usually visibility. You risk severe spinal injuries if you dive into cloudy water without first checking its depth.

The beds of lagoons and rivers are often soft and weed-covered—oozing mud and tangled weeds can trap swimmers just as securely as heavy branches. Panic and quick, jerky movements may only tighten the grip of weeds. If trapped, gently unravel the weed with as little agitation of the water as possible.

Muscle cramp can disable a swimmer in deep water or rough surf and can cause drowning.

Cresting or spilling waves are ideal for body surfers and board-riders. The waves break from the top with foaming crests which tumble down their faces

Plunging waves or dumpers break dangerously by curling over into a tube before thumping down into shallow water. They should be left to experienced surfers

Surging waves often run ashore without breaking, and they can suddenly swamp children playing around rocks, or break on them near the water's edge unexpectedly

Three types of waves—spilling, plunging and surging—are commonly seen on ocean shores. Never underestimate the power of waves which can often appear small when seen from the shore. Dive under waves when surfing—trying to keep your head above water wastes energy

These painful spasms usually occur in the legs, and are more likely to happen to people in cold water and after strenuous exercise. Eating always impairs physical performance because greater quantities of blood are diverted to the digestive system, leaving less for other muscles that need it during physical exertion. Light refreshments or snacks, rather than a full picnic meal, are better for a day at the beach. If attacked by cramp either float on your back or scull gently with your hands in a breast stroke motion and signal for help. Relieve the pain of cramp in the thigh by straightening your knee and raising your leg to stretch the muscle. For cramp in the lower leg, straighten your knee and draw you toes upwards towards your shin. Apply a cold-compress or ice-pack wherever possible, and in hot conditions drink a tumbler of water containing half a teaspoon of salt to aid recovery.

Water safety signs
A new set of standard symbols is being introduced on Australian beaches to replace the multitude of different symbols and word signs used by local authorities. When the symbol is shown in blue it indicates that the nominated sport or activity is permitted and that the area is considered safe. When the symbol is shown in a red circle with a diagonal line through it, the sport is prohibited because conditions are unsafe or there may be danger to other people. On patrolled beaches swimmers must remain in the supervised area which is marked by red and yellow flags. Leave the water when the shark flag is shown or its accompanying siren is heard

Swimming

Fishing

Water skiing

Surf craft riding

Scuba diving

Shark alarm flag

Patrolled swimming area

Fishing for leisure/1 Where and when to find the fish

Fishing is by far the most popular water sport in Australia. An estimated 30 per cent of Australians are recreational anglers. A survey held in NSW in 1977 revealed that 26 per cent of the population had fished in the sea at least once within the year. Sixty per cent of New South Wales boys between the ages of 13 and 17 fished for leisure, and altogether New South Wales fishermen spent 20 million days a year fishing for fun. Wherever there is reasonable access to the bays, beaches and rock platforms around the Australian coast, someone can usually be found waiting optimistically for a bite. However, two basic problems confront the amateur angler—where to find the fish, and what tackle to use.

The most popular recreational fishing areas are the thousands of estuaries and bays around the coast, where lines are cast from the shore, jetties, wharves, rock retaining walls and boats. From boats the best fishing is in the main channels of rivers, streams and inlets. Spots near weeds, rocks and mangroves attract fish, as they are major feeding areas. Around wharves and jetties the supporting piles may be heavily encrusted with mussels, sea squirts, weeds and the other marine life that fish feed on. The species commonly caught within these partly enclosed waters are flathead, bream, tailor, mulloway, whiting, luderick, garfish, leatherjacket, and flounder, all of which make excellent eating.

Surf fishermen will catch most of the species above, but success among the waves requires an ability to recognise the water conditions each fish is likely to favour. Patches of dark water usually indicate the deep channels, where tailor and Australian salmon search for food along the

edges. Mulloway travel the rips and gutters of a beach where they can feed on unwary tailor and whiting, and they may also move along the water's edge seeking out one of their favourite foods—beach worms. Flathead and whiting partly bury themselves in the sandy bottom of shallower zones, covered by the froth and foam of breaking waves, and often within a few metres of the shore. Bream spend most of their time foraging for crustacea, molluscs and worms dislodged by pounding waves, particularly among submerged rocks at the corners of beaches.

Rock fishermen can hope to catch snapper, rock cod and bream, while the more experienced and adventurous will attempt to catch tuna, kingfish, mulloway, and even marlin. Rock fishing can be hazardous, and great care should be taken to make sure the area is safe before stepping on to an exposed rock platform or ledge. Spend some time watching the sea's behaviour to see if the platform is a safe one. Even an apparently placid sea can produce freak waves which will submerge areas that were previously merely splashed by spray. Boots fitted with spiked metal strips give a better foothold on slippery rocks than rubber-soled shoes. Wet granite is extremely dangerous, no matter what footwear is worn. If a wave sweeps across the rocks, stand on one leg to present less surface area to the water, and so reduce the chance of being knocked over. If washed into the sea, do not remove shoes or boots as they will be needed to get a purchase on the rocks when clambering ashore. In smooth waters it may be safe to allow a rising swell to wash you back on to the rocks. But in rough seas swim away from shore to avoid being pushed

under the waves, or dashed against the rocks.

Most fishermen choose a rod and reel rather than the simple handline wound on to a cork or bottle. Whether a rod or handline is used, choose tackle that suits the kind of fishing being carried out. No outfit is suitable for all conditions.

Surf and rock fishermen usually use hollow glass-fibre rods, 3.4 to 3.8 metres long. Any of the three basic reel types—threadline, overhead revolving spool, and sidecast—can be used, provided that the spool has a minimum line capacity of at least 250 metres of nylon line with a breaking strength of 10 kg. The position of the reel on the rod should suit the reel type—low for the sidecast, medium for the threadline, and high for the overhead. Estuary fishermen find shorter rods ranging from 2 to 3 metres best. Reel size, too, can be smaller—use any of the basic types with a spool capacity of 250 metres of 5 to 7 kg nylon. The most popular reel is the threadline because it is easy to use.

There are few poisonous fish in Australian waters. Nevertheless, if you cannot identify a fish, or find advice on its edibility, it is safer to throw it back. In tropical areas a type of poisoning known as ciguatera can kill people who eat the flesh of some reef species (see page 67). In southern waters the spiky toad fish, also known as the puffer, should never be eaten as its flesh is highly toxic and can cause a rapid death.

Some fish have venomous spines which can cause violent pain if they penetrate the skin. Catfish, bullrouts, fortescues and stonefish are common species that may be encountered. Do not even handle these fish. Release them by cutting the line just above the hook, which will event-

Choosing the best rig

IT is important to find the best rig—a combination of hooks, swivels, sinkers and traces—to attract, play and land each species of fish. Fish behave differently as conditions change, so one rig will always be better than others in any set of circumstances. All the rigs shown have been successful, but they should only be used as a starting point for more experiments.

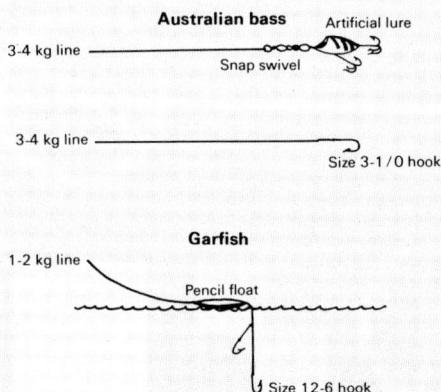

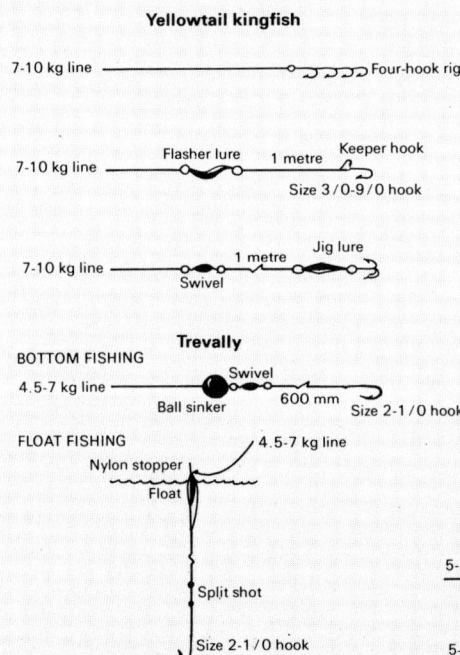

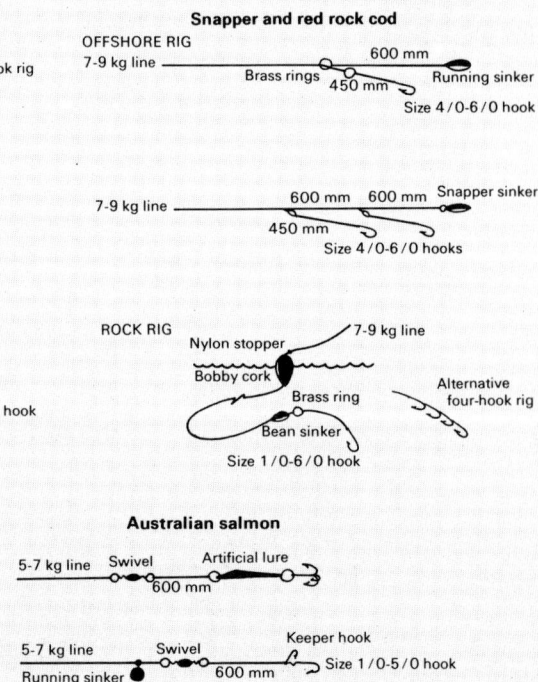

Australian bass

3-4 kg line — Snap swivel — Artificial lure

3-4 kg line — Size 3-1/0 hook

Garfish

1-2 kg line — Pencil float — Size 12-6 hook

Yellowtail kingfish

7-10 kg line — Four-hook rig

7-10 kg line — Flasher lure — 1 metre — Keeper hook — Size 3/0-9/0 hook

7-10 kg line — 1 metre — Jig lure — Swivel

Trevally

BOTTOM FISHING
4.5-7 kg line — Swivel — Ball sinker — 600 mm — Size 2-1/0 hook

FLOAT FISHING — 4.5-7 kg line
Nylon stopper — Float — Split shot — Size 2-1/0 hook

Snapper and red rock cod

OFFSHORE RIG
7-9 kg line — Brass rings — 600 mm — 450 mm — Running sinker — Size 4/0-6/0 hook

7-9 kg line — 600 mm — 600 mm — Snapper sinker — 450 mm — Size 4/0-6/0 hooks

ROCK RIG
Nylon stopper — 7-9 kg line — Bobby cork — Brass ring — Alternative four-hook rig — Bean sinker — Size 1/0-6/0 hook

Australian salmon

5-7 kg line — Swivel — Artificial lure — 600 mm

5-7 kg line — Swivel — Keeper hook — 600 mm — Size 1/0-5/0 hook — Running sinker

ually rust and drop out without harming the fish.

The 22 fish species most commonly caught in Australian coastal waters must each be fished for differently. Behaviour patterns differ widely, so a knowledge of where and when fish are likely to be feeding, and what the most tempting bait is will all increase the chances of success. The best arrangement of tackle may differ with location, so experiments are recommended. The size and placement of swivel, rings, hooks and other tackle shown in the illustrations below have all proved successful.

Dusky flathead Mud flathead, Estuary flathead, River flathead, Black flathead *Platycephalus fuscus*
Sandy bottoms, sparsely patched with weed beds, are the favourite haunt of flathead. These fish move slowly across the bottom searching for food, or lie partly buried waiting for small food fish to swim by. Boat owners can drift with the current and allow the bait to drag along the bottom. Flathead frequently lie on the edges of sandbars waiting for fish that retreat to deeper water as the tide recedes. Small, live poddy mullet and yellowtail, yabbies and prawns are excellent baits, as are fillets of fresh mullet, and whole garfish or blue pilchards. Any artificial lure that resembles a small baitfish, either in shape or action, will attract flathead. Their large mouths will easily accept big hooks, sizes 5/0 to 7/0 are popular. Do not use a wire trace, and the breaking strength of the line need be no higher than 7 kg.

Silver bream Yellowfin bream, Sea bream, Black bream, Surf bream *Acanthopagrus australis*
The delicate flavour of its flesh makes the bream a keenly sought species. They are very timid fish, and are more active after dark, when they should be fished for on a rising tide. Bream roam the shoreline, especially where there are oyster and mussel covered rocks, and they are often taken alongside bridge and wharf pylons. The edges of sandbars and weed beds are other worthwhile hunting grounds. Baits are many, but the best are blood worms, live saltwater yabbies and prawns, fresh mullet or garfish fillets, mullet gut and dough. Small hooks are best—sizes 2, 1, 1/0 or 3/0—and the breaking strength of the line should not exceed 7 kg.

Tailor Skipjack, Tailer, Chopper, Bluefish *Pomatomus saltatrix*
Recognised as one of the most voracious fish in the sea, tailor roam constantly at all depths in search of food. They have no specific habitats, but their presence is often betrayed by gulls and terns as they fight over scraps of torn fish, chopped to pieces by a passing school. Tailor will readily take pilchards and sea garfish, and are easy to catch with silver spoon or minnow-type lures. They invariably attack the tail of the bait, intending to disable their prey and make it easier to devour in a subsequent attack. The sharp, constantly chopping teeth can easily sever a nylon line, and a wire-trace between the main line and the hook is essential when single hooks are used, but not necessary when using a lure or ganged hook. Tow a lure, or bait, 10 to 12 metres behind a slow-moving boat. If fishing from a stationary platform, keep the bait moving by slowly winding it back in. Hook size depends upon the bait. With blue pilchards or garfish baits, gang three or more size 3/0 to 5/0 hooks by passing the point of one through the eye of another. A 5/0 hook is not too big for fillet baits. Use a 7 kg breaking strength line.

Mulloway Jewfish, Silver jew, Soapie (when small), School jew, Kingfish (Vic.), Butterfish (SA), River kingfish (WA) *Argyrosomus hololepidotus*
A prize mulloway can weigh over 50 kg. In estuaries these fish can travel beyond tidal influence, and many are captured several kilometres from the sea. They favour the deeper water of holes and the stream centre, feeding on small luderick, whiting, squid, mullet, tailor, octopus, prawns, and yabbies. Blue pilchards, garfish, and fillets of fresh fish can also be used as bait. One of the best times to fish is at night when the tide is rising or slack. Large hooks, up to size 9/0, and lines of 15 kg breaking strength are necessary for big mulloway.

Sand whiting Bluenose whiting, Summer whiting, Silver whiting *Sillago ciliata*
Small in size but tough fighters, whiting are much sought after. Their habitats are similar to those of flathead, but they are often found in much shallower water. Whiting will seldom take a fish bait, preferring worms, yabbies, or cockles. Light lines of up to 3 kg breaking strength and small hooks, sizes 6 to 1, are best. Keep the bait moving by winding the line in, casting out again, and repeating the process. Morning and evening are good fishing times. A tide rising over sandflats will flush out worms and small crustacea which attract these fish.

Luderick Blackfish, Nigger, Darkie, Black bream, Sweep *Girella tricuspidata*
Luderick will test any angler's skill. They feed mainly on green weed, sea lettuce and the minute marine organisms that cling to them, but they also occasionally take live yabbies and worms. Luderick are found close to shore near weed beds, reefs, rock retaining walls, and wharf or bridge pylons. The fish have very small mouths and dainty feeding habits so a size 8 or 12 hook must be used. Plait the hook with wisps of green weed and suspend it beneath a slim boat at a depth determined by trial and error. Fish on a rising to full tide. When a fish has been caught, cut its throat immediately to bleed it, or the flesh will deteriorate.

River garfish *Hyporhamphus regularis*
Eastern sea garfish Beakie *Hyporhamphus australis*
The flesh of these small fish is good to eat and well worth the trouble of removing tiny bones. They are usually found over weed beds or around jetties and wharves, and take small pieces of fish, worms, prawns, squid, bread crust or dough. Use a small hook, around size 12, and suspend it about 300 mm under a slim, lightweight float. Flashing silver or gold tinsel attract the fish to small artificial flies. To remove the bones prior to cooking, lay the cleaned fish gut down on a board and roll a milk bottle along the backbone. Turn the fish over and gently work the backbone and attached bones free of the flesh. Sea garfish make excellent bait for tailor.

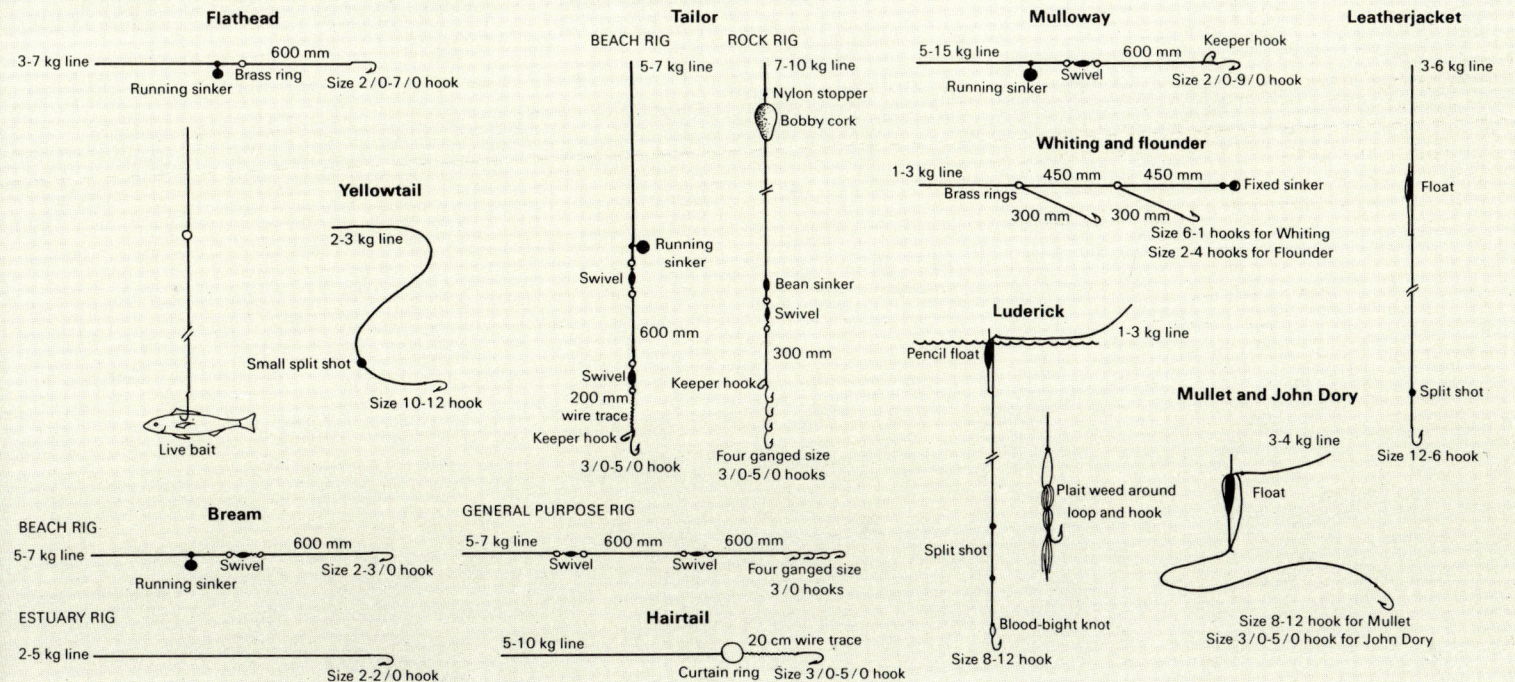

Flathead
3-7 kg line — Running sinker — Brass ring — 600 mm — Size 2/0-7/0 hook

Yellowtail
2-3 kg line — Small split shot — Size 10-12 hook — Live bait

Bream
BEACH RIG
5-7 kg line — Running sinker — Swivel — 600 mm — Size 2-3/0 hook
ESTUARY RIG
2-5 kg line — Size 2-2/0 hook

Tailor
BEACH RIG — 5-7 kg line — Swivel — Running sinker — 600 mm — Swivel — Swivel — 200 mm wire trace — Keeper hook — 3/0-5/0 hook
ROCK RIG — 7-10 kg line — Nylon stopper — Bobby cork — Bean sinker — Swivel — 300 mm — Keeper hook — Four ganged size 3/0-5/0 hooks

GENERAL PURPOSE RIG
5-7 kg line — Swivel — 600 mm — Swivel — 600 mm — Four ganged size 3/0 hooks

Hairtail
5-10 kg line — Curtain ring — 20 cm wire trace — Size 3/0-5/0 hook

Mulloway
5-15 kg line — Running sinker — Swivel — 600 mm — Keeper hook — Size 2/0-9/0 hook

Whiting and flounder
1-3 kg line — Brass rings — 450 mm — 450 mm — Fixed sinker — 300 mm — 300 mm — Size 6-1 hooks for Whiting — Size 2-4 hooks for Flounder

Luderick
Pencil float — 1-3 kg line — Plait weed around loop and hook — Split shot — Blood-bight knot — Size 8-12 hook

Mullet and John Dory
3-4 kg line — Float — Size 8-12 hook for Mullet — Size 3/0-5/0 hook for John Dory

Leatherjacket
3-6 kg line — Float — Split shot — Size 12-6 hook

Fishing for leisure/2 Practical advice on bait and tackle

Chinaman leatherjack Yellow leatherjacket *Nelusetta ayraudi*
Scribbled leatherjacket Fantail leatherjacket, Fan-bellied leatherjacket *Alutera scripta*
Well-known scavengers, leatherjacket are found near jetties and wharves, around boat moorings, and in large weed beds. They will respond to any flesh bait, as well as to bread and cheese. They have a small mouth and incisor-like teeth so use a small hook with a long shank to prevent the fish from biting through the line. Float fishing is the most efficient method—suspend a baited hook, size 12-6, just above the sea floor. The flesh of a leatherjacket is tender and delicious. It makes an ideal food for invalids and children because the large bones are easy to see and remove.

Large-toothed flounder *Pseudorhombus arsius*
Considered a delicacy wherever it is served, flounder is principally a bottom dweller which feeds on worms, small crustacea and shellfish. Best baits are live yabbies and prawns used on size 2 to 4 hooks. The fish are poor fighters, and are often found to be hooked only when the line is reeled in to check the bait.

McCulloch's yellowtail Yellowtail, Yakka, Scad *Trachurus mccullochi*
Small yellowtail are abundant in most estuaries around the Australian coast and they are a popular bait fish.

They can be found around wharves and jetties, among moored boats, in weed beds, and close to underwater reefs in sheltered waters. The fish rarely exceed 200 mm in length, and they have a small mouth so a size 10 or 12 hook is adequate. Handlines are recommended. Best baits are small pieces of squid—which are tough and stay on the hook longer—peeled prawns, and worms. Yellowtail also respond well to small white lures hung in clusters from short leaders attached to the main line. As many as five or six fish can be caught at the one time by jigging the lures up and down. Mashed potato used as a berley will attract and hold yellowtail in the immediate fishing area, but it should be used sparingly—a teaspoon every 10 to 15 minutes—or they may stop biting. The fish may be kept alive in a tank, provided the water is changed regularly and adequate aeration is provided. Small battery-operated aerators can be used, but a constant flow of fresh seawater through the holding tank is more successful. Parents should not be concerned if their children, having caught a number of small yellowtail, want to cook and eat them. The flesh is delicious, although the bones must be removed carefully under adult supervision.

Silver trevally White trevally *Pseudocaranx dentex Pseudocaranx wrighti Caranx nobilis Usacaranx nobilis*
Silver trevally are a popular sporting fish because they are tough, determined opponents that never give in. They are caught in estuaries, off beaches and rocks, and

from the open sea near wrecks and reefs. Trevally are good table fish, but they must be bled immediately upon capture. To do this, simply cut the fish's throat. When fishing from a boat use a short 2 to 2.5 metre rod, and a reel holding about 200 metres of 4.5 kg breaking strain line. Fish weighing up to 2 kg can be caught with this equipment, but stronger line must be used for bigger fish. Rock fishermen should use long, light rods with reels carrying 6 to 7 kg breaking strain line. Good baits are fresh prawns, live saltwater yabbies, worms, and fillets of mullet, pilchard and garfish. Saltwater flies, metal spinners, or small lead-head jigs with a hair body are successful lures. Use a hook between sizes 2 and 1/0. Trevally have soft mouths and should be played gently to prevent the hook pulling out. Do not overcook the fish or the flesh will be dry.

Australian snapper Schnapper, Cockney bream-Red bream-Squire, as size increases *Chrysophrys auratus*
Young snapper are called cockney bream until they reach a weight of about 750 g. Adult snapper, with a fully developed snout bulge and bump on top of the head, can weigh up to 20 kg. Most large snapper are caught around coastal rocks and near offshore reefs, although the occasional stray can be caught from an ocean beach. Rock fishermen should use a medium to fast taper rod up to 4 metres long, a reel holding 7 to 9 kg breaking strain nylon line and hooks of sizes 4/0 to 6/0. Good baits for snapper are skinned octopus leg,

Gathering and preparing fresh bait

WHERE IT is difficult to buy bait, or to store it for long periods, anglers can successfully make their own or gather it around the shoreline. This not only saves money, but also provides the freshest bait possible. Stale bait is only useful as an ingredient in a berley—a mixture of various foods thrown on to the water to attract fish and hold them in the immediate fishing area. Mixtures of minced fish-flesh, bran, soaked wheat, minced prawns, stale bread, crushed shellfish, and a small quantity of tuna oil will produce a good, general-purpose berley.

Dough is one of the most popular baits for bream. Prepare it from flour and water and add a dash of tuna oil and a little cotton wool. The oil gives the dough a putty-like consistency, helps to keep it moist, and attracts fish, while cotton-wool keeps the dough on the hook. Use only sufficient to fill the bend of the hook.

Green weed and sea lettuce attract fish that live on marine algae. Sea lettuce grows abundantly on ocean rocks constantly washed by waves and can also be gathered in estuaries from submerged wharf pylons and rocks. It is normally plaited around the hook shank leaving a short piece hanging below the bend.

Pinkish-white saltwater yabbies are found in estuaries, where they live in burrows beneath sand and mud flats. They are caught with a specially made cylindrical pump. Place the mouth of the pump over a finger-sized yabby hole

and push it into the sand with one hand, while pulling the plunger with the other. This sucks sand, water, and yabby into the pump body. The contents are then ejected into a floating sieve, or on to the sand surface if the tide is out, from where the yabby can be collected.

Cunjevoi, or sea squirts as they are commonly known, are marine animals which grow on ocean rocks in the intertidal zone (see page 17). The animal's rough, leathery covering conceals a soft red flesh that is highly prized as bait. To reach the flesh, cut the cunjevoi from the rock with a knife and pull out the tough muscular tissue inside. The softer parts are difficult to keep on the hook, but can be toughened and preserved by salting down.

Beach worms grow to over 2 metres long and live in the sands of ocean beaches (see page 11). An hour either side of low tide is the best time to search for them. Wave a piece of fish flesh, attached to a cord, or in a stocking, in the water as a wave recedes. The worm's head will emerge from the sand as it searches for the bait, and it can be lured further from the sand using a smaller piece of bait held near its head. Quickly grip the worm behind the head with your thumb and forefinger and pull it firmly and steadily from the sand. Practice is needed to perfect the technique, as the worms are very quick at retreating.

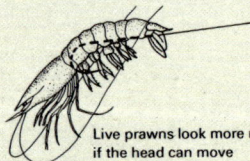

Live prawns look more natural if the head can move

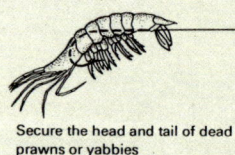

Secure the head and tail of dead prawns or yabbies

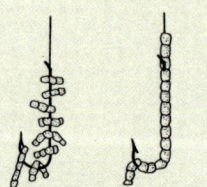

Allow the ends of worm sections to move on the hook

Allow the fronds of baited sea lettuce to move freely

Arrange a strip of fish flesh on the hook so that the end is left free

Feed a small crab on to the hook to give it a natural position in the water

Break large crabs into small pieces so they can be used as bait

Bait live fish through the mouth, or in fleshy parts, to avoid damage to the spine

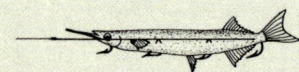

Make sure enough of the hook on ganged-rigs is left to penetrate the catch

squid, pilchard, garfish and slimy mackerel, live yellowtail, fresh prawns, crabs, and fillets of fresh mullet, bonito and striped tuna. Wherever possible do not use a sinker. A floating bait such as a blue pilchard on a series of ganged hooks, slowly reeled in, is most likely to attract snapper. If possible use a berley of chopped fish-flesh, crabs, prawns and squid mixed with stale bread and a dash of tuna oil. When rock fishing use a long-handled gaff to land the fish and reduce the risk of being washed into the water.

Red rock cod Cardinal scorpionfish, Red scorpion cod, Fire cod, Prickly heat *Scorpaena cardinalis*
Mottled reds, browns, and yellows decorate the red rock cod and camouflage it for life among rocks and seaweed. These fish are poor fighters but they can offer considerable resistance by opening their large mouths, expanding their pectoral and ventral fins and curling their tails to one side. The pressure of water against the fish's body has been known to snap light lines. The rock fishing rig for snapper will attract and hold the cod, but they will take almost any flesh-baited rig with hooks ranging from size 1/0 up to size 6/0, and even larger. The cod's mouth is so big that it has earned the nicknames swallow-all and mouth almighty. Venomous spines on the cod's fins can inflict a painful wound, so it should be handled with care, even when dead. The flesh is delicious, especially if lightly cooked and eaten cold.

Australian salmon Salmon trout *Arripis trutta*
These powerful fish grow to about 8 kg, but they are not a popular food fish because the flesh has a strong flavour. Juveniles are often caught in estuaries and bays and are called, colloquially, salmon trout or bay trout. Adults live in the open ocean and are popular sportfish with surf fishermen who find them one of the toughest adversaries. Use a 3 to 4 metre surf rod, a reel carrying at least 200 metres of 5 to 7 kg breaking strain nylon line and hooks of size 1/0 to 5/0. A sinker weighing 70 to 84 g will enable a long cast to be made. When fishing from a boat offshore use a 2.1 m rod and a line with a breaking strain of up to 6 kg. Best baits are sea garfish and blue pilchards, attached whole on ganged hooks, or small fillets used on single size 3/0 to 5/0 hooks. Chrome-plated hexagonal or round, sliced lures will also tempt Australian salmon. When fighting the fish it will be necessary to wind the line in quickly, so use a reel with a gear ratio around 4 to 1. Schools of migrating salmon encountered offshore will bite on a blue plastic squid lure, saltwater flies and feather jigs, cast from or towed behind a boat.

Sea mullet Bully mullet, Mangrove mullet, Hargut mullet, Poddy mullet, River mullet, Bullnose mullet *Mugil cephalus*
Mullet are one of the most common fish in the sea, but also one of the hardest to catch. They can be found in most estuaries and bays around Australia, and usually roam close to the shore or along the edges of sandbars where the juveniles, known as poddy mullet, fall prey to flathead, tailor, and mulloway. The gut of an adult mullet is a good bait for bream, and fillets of fresh sea mullet are a popular bait for most carnivorous fish. The mullet's basic diet is algae, but they can be caught using small pieces of prawn, fish flesh, and worms. Dough is an easy bait to prepare and is eagerly taken by mullet, especially if a berley of bread crumbs is used as well. Fly fishing, using small white or pink flies, is also successful. Use a size 8 to 12 hook suspended 200 to 300 mm below a float on a line of 3 to 4 kg breaking strength. A short spinning rod and reel are adequate. Mullet are determined fighters and skill is required to land them. The flesh has an excellent flavour, but when preparing it for the table make sure the black stomach lining is removed, because it can affect the taste.

Basic fishing knots

WELL-TIED knots distribute strain on a line through the knot, and avoid weak spots that might break under pressure. To obtain the utmost strength make sure the correct number of turns are completed, and that turns do not cross over one another, or slip out of place as the knot is being closed.

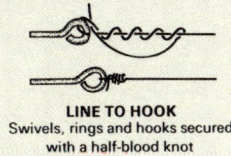

LINE TO HOOK
Swivels, rings and hooks secured with a half-blood knot

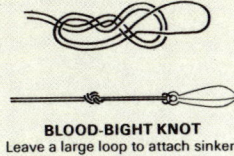

BLOOD-BIGHT KNOT
Leave a large loop to attach sinkers

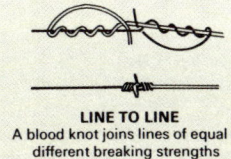

LINE TO LINE
A blood knot joins lines of equal or different breaking strengths

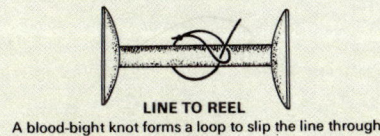

LINE TO REEL
A blood-bight knot forms a loop to slip the line through

Yellowtail kingfish Kingfish, Kingie, Amberjack, Southern yellowtail *Seriola lalandi*
Strong, vigorous sporting fish, yellowtail kingfish can grow to 65 kg, but the average size encountered by most fishermen is about 5 kg. They can be caught with a fish bait, or with a lure towed behind a boat. Yellowtail are a good live bait, and small kingfish are sometimes used to catch the large record breakers. Strong size 5/0 to 9/0 hooks are needed to hold a large fish when live bait is used, and it pays to use a length of heavier line between the hook and main line when fishing over reefs. Kingfish have a habit of diving for the bottom where the line may be snagged and broken. Kingfish may also be caught with a jigged lure—a lure repeatedly dropped to the bottom and rapidly retrieved with a jerking pull. Metal jigs vary in weight and shape, but most are thin and long, with an average weight of 200 g. Colour does not seem to be important. Schools of kingfish roaming surface waters will readily attack red and white feather jigs or a pink plastic squid lure towed at speeds from 5 to 30 km/h. When one kingfish is hooked, the rest of the school generally follows and a large surface popper lure, cast to the surfacing school, should result in a strike. Kingfish can sometimes be caught with live bait cast into deep water from rocks along the ocean front.

Australian hairtail Ribbonfish *Trichiurus coxii*
Despite its forbidding appearance, hairtail is an excellent table fish which requires little preparation for cooking, as it has no scales. The undershot jaws of the fish's angular head are studded with razor sharp teeth and care must be taken to avoid a nasty cut. When a fish is landed, hold the line with a finger through the curtain ring near the end of the rig, grip the fish firmly behind the head and place it in a strong bag to prevent accidents. Hairtail are usually found in the deep water of bays and estuaries. When fishing from a boat use a stout handline of up to 10 kg breaking strength, and size 3/0 to 5/0 hooks. Rod and reel fishermen will find this an exciting fish to catch as it does not give in easily. Best baits are live yellowtail, prawns, gang-hooked garfish and blue pilchards. A steady supply of minced fish berley will attract and hold a school in the fishing area. The best depth for fishing can only be found by trial and error, but a good starting point is 6 to 7 metres. Hairtail take hold of a bait gently and move slowly away with it. If a fisherman strikes too early, the bait will be pulled from the fish's mouth. The best strategy is to let out a metre of line, and then strike. Use a wire trace as the hairtail's teeth will quickly sever even heavy nylon line.

Australian bass Australian perch, Estuary perch, Gippsland perch *Macquaria colonorum*
The sturdy fighting bass is found in coastal streams below tidal influence along the eastern seaboard from the Pumice Stone Channel in southern Queensland to the Gippsland lakes in Victoria. Above tidal influence, a similar fish—*Percalates novemaculatus*—can be caught using the same tackle and approach. Two good fishing outfits are a threadline reel spooled with nylon line of 3 to 4 kg breaking strength mounted on a light spinning rod, or a pistol-grip rod with a closed-face or baitcaster reel. The different kinds of bass lure are designed to move like food fish, frogs and insects, or small animals which have fallen into the water. Some lures are made to dive deep when they are reeled in, while others splash across the surface and are more popular for night fishing. Lines are best cast from a boat drifting close to the shore, slowly retrieved, then cast again until there is a strike. The lure should be dropped as close as possible to weed beds, overhanging trees, submerged logs and rocks where bass are likely to be waiting.

John Dory *Zeus faber*
John Dory consistently commands a high price at Australia's fish markets, and is always in demand for restaurants. This greenish brown fish is easily identified by the large dark grey spot on each side of its body just above and behind the small pectoral fins. They can grow to a weight of 4 kg, but most specimens are about 500 g. Their bodies are tall and thin and the head accounts for almost one third of the total length. The huge mouth is capable of wide and rapid extension. The best bait for John Dory is live yellowtail. Use a hook between sizes 3/0 and 5/0, and a light line with a breaking strength of 3 to 4 kg. Rod and reel fishing is usual, and it is worthwhile using a float to keep the live bait in mid-water. John Dory are poor fighters. They are often taken around wharf and jetty piles, in weed beds and over reefs where they feed on small yellowtail, hardyheads, cockney bream, and other bait fish. The fish's skin is smooth and scaleless, so it is only necessary to remove the large head and intestines before cooking.

Prawn family *Penaeidae*, various species
Prawns mature in tidal estuaries and lakes in summer and are caught in shallow water at night as they move towards the sea. Carry a strong light so that prawns stationary on the bottom can be spotted easily, and use a triangular-framed net. Place the net behind the prawn and scoop it up quickly, or startle it with a movement of your foot so that it shoots backwards into the net. Drag longer nets against the current, with one prawner wading into waist-deep water.

Identifying your catch

Of the thousands of species of fish living in the waters around Australia's coast only a small percentage end up in an angler's creel. Many are considered unfit for eating and are simply thrown back into the sea when caught. On the Great Barrier Reef alone there are around 1400 species to be found. Most of these, however, are small fish, more suitable for an aquarium than for the dinner table. Some fish are toxic and if eaten can cause sickness and even death, so it is important to be able to identify your catch. The 22 fish illustrated below are the ones most commonly fished for and caught, either for sport or for eating. Many fish are known by a variety of common names, and these vary from place to place. Even scientific names can change when species are reclassified.

Scribbled leatherjacket
Fantail leatherjacket, Fan-bellied leatherjacket
Alutera scripta

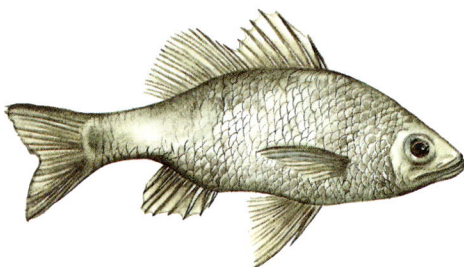

Australian bass
Australian perch, Estuary perch,
Gippsland perch *Macquaria colonorum*

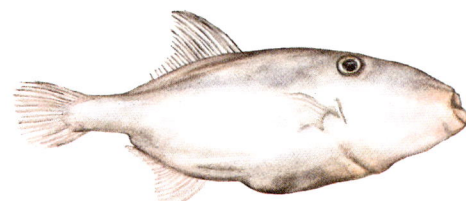

Chinaman leatherjacket
Yellow leatherjacket *Nelusetta ayraudi*

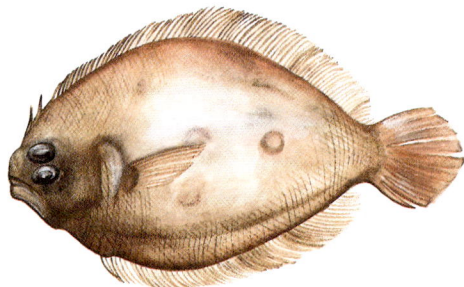

Large-toothed flounder
Pseudorhombus arsius

Red rock cod
Cardinal scorpionfish, Red scorpion cod,
Fire cod, Prickly heat *Scorpaena cardinalis*

Eastern sea garfish
Beakie
Hyporhamphus australis

River garfish
Hyporhamphus regularis

McCulloch's yellowtail
Yellowtail, Yakka, Scad
Trachurus mccullochi

Sand whiting
Bluenose whiting, Summer whiting,
Silver whiting *Sillago ciliata*

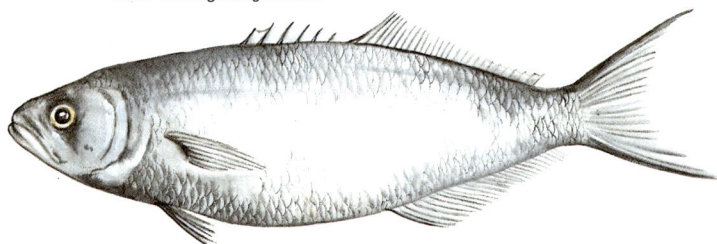

Mulloway
Jewfish, Silver jew, Soapies (when small),
School jew, Kingfish (Vic.), Butterfish (SA), River kingfish (WA)
Argyrosomus hololepidotus

Tailor
Skipjack, Tailer, Chopper,
Bluefish *Pomatomus saltatrix*

Yellow kingfish
Kingfish, Kingie, Amberjack,
Southern yellowtail
Seriola lalandi

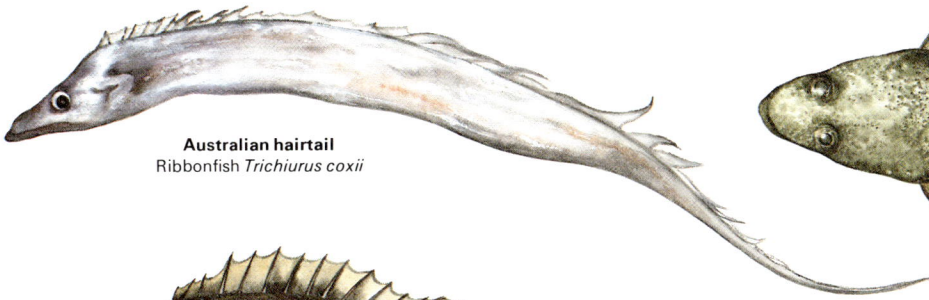

Australian hairtail
Ribbonfish *Trichiurus coxii*

Dusky flathead
Mud flathead, Estuary flathead,
River flathead, Black flathead
Platycephalus fuscus

Luderick
Blackfish, Nigger, Darkie,
Black bream, Sweep
Girella tricuspidata

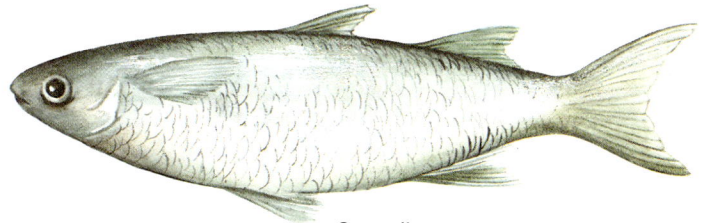

Sea mullet
Bully mullet, Mangrove mullet, Hardgut mullet,
Poddy mullet, River mullet, Bullnose mullet
Mugil cephalus

Australian salmon
Salmon trout *Arripis trutta*

Silver trevally
White trevally *Pseudocaranx dentex*
Pseudocaranx wrighti, Caranx nobilis, Usacaranx nobilis

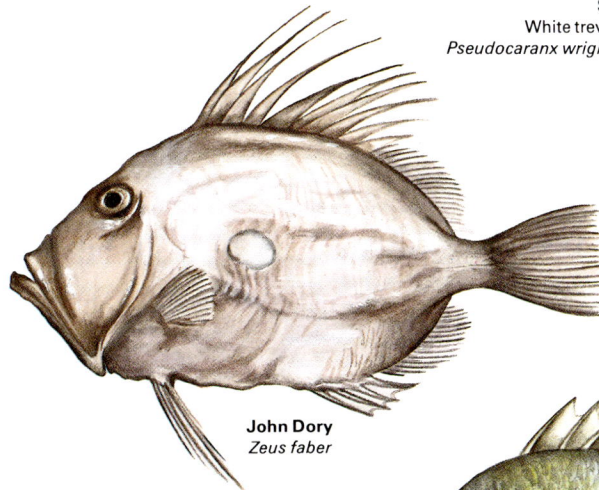

John Dory
Zeus faber

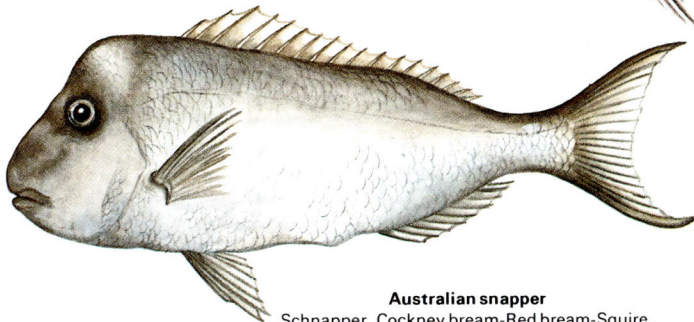

Australian snapper
Schnapper, Cockney bream-Red bream-Squire,
as size increases *Chrysophrys auratus*

Silver bream
Yellowfin bream, Sea bream, Black bream,
Surf bream *Acanthopagrus australis*

Inshore boating Vital preparations for a day on the water

Nearly 700,000 Australian families own a craft for sailing, paddling or power boating. Most are small and low-powered, used mainly for weekend recreation on bays and estuaries where boat owners are attracted by fine conditions and placid waters. But behind the apparent safety of sheltered waterways lie potential hazards which must not be disregarded. To prevent a holiday turning into a nightmare, every boat owner must be aware of the problems that can arise, and the steps that may be taken to avoid them.

The anchor, one of the principal pieces of equipment on the boat, is thought by many to be of use only for holding the boat in position while fishing over a favourite spot or picnicking on the shore. But the anchor is more than that—it is a vital safety aid. In the wide estuaries common to most of Australia's big rivers mechanical failure may result in a boat being caught in a strong out-running tide and swept on to a dangerous bar at the entrance. Because most boats are too heavy or cumbersome to be rowed against such a tide, or against a strong wind, the only way to avoid disaster is to drop the anchor as quickly as possible. With the correct anchor and gear, a boat can be halted and held in position while repair work is carried out, or signals are sent for help.

Anchors of inappropriate design and weight, however, will not catch in the sea bed, and an anchor line which is too short will constantly pluck the anchor out before it can take a firm hold. While a sand-anchor may sometimes hold on a rocky bottom, a reef-anchor will not hold properly in sand or mud. A short anchor line which is quite adequate in a sheltered bay will be insufficient in deep water or against a strong current.

The best anchor lines are made of nylon or other synthetic materials and must be long enough to allow at least five or six times the water's depth to be paid out. The longer and heavier the anchor line, the greater the anchor's holding power. A length of chain about 3 metres long between the anchor and the line adds weight and prevents the line chafing on the sea bed, particularly over reefs. Any reputable dealer will advise on the correct type and weight of anchor for your particular craft.

A boat which is overloaded may appear stable in sheltered nearshore waters, but the wash of a passing vessel or a turbulent rip sweeping around

Long mooring lines must be used in areas where the tide range is large. Secure a boat at both bow and stern so that it can rise and fall with the water level

A long line, with a length of chain attached, helps the anchor to lie on the sea bed and dig in securely. The length of line hanging in the water forms a buffer against the tugging of the boat as it is buffeted by wind and waves—small shocks are absorbed by the line before they reach the anchor

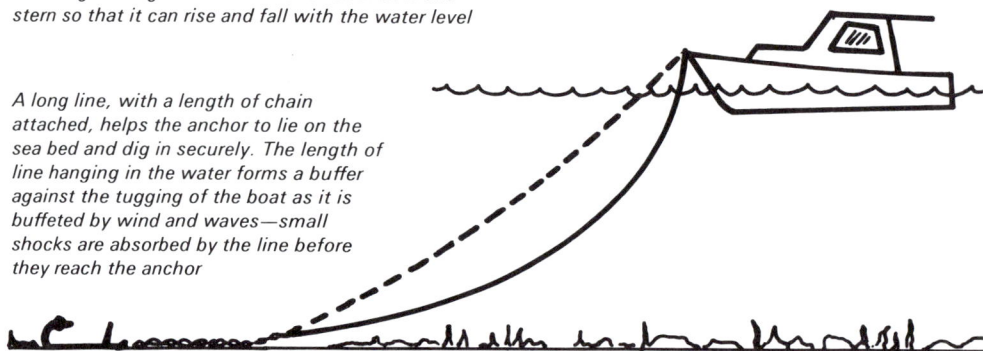

a headland may push a wave aboard. When the boat's stability is upset it may be impossible to avoid further waves and the boat may soon be swamped. All boats should carry a notice indicating the maximum number of people to be carried, and this figure must be sensibly balanced with the amount of gear taken on board.

The effect of bad trimming is much the same as overloading. Move passengers or gear so that the boat is neither down at the bow nor at the stern—conditions which make any craft difficult to handle and impair its performance. A badly trimmed boat will use more fuel, strain the motor and provide an uncomfortable ride. In small boats correct trim is easily achieved by adjusting the positions of passengers or luggage, but larger craft need adjustable trim controls.

Naval charts and boating maps can help sailors avoid the hazards hidden in many deceptively safe waterways. If a boat is grounded on a mud-

bank it may result in little more than a scratched bottom, but to hit a reef, particularly at high speed, can cause serious damage to the craft and injury to the occupants. The reefs, sand banks, shoals and channels shown on maps allow sailors to plot a safe course, and prominent landmarks are shown to aid navigation.

For anglers, the location of wrecks and the contours and composition of the sea bed may give a good indication of the sorts of fish likely to be found in an area. Charts produced by the hydrographic office of the Navy are readily available for most major waterways, and boating maps produced by local authorities cover many popular rivers, lakes and estuaries.

In unfamiliar waters boat owners must seek local advice on sand bars and channels, as these may change considerably depending on the weather, the tide and the volume of water flowing into rivers and lakes.

Signalling for help

THERE are a number of internationally known distress signs that can be used in emergencies. These include raising and lowering outstretched arms, firing red flares or rockets and regularly repeated signals from a foghorn or gun. Flames and smoke from a container of burning tar or oil will attract attention by day or night. Distress sheets—bright orange rectangles marked with a black 'V', or a black square or circle—are valuable for attracting the attention of aircraft.

The gradient of any specially constructed launching ramp usually provides sufficient depth of water over a normal range of tides, so that a boat can be launched and retrieved without damage to its hull. Take care not to immerse the trailer's wheel hubs because bearings will rapidly corrode in the salt water, and this is potentially dangerous. Most ramps have areas nearby where preparation for launching can be carried out. Release tie-downs, check the motor, and load all equipment to prevent unnecessary delays on the ramp itself

Nothing has a greater effect on boating holidays than the weather. Apart from comfort, the weather can greatly affect the safety of any vessel. Check the forecast before setting out to avoid being caught in bad weather. This is particularly important for small boats in open waterways such as Melbourne's Port Phillip Bay and Brisbane's Moreton Bay, where choppy seas can quickly develop that will threaten all but the most seaworthy craft. However, local conditions can change rapidly and forecasts can be wrong, so it is wise to learn to recognise threatening weather patterns.

Most dangerous weather conditions give an indication of their approach with unmistakable sky signs. A cold front is usually accompanied by a build up of giant towering clouds. A line squall can appear as a fast-moving roll of cloud stretching across the sky. Local weather patterns may have their own peculiar signs which, if recognised early enough, give sailors time to make for port or for the shelter of a headland. Coast guards, members of yacht clubs and commercial fishermen are always willing to provide helpful information to visitors.

Many of the rules governing safe boating are covered by regulations and enforced by law. Speed limits apply in most popular waterways and around moorings, and boating may be prohibited altogether in swimming areas. One life jacket per passenger is obligatory on all craft, from the smallest dinghies to ocean-going yachts. An anchor, paddles and fire extinguisher may also be considered to be standard equipment in some areas. Alternative means of propulsion—a secondary outboard, sail, oars or paddles—are useful in case a motor fails or winds become too light to propel a yacht. A good sailing day with a brisk breeze can become a dead calm by the middle of the afternoon, and the shore may be a long way off. Carry a spare length of rope to repair rigging, or a shear pin in case the propeller hits an obstruction in the water. Such precautions can mean the difference between getting back to shore on time or spending hours waiting for a tow. Report trips into offshore waters to the water police or coastguard. Detailed plans of the route to be travelled and expected time of arrival are necessary, so that a search operation can be started if a boating party fails to confirm its safe arrival.

Four basic knots that boat owners must master

Boats must be securely tied to anchors and mooring points for safety. The knots that are used must remain firm whether the rope is wet and taut, or dry and slack. Modern synthetic ropes have a slippery surface and this must also be taken into account. A good knot must release easily when the direction of pressure is reversed, so that a quick reaction to emergencies is possible. Each knot serves a different purpose—everything from mooring a boat to a jetty to joining two pieces of rope together—and all boat owners must be familiar with the four most common ones. These are the reef knot, the clove hitch, the bowline, the round-turn with two half-hitches. Practice tying the knots at home until the sequence of operations becomes second nature.

Reef knot
Joins two pieces of rope of similar size. Will not jam. Release by pushing strands of one rope into the knot

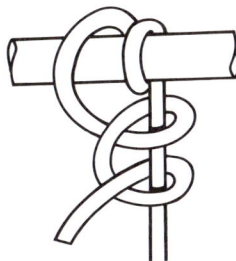

Round-turn and two half-hitches
Safe, efficient way to securely fasten a rope to small fixtures such as jetty rings and nails

Clove hitch
Simple knot used to attach a rope to a fixed object. Release knot by easing pressure on either end of the rope

Bowline
Mainly used at the end of a rope to make a non-slip loop for dropping over mooring posts on a wharf or jetty. Release by pushing rope into knot

Coastal hazards   Dangers that can be avoided

Coasts are risky places—mainly because so many people using them are visiting unfamiliar territory and experiencing an unaccustomed climate. Often people are literally out of their element, venturing on and into water that holds its own menace, as well as concealing dangerous creatures. But nearly all trouble can be avoided with some knowledge of where hazards may be found, and the exercise of common sense and caution. The problems that most frequently lead to drowning are discussed earlier in this section, and resuscitation is dealt with overleaf, as are other first aid treatments, including those for many stings and bites. Two special menaces of tropical coasts are saltwater crocodiles, which can kill with a blow from their tails, and box jellyfish, whose stings require trained assistance.

Sun effects—sunburn, sunstroke and heat exhaustion—are characteristic of coasts only because most people wear less clothing and spend more time basking than usual. Screening creams provide the best protection against burning. If washed off by perspiration or bathing, they should be reapplied at once. Sunstroke is a breakdown of the body's heat-regulating system: victims do not sweat. Heat exhaustion is a failure of blood circulation to the extremities, caused by loss of body salt and fluid, and is more common among the chronically ill or elderly. People prone to either sunstroke or heat exhaustion should seek shade and cooler air, and perhaps limit their travelling to temperate regions.

Infections start easily from coral cuts in the tropics, from wounds inflicted by some of the relatively harmless marine stingers or spiked fish, and from insect bites. Shoes should be worn on reefs and in tropical waters. The use of insect repellents is advisable, even by people who are not irritated by itching bites. Mosquito-borne

Cone shells must be left alone—the poison injected by tropical species is usually fatal

diseases include dengue fever in the tropics and the related Ross River fever in subtropical Queensland. And in remote parts on the north coast, pockets of malaria may still be found.

Stinging jellyfish, other than the tropical box jellyfish, are unlikely to cause death. But heavy doses of their venom can cause severe and prolonged pain and may bring about collapse. Corneal scarring may result from a sting across an eye. Swimmers should note that the prevalence of most such jellyfish increases with the water temperature: risks are greatest in late summer. At least six Australian species of *Conus*, the **stinging shellfish,** are known to be dangerous. They shoot out hard, barbed spears that pump venom. The most lethal are found on tropical reefs, where they bury themselves in sand by day. All known species contain some venom and none should be handled before making certain that the living animal is not still inside.

Of dozens of species of venomous **stinging fish,** the deadliest are stonefish, *Synanceia*. Though big—up to 500 mm—and bulky, they are virtually impossible to see in their coral reef or mudflat habitats, because they are coated with slime and algae and sometimes partly buried in sand. They have 13 sharp spines along their backs, each

linked to two venom glands. Stonefish are distributed throughout the tropics and south to Brisbane, most stings occurring at Easter or during the August school holidays. Strong footwear is the best protection. Fishermen should learn to identify stonefish, and not grab too quickly at whatever they hook or net. Stinging fish common in cooler waters—catfish, bullrout, fortescue, cobbler, red rock cod, flathead, goblinfish, old wife and many more—do most harm to anglers and trawlermen handling them accidentally, especially at night. Their venom is much less dangerous than that of the stonefish and other tropical species, but it may cause a collapse leading to drowning. Stingrays, though venomous, do most of their damage by the wound they inflict. Feeding on the sea bed and often motionless, a stingray drives its long, spiny tail directly up at anyone treading on it. Some species are found all around the coast. They are unlikely to feed where many people are swimming, but a close watch should be kept in lonely waters. One species of shark, known as the Port Jackson but

Camouflage renders the stonefish almost invisible

The ocean's most feared menace

THE POSSIBILITY of shark attack probably worries Australian surf bathers more than any other seaside hazard. Yet the chances of being bitten are extremely remote. In the decade from 1970 there were only 20 attacks in Australian waters, of which five were fatal. Many city beaches have now been made even safer by meshing—with a net suspended in the water a few hundred metres from the beach for part of its length. The net is not intended to seal off the beach completely, but to provide a trap for any sharks in the area. Sharks must keep moving so that water can circulate through their gills; if they are caught in a net and immobilised they quickly drown. Nets are retrieved at regular intervals, dead sharks removed and damage repaired. Since meshing was introduced in Sydney in 1937 there has not been a fatal attack on any of Sydney's 60 km of ocean beaches. In recent years the number of sharks caught in nets has declined considerably, in Sydney from 224 in 1951 to 43 in 1969, and some experts think that the nets may discourage sharks from establishing territories. Attacks are very rare in waters where the surface temperature is below 21°C, so the seasonal patterns of water temperature variations are a good guide to the periods when bathing is most likely to be safe.

Shark attacks follow the seasonal warming of southern waters. Bathers should remember that shallow bays are often warmer than the surrounding ocean

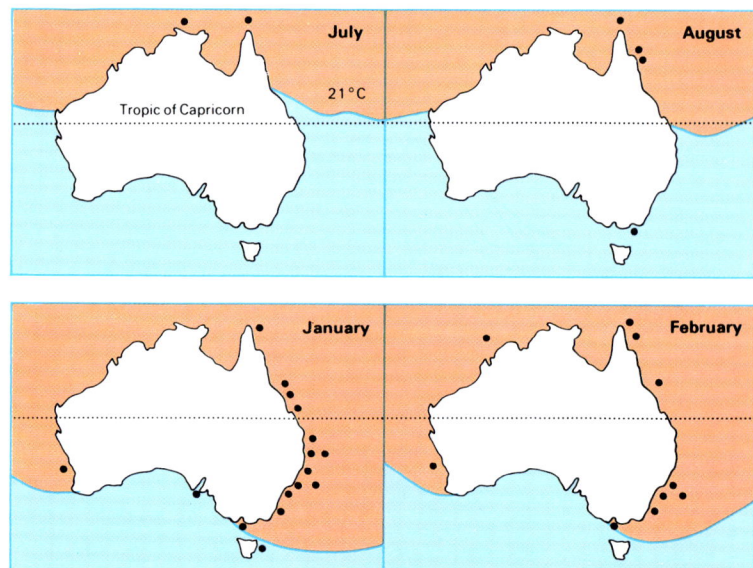

Temperature above 21°C   Temperature below 21°C   ● Shark attack sites

Vivid circles of colour make the blue-ringed octopus easy to identify. These creatures are very common

When a fish feast may be poisonous

CIGUATERA poisoning, much publicised since the late 1970s, has always been a risk on tropical coasts and islands. Toxins originating in coral reef algae and small marine animals are passed from fish to fish in the reef food chain. The bigger the fish, the greater the accumulation of poison. More than 300 species could have it, but the highest concentrations are believed to be in the liver and other internal organs of red bass, chinaman and paddletail—none of which are permitted to be sold commercially—along with barracouta and moray eel.

Symptoms of ciguatera poisoning usually include numb and tingling fingers, numbness around the mouth, burning or tingling of the skin in cold water, muscle and joint pain, vomiting, diarrhoea and headache. Death is unusual but a lengthy treatment in hospital may be necessary. The disease can have a debilitating effect for months. Fish eaters visiting the tropics should not eat large portions from the bigger reef fish, and they should never eat repeated meals from the same fish. Whatever the species, the internal organs of reef fish should never be eaten.

distributed throughout temperate waters, has a venomous spine in front of each of the two fins on its back. Its struggles when hooked or speared can drive a spine centimetres into a fisherman's flesh. Pain and muscle weakness from the poison may last only a few hours, but the ragged wound is easily infected. Both the tiny southern blue-ringed octopus and its bigger tropical relative have been known to kill humans with the venomous bites of their beaks. The deaths were entirely avoidable. This easily identified animal is harmless in the water—it bites humans only if it

is picked up, usually after having been stranded in a rock pool by low tide.

More than 30 species of **sea snake** are found in tropical Australian waters but only two are distributed as far south as Cape Leeuwin or Bass Strait. Their fangs deliver meagre amounts of venom but it can be extremely toxic, causing death by muscle destruction. No one inexperienced in handling snakes should pick one up, and prawning or fishing nets should be handled with care, especially at night.

Coastal **land snakes** in temperate regions

include the Western Australian dugite and the Sydney broad-headed snake, both of which are highly venomous though unlikely to cause death. The broad-head likes to hide in dry rock crevices or under boulders and slabs. The taipan—the longest venomous snake in Australia, and invariably lethal with its bite until an anti-venom was developed in the 1950s—inhabits north-eastern and northern coastal areas. Normally timid, it flees when approached, but is likely to strike if cornered, snapping three or four times with fangs up to 13 mm long.

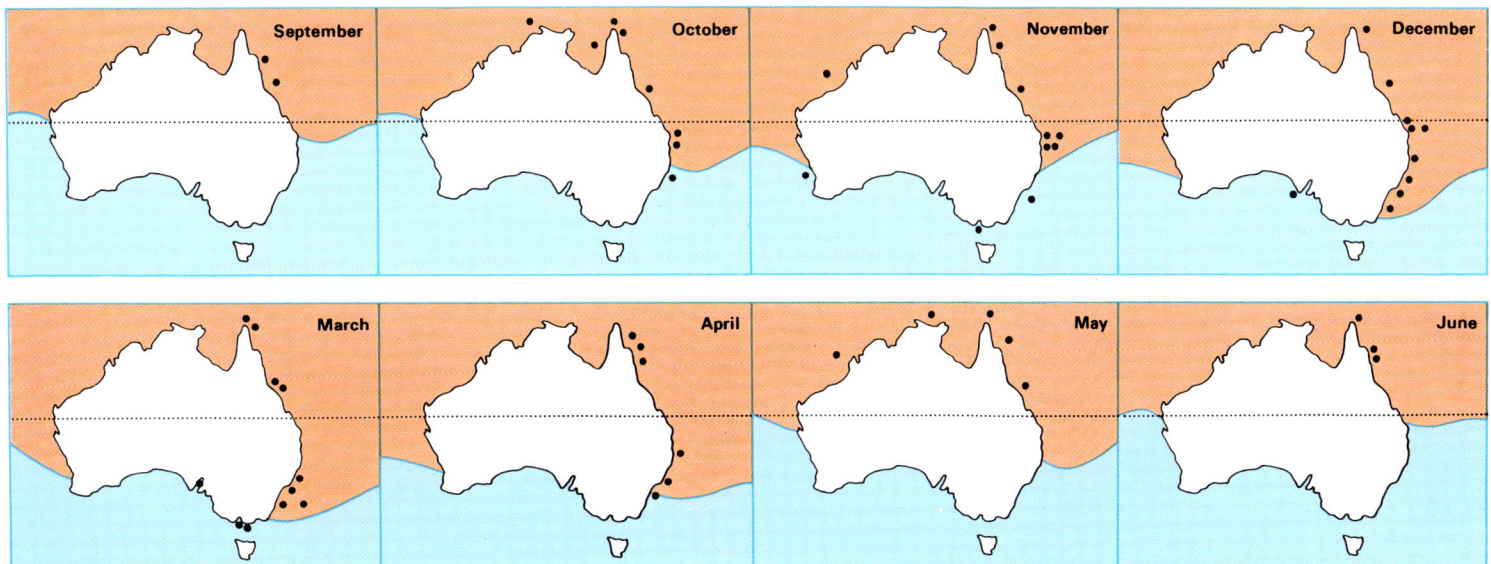

Emergency action Skills to save a life

A drowning person's breathing and heartbeat may stop, but they can still be revived. Resuscitation has to begin as soon as possible—in the water if necessary—to restore the supply of oxygen to the blood, restart the heart and keep the blood circulating around the body. Victims of suffocation, electric shock, heart attack and some poisons and venoms can also be kept alive.

Place the victim on their side on a firm, level surface and clear the throat to prevent any food, blood or mucus going down into the lungs. If the patient is unconscious, make sure the tongue does not fall backwards and block the throat. Use your fingers to scoop out any particles behind the tongue. Take out any false teeth. Tilt the head backwards while supporting the jaw with the other hand, keeping the face pointing slightly down so that any mucus or fluid can drain out of the mouth. Then put the person on their back. Kneel at the head and put the palm of one hand on the top of the victim's head while supporting the chin with the other, and tilt the head back so the tongue will keep out of the way and air will be able to enter freely.

Pinch the victim's nostrils closed with your thumb and forefinger, all the time keeping the head tilted back. Take a deep breath, open your mouth as wide as possible and put it over the victim's mouth, making an airtight seal. Blow into the mouth strongly.

Take your mouth away. If the victim's chest is not rising, check if the airway is clear. Then put your mouth back over the victim's and breathe into the victim five times, as fast as you can.

Check if there is any pulse beat by feeling for the carotid pulse in the neck (as shown). If there is a pulse beat, continue with mouth-to-mouth respiration at 12 breaths a minute. It may be necessary to continue for a long time. Check the carotid pulse every two minutes.

If there is no carotid pulse, mouth-to-mouth respiration should go on and heart massage should begin immediately. Kneel beside the victim. Find the lower half of the breastbone. Put the heel of your other hand over the first hand. With arms straight, lean forward and press down on the breastbone so it goes down about 50 mm. Keeping your hands in position, lean back and release the pressure. Continue the process rhythmically, pressing down *at least* once a second. The best rate would be around 80 times a minute.

If you are alone with the victim, after 15 chest presses move to the head and use your mouth to inflate the lungs twice. Continue with 15 chest compressions then two lung inflations in turn.

If there are two people available they should kneel on opposite sides of the victim. One person does five chest presses, one every second—to get the timing right, count out loud 'one thousand, two thousand' and so on. The other person then makes one chest inflation using mouth-to-mouth.

If the victim is a child, only one hand should be used for chest compressions, and they should be given a little faster. The breastbone should be pressed down only 20 mm. Do not press a baby's breastbone down more than 10 mm.

If breathing begins, put the victim quickly into the recovery position (as shown). Vomiting will often occur now. Keep the throat clear. Watch the person continually to check if the breathing is satisfactory. If not, replace on the back and begin resuscitation again. Check the pulse every 2 to 3 minutes. To stop loss of body heat, cover the victim with a coat or blanket. Stay with the victim until qualified help comes.

How to give mouth-to-mouth resuscitation

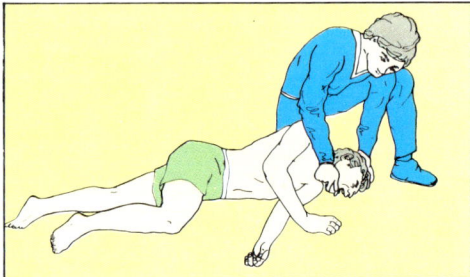

1 Resuscitation can begin in the water if necessary. Once out of the water, place the victim lying on their side on a firm, level surface. Keep the head tilted to help clear the airway

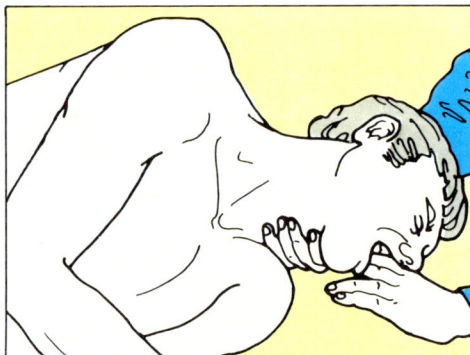

2 An unconscious person cannot prevent food or mucus passing down the throat into the lungs, so clear the mouth behind the tongue

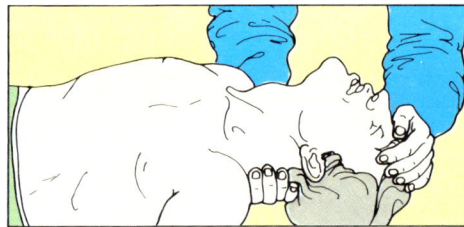

3 Once the airway has been cleared, turn the patient on their back. Supporting the chin, tilt the head so that the tongue is clear and air can enter the lungs

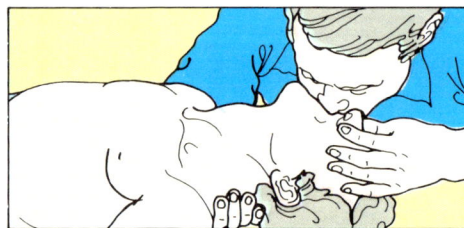

4 While the head is still tilted back, pinch the patient's nostrils. Take a deep breath, hold it, then put your mouth firmly over the victim's and blow strongly

5 When you take your mouth away, check to see if the patient's chest is rising, and listen for any exhalation of air. Repeat resuscitation until breathing resumes

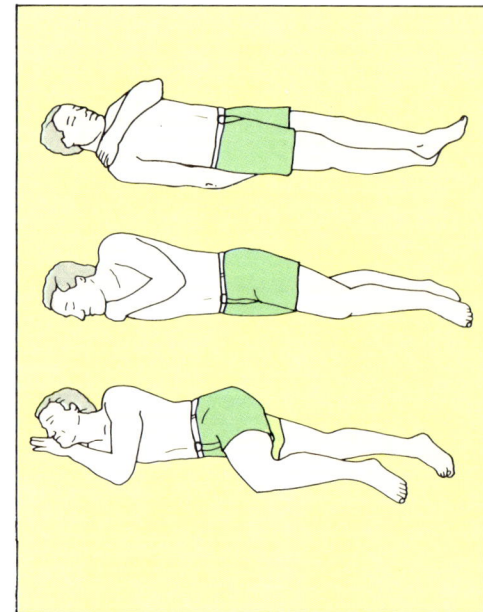

6 The recovery or coma position keeps the airway clear and stops vomit getting into the lungs. If you have given mouth-to-mouth resuscitation and heart massage and restored a victim's breathing and heart beat, they will be lying on their back.

To put the victim in the recovery position, kneel at the victim's side and pull their further leg over the one nearest to you. Then place the arm further from you across the chest to the shoulder area. Position the other arm down along the torso (with the palm upwards). Next pull the victim on to the side that is nearest to you. Pull the underneath arm down behind the back. Bend the top leg. Put the arm of the top hand under the chin, supporting the chin but with the hand clear of the mouth. Tilt the head slightly backwards to keep the airway clear

The technique of heart massage

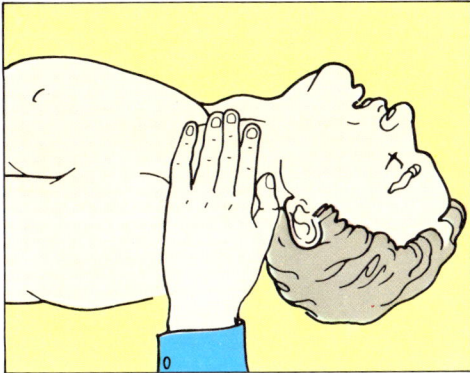

1 To check for heartbeat, place your hand palm downwards across the side of the victim's neck and feel for the carotid artery pulse between the Adam's apple and the neck muscles

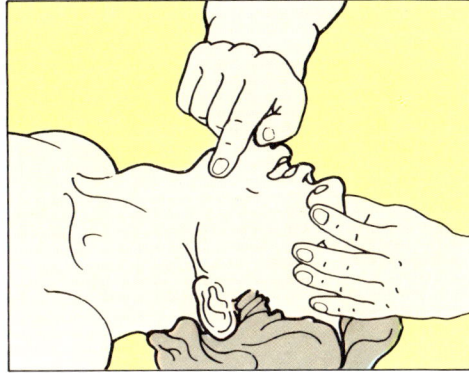

2 Before applying external cardiac compression, place the patient on their back on a flat, firm surface and remove any restricting clothing. Check that the airway is clear, then tilt head well back

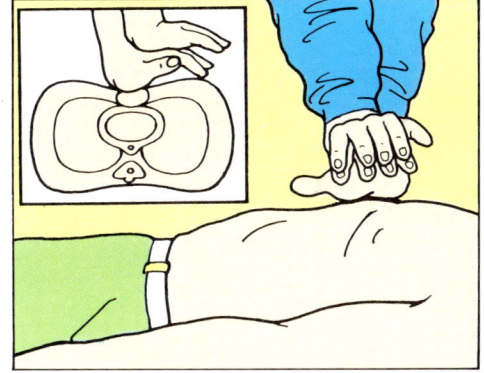

3 Kneeling to one side, place the heel of one hand on the middle half of the patient's breastbone. Keeping palm and fingers raised above the chest, place heel of other hand on top of first hand

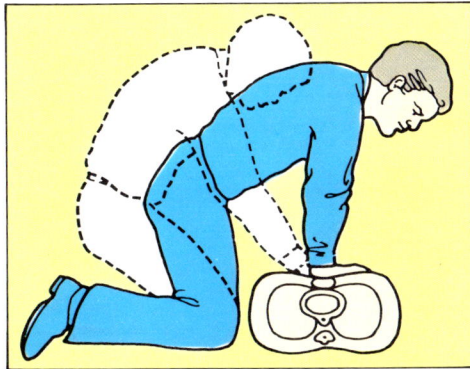

4 Straighten arms and push down on the breastbone, depressing it about 50 mm. Keeping your hands in position, lean back and release pressure on chest. Repeat at least once a second

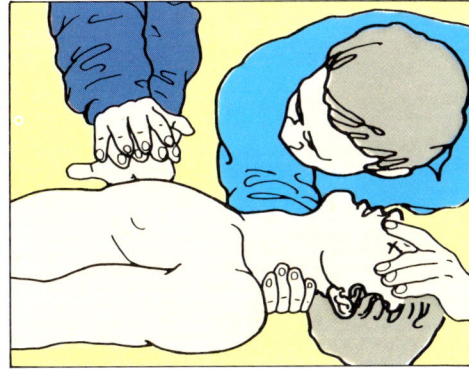

5 If two people are available, one should apply mouth-to-mouth resuscitation while the other continues heart massage, working together at the rate of 1 air inflation to 5 compressions

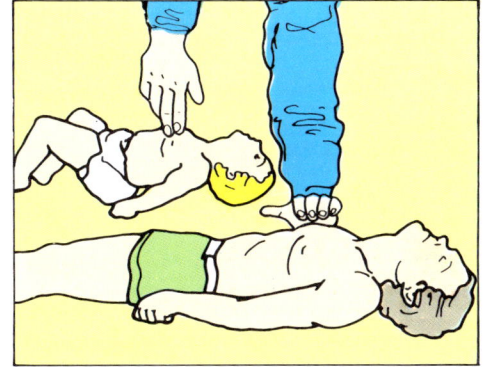

6 On a child, use only one hand and increase the adult rate of cardiac compressions, with less depression of the breastbone. Do not depress a baby's breastbone more than 10 mm

Aiding a shark attack victim

MOST shark attacks are survivable if help is at hand. Rescuers are hardly ever harmed. But people must condition themselves to the horrifying appearance of some wounds, to avoid panic.

Bleeding must be staunched quickly. If the victim cannot be brought ashore immediately, use your fingers to press hard into or just above any point where blood is spurting. Once ashore, do NOT try to get the victim to hospital. Move him only out of reach of waves and lay him on the sand with his head lowermost.

Apply a tourniquet above the wound, over a long bone—not a joint. You can use a belt or a strip of cloth or rubber, but nothing as narrow as string or shoe laces. If heavy bleeding continues, use pressure by hand or pack cloth of any kind over the wound. Do NOT remove blood-soaked dressings—press more cloths on top. Then call an ambulance.

While waiting, cover the victim lightly but give him nothing to eat or drink. If he is wearing a wetsuit, leave it on. Monitor the victim's breathing and be ready to give mouth-to-mouth resuscitation.

Venomous bites and stings

Snakebites and most serious marine stingings can be combated with good first aid. The aim is to slow the spread of venom and the onset of paralysis until qualified medical treatment can be given.

Never cut into a snakebite wound or cut away injured tissue. That does more harm than good. Do NOT try to remove clothing covering the wound—movement will spread the venom. Do NOT wash the wounded area. Surplus venom splashes on the skin cannot hurt the victim and it will help in quick identification of the snake type. Do NOT try to kill the snake at the risk of further bites. And do NOT tie an arterial tourniquet above the wound.

Wrap a wide bandage directly over the bitten area, as firmly as if you were binding a sprained ankle. Extend the binding as high as you can—to the thigh if a foot or leg is bitten—and secure a splint to the whole leg. If the bite is on a hand or forearm, apply bandages and a splint as far as the elbow and place the arm in a sling.

Keep the victim warm and as still as possible.

Check regularly for breathing. If first aid comes too late and paralysis sets in, mouth-to-mouth resuscitation may be necessary. If the victim must be moved, it should be done gently—preferably on a stretcher.

Exactly the same pressure/immobilisation first aid works for funnelweb spider bites. It is not necessary for the bite of the redback spider, which has a slower-acting venom. Pressure on a redback bite only increases pain, and that can be eased by cooling the wound with a mixture of ice cubes and water in a plastic bag—but do NOT apply ice directly to a wound.

Warm water, on the other hand, is often a pain-reliever for the victims of stinging fish. Cone shell stings and blue-ringed octopus bites are dealt with by the pressure/immobilisation method. Jellyfish stings can be neutralised to some extent with vinegar—NOT methylated spirit or other alcohols. The main risk of marine stingings is for a person to collapse and drown—but be as gentle as possible in removing a victim from the water.

PART 4

Discovering the coast

Faced with the immensity of the seaboard, travellers must be selective. For every person who seeks reassuring surroundings and familiar activities at journey's end, there is another who hopes for surprise and challenge.

Fascination may lie in landscapes and wildlife, or the ocean itself may be the lure.

Coastal towns can command attention in their own right, or be seen as mere resting places. Choice is a matter of personal taste and circumstances.

In this part of the book the options are left open. With the widest range of interests in mind, priority is given to solid, serviceable information about scores of localities.

Most of the places described are illustrated with aerial photographs, and wherever possible these have been joined together to give the broadest possible view, even if there is a shift in colour.

These sweeping panoramas could otherwise be photographed only from a great altitude, where atmospheric haze reduces clarity.

The photographs provide a remarkable new perspective of even familiar areas. Mysteries of local topography, access, vegetation and waterways all become clear.

Even individual houses can be easily identified.

Evening clouds gather over a coastal mountain range

Aerial photography A bird's eye view of the shore

Nearly all of the illustrations in the following guide sections are reproduced from specially commissioned vertical aerial photographs. The technique of taking them is a demanding one, calling for exceptional precision in navigation and timing. But nothing else is so effective in showing the positions of ground features in relation to one another. The pictures work as living maps. And some incidental points of information emerging from them could not be conveyed even in the most elaborate formal mapping.

Aerial cameras work the same way as those used in conventional photography. But they are exceptionally big. They take rolls of film on which each frame is more than 225 mm square— almost the size of this page—and each roll has room for more than 100 frames. The film magazine alone is bigger than a typewriter and almost as bulky. High-performance light aircraft are modified—their hydraulic systems and electrical wiring may have to be shifted—so that the camera can be mounted in the belly of the fuselage with a lens cone protruding downwards through the hull. Normal or wide-angle lenses may be fitted. The mounting allows the camera to be swung out of line with the heading of the aircraft, or to be tilted if the aircraft is not in level flight.

The requirements of the picture—always a compromise between the detail that can be shown and the area that can be covered— determine the shooting altitude. Reader's Digest decided on 3000 metres, giving a ground spread of about 4.5 km in each full frame. Each area was plotted on detailed maps, allowing for overlaps where it was intended that pictures be joined up. Then it was up to navigator-cameramen to direct pilots over exactly the right spot while maintaining the right height. Taking their bearings from the most prominent ground features, they set a course to the centre of the plotted area. Sighting instruments enabled them not only to trigger their cameras with split-second timing, but also to

Only the centre of an aerial photograph is a truly vertical view—features at the edges lean outwards

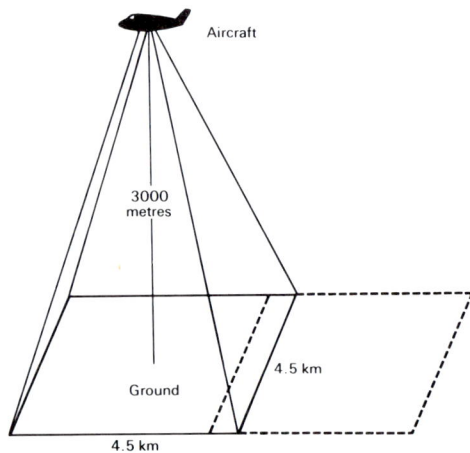

A normal lens used at an altitude of 3000 metres covers a ground area of 20.25 sq km. Pictures are overlapped to reduce the contrast in angles when they are joined

observe wind-drifting or tilting so that camera angles could be adjusted. The precision achieved far excels that of wartime bomb-aiming.

Because the distance between the camera and the ground is greater at the edges of each picture, angles are created that slightly distort the image. Tall features appear to lean out at all sides of a picture—most noticeably in city shots. Angling at the edges may also affect coloration, so that pictures that are joined with a considerable overlap do not match well. Readers will see some pictures that are much more obviously mis-matched: the hues of water and sometimes of vegetation seem to change completely. That is because they were not taken on the same aerial run. Flight plans are subject to sudden change for many reasons—for example, the requirements of air traffic control. And a delay even of minutes means a change in sun angle and perhaps in light intensity. If the delay is extended to days or weeks by bad weather, then water conditions and vegetation will almost certainly be different.

Given that pictures are taken in the desired place, the only yardstick of success in aerial photography is the sharpness of ground details. Good definition requires very strong sunlight. A picture taken in poor light will come out, but ground features do not stand out starkly enough for it to be of much use. So aerial photographers are much more subject to weather limitations than most other aviators, whose only concern is getting safely from place to place. Overcast con-

ditions, even if the air is perfectly calm, mean no work can be done. Just a thin layer of light cirrus cloud above the aircraft softens the details in a picture. Isolated, fluffy cumulus clouds cast shadows that may obscure important features, interrupting or spoiling a run at the last moment. Clouds scattered below the plane may be less of a problem because their positions are more easily observed. But haze or extensive smoke—conditions that other fliers could avoid or ignore —rule out photography altogether.

Angling of the sun shortens an aerial photographer's productive hours, even in totally clear weather. The light cast below the plane is inadequate if the sun is within 30 degrees of the horizon—within three hours, say, of dawn or dusk around the latitude of Adelaide in mid-spring. Mid-winter work is scarcely worth attempting in the far south, not simply because of bad weather but also because the sun passes so far to the north that it is at a poor angle nearly all day.

The time of year is also important if the purpose is to assemble knowledge of vegetation, or to record slight contour variations that could be obscured by vegetation—for example, a flush of tall grass in late spring. In areas such as the far north, where there are big tide ranges and tidal flats kilometres wide, a set of pictures makes little sense unless the tide level is consistent. In that case the photographer can only work on certain days, regardless of weather and light conditions.

What the guide sections do

Information on virtually every place on the coast where travellers are likely to stay has been compiled from on-the-spot reports. In the descriptive material, every attempt has been made to bring out the points that give each place its own character, whether they be aspects of scenery, activity or historical interest. But the guide entries are not intended to amount to recommendations. Personal tastes vary as widely as the places. It is for readers to weigh up their own preferences and judge—from the pictures, from the descriptions and from the details of facilities and access—where the effort and expense of travel may produce the greatest reward.

Key maps are included with all entries. They place each locality in the context of its surrounding district, to assist travellers to find their bearings and to make sure that they do not overlook nearby points of possible interest. Minor roads, except for those essential to reach destinations discussed in the text, are omitted for the sake of

Key to town facilities

Hotel or motel · Holiday letting · Caravan park · Camping ground · Petrol · Chemist · Cinema · Public bar · Licensed club · Restaurant · Takeaway food · Boat hire · Bait · Swimming pool · Golf · Tennis · Bowls · Launching ramp

clarity. All key maps are designed with north to the top of the page. Shaded parts represent the areas covered in the accompanying aerial photographs. Some variation in the scale of the photographs has been dictated by space restrictions. The white northward arrow appearing on each picture indicates not only its alignment with grid north but also its scale: the arrow's length represents an actual ground span of about 250 metres.

Secrets unlocked from above

AERIAL pictures speak volumes to scientists. Botanists use them to classify vegetation—not only the dominant land plants but also seagrass beds and seaweeds. Zoologists can tell what animal life is likely to be found. Geologists are able to distinguish rock types, and by picking out ancient dunes and beach ridges they trace changes in sea level. Oceanographers discern currents, and 'fronts' of different water temperature. From wave patterns they can read the contours of the sea bed.

Laymen, too, can learn more—even of their home shores. Bushwalkers can spot unknown tracks, surfers can note unusual wave breaks, and boat owners can see the twists and turns of channels. Submerged reefs and bars and tricky currents show up. So do flood-prone areas.

Right: Contrasting colours of river and tidal waters at Burnett Heads, Qld, mark a 'front' where fish feed intensively

Travelling sand bars off Busselton, WA, go westward in storms, averaging a few metres each year. Beach sands move with them, perpetually altering the shoreline

Details of motoring access and of public transport availability are not exhaustive. They are based on the usual travel routes and practical requirements of most people. Other routes and services may be found, particularly from inland centres. Some hotels and motels operate pick-up services for booked guests arriving at railway or coach stations and airports. And once in a seaside township, visitors may find that they can avail themselves of local transport arrangements that are too variable to be listed.

Hours stated for surf club patrols, and for some other institutions such as museums and historic buildings, are subject to change, in most cases from year to year but sometimes at shorter notice. Weekday lifeguards, paid from council grants or business donations, may augment the part-time protection afforded by surf club volunteers in some beach towns. The financial basis of such services was considered too uncertain for them to be included in a book which it is hoped readers will use for many years.

Coastal conditions are subject to change, both gradual and sudden. References to the popularity of certain beaches for swimming, or to the suitability of certain spots for boating or fishing, should not be taken as absolute assurances as to their safety. It is always advisable for visitors to take every opportunity to borrow local knowledge, not only to avoid hazards but also to gain the maximum enjoyment from their stay.

The metropolitan sections do not include listings of transport details and other localised information. It can be presumed that all facilities will be found within a reasonable distance of the places dealt with in the text and that ample information on access and public transport will be easily obtainable by visitors.

The introduction to each regional section includes some discussion of general climatic factors, especially those that bear on the times of year when visits are likely to be most enjoyable. Charts showing the year-round averages of meteorological readings are included with some individual entries. They give a guide to seasonal trends in temperature, sunshine, rainfall and 3 p.m. relative humidity. But they have a most limited application. Actual weather conditions vary widely at any time, and quite small differences in distance or altitude from the site of the weather station could produce a markedly different climatic pattern. Figures are given only where they are of some relevance because the weather station is nearby.

Brisbane and the Gold Coast

Nearly two million visitors flood into the Gold Coast every year, clear evidence that the area's promoters know exactly what holidaymakers want. Brisbane surfers must also travel there for their waves as the muddy waters of Moreton Bay, although excellent for sailing and fishing, have little appeal for swimmers.

Team riding in the waterski show, Sea World, Southport

Northern beach suburbs of Brisbane, on Redcliffe Peninsula

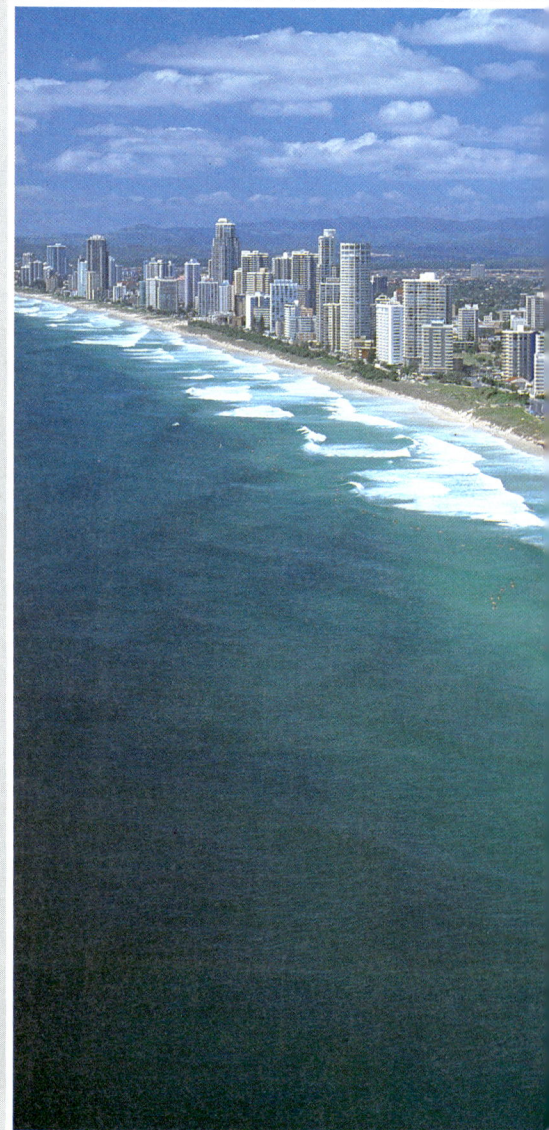
High life beside the Nerang River, Surfers Paradise

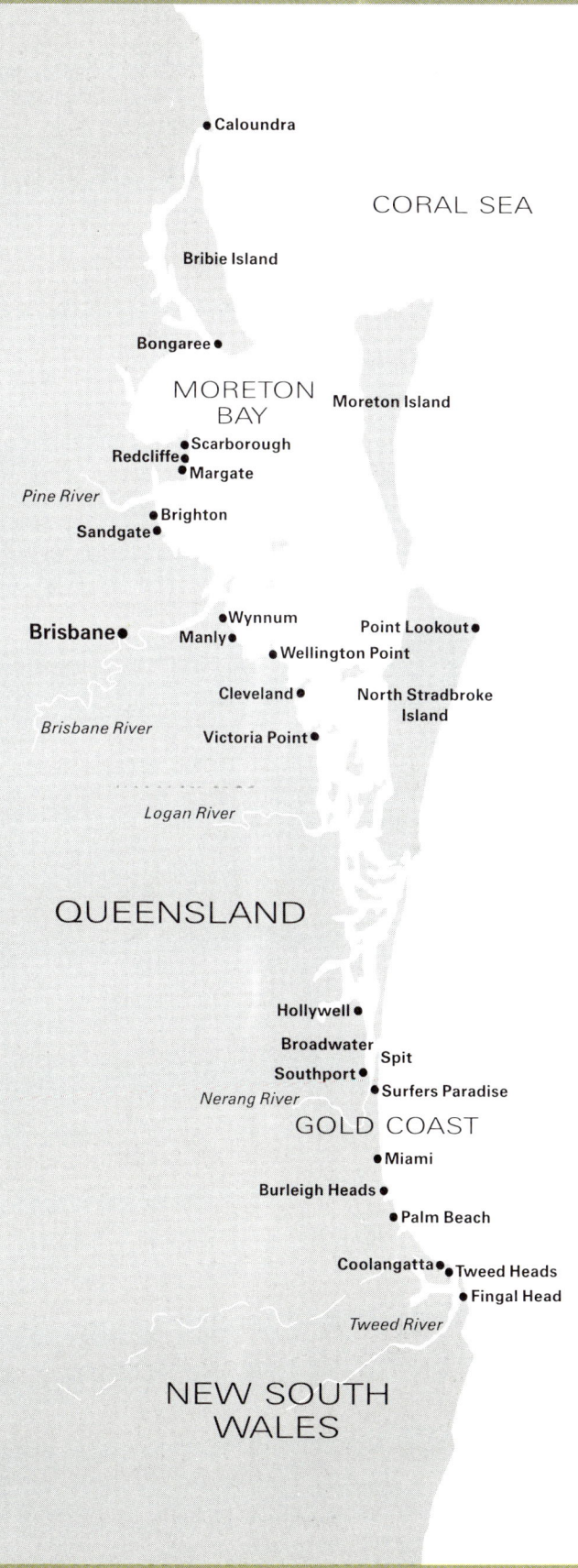

CORAL SEA

Caloundra

Bribie Island

Bongaree

MORETON BAY

Moreton Island

Redcliffe
Scarborough
Margate

Pine River

Brighton
Sandgate

Wynnum
Brisbane
Manly
Wellington Point
Point Lookout

Cleveland
North Stradbroke Island

Brisbane River

Victoria Point

Logan River

QUEENSLAND

Hollywell

Broadwater
Spit
Southport
Surfers Paradise

Nerang River

GOLD COAST

Miami

Burleigh Heads

Palm Beach

Coolangatta
Tweed Heads
Fingal Head

Tweed River

NEW SOUTH WALES

Bayside stillness and hard-sell surf

BRISBANE'S environs encompass a range of landscapes and coasts from the rainforests of the Great Dividing Range to the sheltered shores of Moreton Bay, and the long, unbroken surf beaches of its barrier sand islands and their counterpart along the Gold Coast, Australia's tourist capital. In Moreton Bay, where the shoreline is protected from the force of ocean waves, wide mudflats and sand bars are exposed at low tide. Swimming is an unattractive proposition then, but enclosures usable at high tide remain scattered around the bay as a reminder of the days when suburban settlements were the city's main coastal resorts. Sailors and anglers are not deterred by the mudflats. Boat ramps, jetties, small-boat harbours and marinas along the bay shores give access to wide expanses of superb sailing water or to narrow channels and over reefs teeming with fish.

Away from the muddy shores of Moreton Bay, Brisbane has found its access to the ocean coast at small resort towns on North Stradbroke and Bribie Islands, and along the burgeoning tourist strip of the Gold Coast. Surfing beaches stretch 35 km from the island-cluttered bay of the Broadwater, past the towering beachfront buildings of Surfers Paradise to the wide lower reaches of the Tweed River. The region's population, scattered and mainly rural before World War II, swelled in the 1950s to around 30 000. The figure has almost doubled in each successive decade.

Brisbane, by contrast, grew away from the coast as a river port chosen in preference to sites on the shores of Moreton Bay. The Brisbane River is subject to siltation and had to be dredged to create its shipping channels. Cleveland Point was favoured by woolgrowers as the site of a port until Governor Gipps paid his first visit to the settlement in 1847. Obliged to land on oozing mudflats at Cleveland,

he soon made his displeasure known with a declaration that the official port was to be upriver. As the volume and size of shipping increased, the city's wharves—originally in the heart of the town—moved to the deeper and wider downstream reaches. After more than 150 years they have found their way back out to Moreton Bay. Four mangrove islands at the entrance to the river, known collectively as Fisherman Island, were amalgamated with land fill in 1976 and have become the Port of Brisbane's main container terminal, capable of handling freighters of up to 60 000 tonnes.

Upstream from the William Jolly Bridge, industrial wharves and the city's riverbank freeway system give way to residential areas with public launching ramps. The river is navigable to its junction with the Bremer River, near Ipswich, but coal and lime barges working seven days a week cause difficulties for small craft. Tourist cruises run from Brisbane's North Quay along banks crowded with historic houses to the industrial development of Hamilton Reach and Gibson Island, and upstream to the Lone Pine Sanctuary at Fig Tree Pocket, which has a large colony of koalas and other native animals.

Inland from the tourist centres of the Gold Coast, quiet country towns serve rich farming land criss-crossed by rivers descending from the Great Dividing Range. To the west and south of Brisbane an arc of 21 national parks, known as the Scenic Rim, preserves ridges and valleys of dense rainforest which once covered the whole area. Cool waterfalls spill from the ranges just a short drive from the sun and sand of the popular ocean beaches. Picnic grounds and camping sites are dotted through the parks, with walking tracks to the falls and rock pools and to lookouts giving views over deep, narrow gorges and across the farming valleys to the coast.

Seen from the mouth of the Currumbin River, the imposing skyline of Surfers Paradise rises from the mists

SANDGATE	Jan	Feb	Mar	Apr	May	Jun	Jul	Aug	Sep	Oct	Nov	Dec
Maximum C°	29	28	28	26	24	21	20	21	23	25	27	28
Minimum C°	20	20	19	16	13	10	9	9	12	15	17	19
Rainfall mm	171	181	154	88	74	70	59	42	48	81	101	134
Rain Days	11	12	13	9	8	6	7	5	6	8	8	9
Sunshine hrs	Summer 7 +			Autumn 7 +			Winter 7 +			Spring 8 +		

COOLANGATTA	Jan	Feb	Mar	Apr	May	Jun	Jul	Aug	Sep	Oct	Nov	Dec
Maximum C°	29	28	29	27	25	22	21	22	23	25	28	30
Minimum C°	23	23	21	19	16	14	14	14	16	16	19	21
Rainfall mm	200	262	240	153	143	131	90	71	55	119	116	144
Humidity %	73	73	67	63	63	61	67	61	65	72	74	72
Rain Days	11	13	14	11	10	8	7	6	6	8	8	9
Sunshine hrs	Summer 7 +			Autumn 7 +			Winter 7 +			Spring 8 +		

The city of Brisbane stretches inland, with commercial and residential areas built on both sides of the river

The first of the blackbirders

QUEENSLAND'S 19th-century traffic in Pacific Island labourers was pioneered not in the tropical far north but south of Brisbane. And it was promoted from Sydney. Robert Towns, a speculator who wanted cheap labour for a cotton plantation beside the Logan River, was first to take advantage of Queensland legislation in 1862 permitting the importation of non-white agricultural workers. He sent Ross Lewin, the master of his schooner *Don Juan*, to recruit men in the New Hebrides (now Vanuatu).

In August 1863 Lewin delivered 67 bewildered Melanesians, indentured to work for three years. They were clothed, sheltered and fed, and at the end of their term were to be rewarded with trade goods. 'Slavery has come to Queensland', a Brisbane newspaper protested. It was not far wrong: although the men were not owned, their services were bought and sold.

During the next 40 years more than 50 000 Islanders were imported; they were referred to as Kanakas, from the Hawaiian word for man. In many cases the recruiters, or 'blackbirders' as they were called, used unscrupulous methods on unsuspecting villagers. Queensland outlawed the traffic in 1885, but breaches went unpunished. Only with the passage of a federal law in 1904 did importations stop.

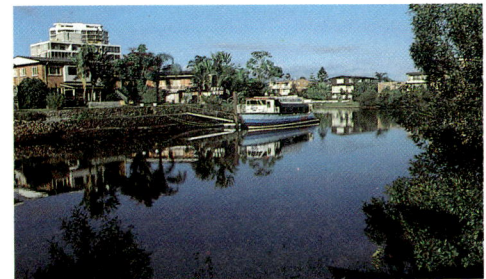

Elaborate canal developments in Surfers Paradise

Tasty harvest from the shallows

MORETON BAY'S calm, shallow waters hold little interest for bathers accustomed to surf. Its most noted swimmers are crabs—big, tasty ones that are sought after by seafood gourmets. Crabbing is an important element of the district's commercial fishery, and many seaside residents set traps as a profitable hobby. Most boat-hire companies offer crabbing equipment so that visitors, too, can try their luck with the delicacies.

Two distinctly different species are fished commercially. The blue swimmer crab, *Portunus pelagicus*—known in Brisbane as the sand crab—frequents open, sandy-bottomed areas and reef edges. Its shell, sharply pointed at each side, may be 180-200 mm wide. The mangrove crab, *Scylla serrata*, is found in muddy estuaries and inlets. Full-grown it is even larger than the blue swimmer, and

markedly more bulky. The shell colour usually ranges from grey-green to brown, but may be blueish. Locals call it the mud crab or muddy.

Traps—either cages like crayfish pots or nets known as dillies—are set from boats below the low-water mark. They are baited daily, usually with shellfish or small pieces of fish, and left overnight. Best results are obtained in warmer water, from December to May. Mangrove crabs can also be caught with a hooked wire when they move seasonally to burrows above low water. This method

is subject to close regulation. However, anyone 15 or over can set up to four pots or dillies and there is no limit on the number of crabs caught, provided that they are males not less than 150 mm across the shell. Females, distinguished by a much broader abdomen flap under the back of the shell, are totally protected.

After capture, crabs can be left alive out of water for a reasonable time—at least until the next meal—if they are kept cool and damp. Queenslanders commonly pack them in moist mangrove leaves with their claws securely tied.

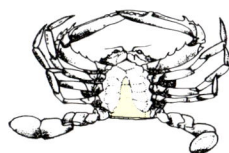

Male blue swimmer crab

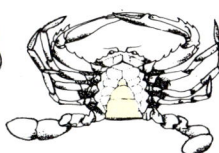

Female blue swimmer crab

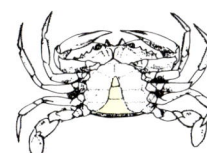

Male mud crab

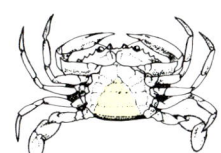

Female mud crab

Northern shores of Moreton Bay

Redcliffe Peninsula's gently scalloped coastline drops steeply to the waters of Moreton Bay to provide the most pleasant swimming beaches in the Brisbane metropolitan area. The firm, sandy shores, broken by scattered rocky outcrops and boat launching ramps, draw busy crowds on fine days and contrast strikingly with the wide, oozing mudbanks which encumber the foreshores to the north and south. At the northern end of the peninsula a small park runs towards the Reef Point boat harbour, where long, man-made breakwaters protect the Moreton Bay Boat Club and a fleet of commercial fishing boats. On the rocks of the point, public oyster beds provide abundant summer supplies of shellfish that can be eaten on the spot but not taken away. A strong blade is needed to prise open the shells. Behind the harbour a caravan park has boats for hire, near a park and children's playground. Offshore, anglers fish from small boats between signs marking dangerous reefs.

Red cliffs fall from a grassy headland to Scarborough Beach, with long beachfront caravan parks sheltered behind the crescent beach's row of towering Norfolk Island pines. These cliffs, from which the peninsula derives its name, were sighted by Matthew Flinders in 1799, but it was not until 1823 that a convict camp was established at what is now Redcliffe Point. The settlement, the first in Queensland, was abandoned a year later in favour of a better harbour and richer soils beside the Brisbane River. The peninsula became known as Humpybong, believed to derive from the Aboriginal words for 'dead houses'—a reference to the deserted settlement.

In front of Redcliffe's main shopping centre,

Redcliffe Peninsula cannot offer surf, but it has the sandiest shores on a mostly mud-lined bay; suburbs from Scarborough to Clontarf started as resorts, long before the family car brought the Gold Coast within reach

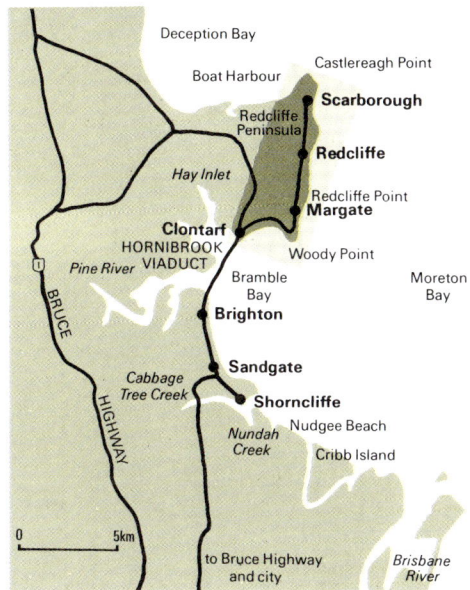

long curved steps run down to the water from beneath big Moreton Bay figs forming a curtain between the bustling city and the peaceful bay. A narrow plank jetty reaching into the bay has the remains of an amusement pavilion, built in 1922, at its offshore end. The jetty was also a passenger ferry stop, until the Hornibrook Viaduct was constructed over the wide mudbanks to the south of the peninsula. Woody Point, with its cluster of bait and food shops, overlooks a concrete jetty and the long thread of the viaduct, parallel to an older bridge which retains the advertising hoardings erected above the roadway. The superseded structure is open to walkers and is a popular spot for handlining over the channels of the Pine River and Hay Inlet. Between Brighton and Sandgate a stone revetment abutting Bramble Bay drops to dark, rippled mud after the ebb tide. From a boat-hire depot just inside the Pine River, boats are launched over the sand and mud for fishing and cruising in the bay. To the south a commercial fishing fleet lines the north bank at the junction of Cabbage Tree Creek and Nundah Creek, with bright blue nets strung out to dry after the catch has been dispatched. At Shorncliffe a fenced, grassy lookout runs along the clifftop overlooking a long wharf and pier popular with fishermen. Parks with swings and barbecues shaded by fig trees and palms line the head at water level.

Brisbane and the Gold Coast 79

Wellington Point reaches out into clear boating waters, beyond the mudflat fringe of Waterloo Bay

The southern bays

Market gardens in the Redlands district flourish on rich, rust-coloured soil above the beaches and island-cluttered waters of southern Moreton Bay. Fruit is abundant—particularly the winter strawberries for which the area is famous. But horticulture is gradually giving way to residential development as Brisbane sprawls southward. Offshore, the low-lying islands of Coochiemudlo, Macleay, Lamb, Karragarra and Russell are dotted with the weekend cottages of city-dwellers. The islands are served by passenger and vehicle ferries, and launching ramps for private boat owners are strung along the mainland shore between Wynnum and Redland Bay.

Boats are launched into Redland Bay just south of the Coochiemudlo Island ferry wharf, in front of a stairway leading up from the deep red earth of Victoria Point. A shaded, log-lined picnic reserve looks down on scattered mangroves below the point's car park, and across Moreton Bay to the long dunes of North Stradbroke Island. To the south, golf fairways spread out along the bay shores and a heavy ramp leads down to rows of massive posts. They steady the ferry carrying passengers and cars to the resort centre of Dunwich on North Stradbroke. At the mouth of nearby Weinam Creek, a ramp with space for

four simultaneous launchings runs into deep water near a water-taxi base and a busy marina with moorings, jetties and a big gravel car park.

Wide mudbanks and mangrove flats surround Cleveland Point, broken only by jetties and launching ramps which allow sailors and anglers out into deeper, unencumbered waters to the north. The road to the point's modern lighthouse passes a sheltered picnic ground and an earlier wooden light tower, in use from 1864 to 1976.

Ormiston House, a splendid colonial mansion in gardens fronting Raby Bay, was built for Louis Hope, who pioneered sugar milling in Queensland. It is now occupied by Carmelite nuns, but the grounds are open on most Sunday afternoons and an open-air classical music recital is given on the last Sunday evening in October.

At low tide a winding sandbar forms a causeway reaching from the park at the tip of Wellington Point to small, scrub-covered King Island, which is an environmental park. Waterbirds join anglers to search the mud around the sandbar for food and bait. Ramps run into the bay on either side of the jetty to the east of the point, by a kiosk and boathouse behind the grassy picnic area. At high tide the beaches on the western side are suitable for swimming.

Market gardens, resisting the tide of residential development around Raby Bay, add touches of patchwork colour to the town of Cleveland

Weinam Creek's muddy mouth separates Victoria Point from the township of Redland Bay, the ferry terminal for travellers to North Stradbroke Island; homes are spreading over the district's red soil

Moreton Bay islands

Pumice Stone Channel cuts a deep, easily navigable course between the mainland and Bribie Island, under the road bridge to Bellara and Bongaree

More than 300 low-lying islands, surrounded by mudflats and sandbars, are enclosed in the calm waters of Moreton Bay by the long sand-barrier islands of North Stradbroke, Moreton and Bribie. Well-marked boating channels lead through the islands and shoal areas in the bay's southern reaches, and commercial passenger and vehicle ferries operate regular services to several of the larger settlements. Coochiemudlo, Russell, Lamb and Karragarra Islands have picnic areas, shelters and jetties where fishermen can pull ashore to barbecue the day's catch. St Helena and Peel Islands are parks where camping is permitted but no facilities or water are provided.

North Stradbroke Island has caravan and camping reserves at the resort centres of Dunwich and Point Lookout, with another small settlement and camping ground at Amity Point. A sealed road leads east of Dunwich, past the pic-

nic grounds and deep, clear swimming water of Brown Lake to Blue Lake National Park (445 hectares). A 2.5 km walk leads from the road through sandy coastal country—southern Queenslanders call it 'wallum'—to Blue Lake for freshwater swimming and overnight bush camping. With a National Parks permit, camping is also possible on Main Beach, 35 km of unbroken sandy shore stretching along the island's Pacific coast. Point Lookout, at the beach's northern end, is surrounded by a picnic reserve overlooking sheltered Deadmans Beach to the west and a patrolled beach to the south.

At Tangalooma on Moreton Island, guests at the holiday resort play tennis on a rooftop court which was once the flensing deck for a whaling station, and toboggan down the bare slopes of high sand dunes just inland from the settlement. The wooded crest of Mount Tempest, at 282

metres, dominates the peaks in the north of the island and tops the highest permanent dune in the world. Day visitors can use the resort's beach and picnic areas or join tours to the surfing beaches and an old lighthouse at Cape Moreton.

The northernmost of the Moreton Bay islands, Bribie, is connected to the mainland by a bridge over the waters of Pumice Stone Channel. Roads connect the thriving townships of Bellara and Bongaree with the holiday settlement of Woorim at the southern end of the island's 47 km surfing beach. Bush walking tracks branch out north from Woorim through country known for its spring displays of wildflowers and blossoming scrub. From the Woorim surf club tower a trail follows the coast north along scrub-covered dunes to the woods and marshes around First Lagoon, a long, narrow body of water attracting a wide variety of bird life. The jetty below Bon-

Deep beaches and dunes surround Point Lookout on North Stradbroke Island

garee's waterfront picnic grounds is a popular spot for handliners, while nearby launching ramps take boat anglers into the sheltered waters of Pumice Stone Channel. It is navigable from shore to shore at its southern end, but becomes a maze of mudflats, sandbanks and mangroves to the north. Areas are set aside for water-skiers and there is deep water suitable for sailing.

NORTH STRADBROKE 10 km from Redland Bay.
TRANSPORT: ferry Cleveland-Dunwich, Redland Bay-Dunwich daily.
SURF CLUB PATROL: Main Beach and Cylinder Beach October-May, Saturday 09.00-17.00, Sunday 07.00-14.00, public holidays 07.00-17.00.

BRIBIE ISLAND (pop. 3023) east of Bruce Highway 59 km from Brisbane (turn off at Caboolture).
TRANSPORT: bus Brisbane-Bribie Island daily.
SURF CLUB PATROL: October-May, Saturday and public holidays 08.00-17.00, Sunday 07.00-16.00.

Blessings at the back door

GOVERNMENT and business investment in central Brisbane, 30 km upriver, has been so lavish that the community may seem to be turning its back on Moreton Bay. But people who find delight on the water—whether drifting and dreaming in a fishing dinghy or straining every muscle in a yacht race—still look east and count their blessings.

Moreton Bay is uniquely protected. The enormous sand masses of North Stradbroke and Moreton Islands enclose a pleasure-boating playground of more than 1000 square kilometres. Beyond the muddy fringes much of it is deep, blue water. Near-tropical temperatures allow enviable scope for relaxation and sport. The bay even boasts game fishing opportunities. Marlin, sailfish, tuna, wahoo and big sharks are hooked here. Whales, too, call in to breed. Until 1962 they were commercially hunted from Moreton Island.

The low inshore islands are popular picnic sites. The barrier islands, offering Pacific Ocean surf along with impressive dune formations and inviting woodlands, are gaining favour as holiday destinations. North Stradbroke is the more heavily used. Already easy to reach by ferries from Redland Bay or Cleveland, it is soon to be linked with the mainland by road bridges. Conservationists are fearful that over-visiting will wreck the island's scenic gem, Lake Kaboora in the tiny Blue Lake National Park.

On Moreton Island, however, nature is to get a second chance. Existing sand mining leases are almost exhausted and no more are proposed. In the 1990s all traces of mining should have disappeared. Apart from three tiny west coast settlements and the resort at Tangalooma—on the site of the old whaling station—the entire island is to come under national parks control.

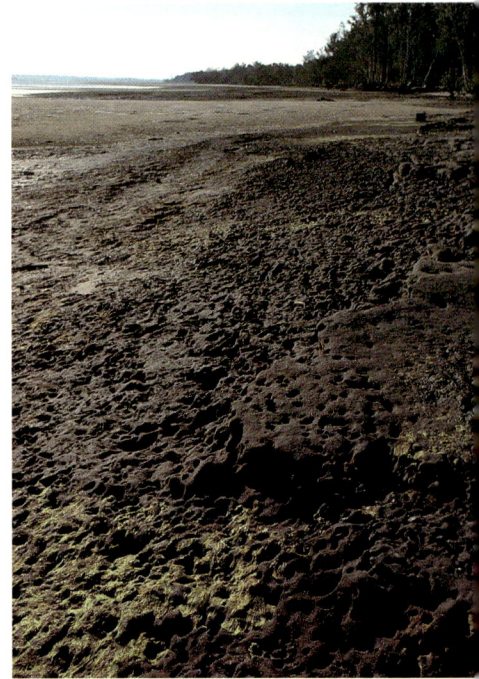

Pumice Stone Channel, Bribie Island

A tidal pool on Moreton Island's northwest coast – soon to be embraced in a national park

Sightseers at Blue Lake – officially Lake Kaboora – are only five minutes from a surfing beach

Spitfire Creek, the outlet of Jabiru Lake on Moreton Island, makes a marshland among high dunes

North Stradbroke Island, looking south toward Jumpinpin Bar

Perfect peace on Moreton Island

Winds build mountains of sand

Waterlily, Jabiru Lake

East coast, Moreton Island

Northern reaches of the Broadwater, sheltered by the long sand barrier of South Stradbroke Island, make a boating playground beyond Lands End

Gold Coast north

From Lands End north, the Gold Coast is a quiet residential area—a break from the glitter and commercial bustle that starts at Southport. The accent here, in the shelter of South Stradbroke Island, is on boating. A tracery of artificial canals and small marinas on the north-western reaches of the Broadwater indicates the locals' enthusiasm. By a concrete ramp west of the Biggera Creek bridge, boats for hire line a sandy bank and cabin cruisers are moored at private jetties which jut into the creek from neat lawns. The creek is navigable for more than 2 km to a cara-

van park on its upper reaches, where pelicans compete with fishermen for a catch.

Hollywell and Paradise Point are well supplied with ramps to give boat enthusiasts access to the shores of Coombabah Creek and the Coomera River, lined with mangroves and scrubby mudflats. In the early morning by the Hollywell caravan park the shallow, sandy water is crowded with bobbing metal dinghies as anglers set off to cruise around the Broadwater's low sand and mangrove islands. Larger craft make out to sea around the Southport Bar, although the

exposed position of the entrance channel makes it a tricky proposition, and there is more than adequate scope for boating along the Broadwater and north into Moreton Bay.

Parks and picnic grounds line the waterways around Paradise Point, opposite Griffin Island. Well-kept lawns, shaded by casuarinas, are dotted with seats, playground equipment, sheltered tables and a stone barbecue. Although only a 15-minute drive, the tranquillity of the point makes it seem much farther from the bustle and clamour to the south at Surfers Paradise.

Even more remote is the long, narrow stretch of South Stradbroke Island. A water-taxi and larger cruisers leave from jetties along the Gold Coast on tours of the Broadwater, stopping off at South Stradbroke for picnic lunches. The water-taxi will also take day visitors to beaches along the island's western shores and return to pick them up at the end of a day's swimming—either on the sheltered side or along the surf beach, which is unpatrolled and subject to rips. Walking trails criss-cross the island. South Stradbroke has only a sprinkling of holiday cottages, two camping reserves and a growing resort clustered around Tipplers' Tavern, leaving much of the island undeveloped. The tavern and reserves generate their own power and rely on plentiful supplies of bore water for drinking. Members of the island's large colony of wallabies can be seen making their way down the bracken-covered shores at low tide to fresh water seeping through the sand into shallow depressions behind the Broadwater beach.

Before 1898, South and North Stradbroke were one island. Now they are separated by the navigable channels of the Jumpinpin Bar. Legend has it that the division began in 1894 after explosives were unloaded from a grounded ship and detonated, destroying the protective scrub covering of the dunes and starting a process of wave erosion.

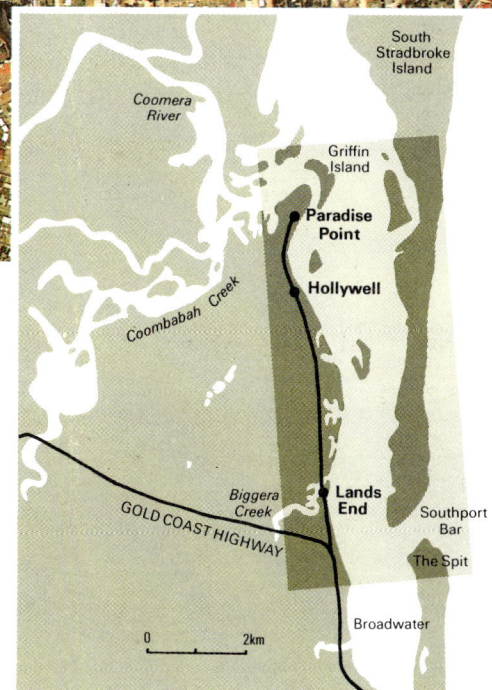

Southport and the Spit

Building sites at Southport—now among the most valuable in Australia—were unwanted when first offered for sale in 1874. The following year a few sections went for £10 and £30. The district was so secluded that Queensland governors used it as a country retreat. Their mansion and extensive grounds, facing Macintosh Island where the Nerang River enters the Broadwater, were vacated at the turn of the century and taken over for what became the Southport School. The original building remains, serving as the preparatory school.

Southport was the first town, and for long the only one, on the Gold Coast. Beachfront resorts to the south did not come until mass motoring in the 1920s brought a bridge over the Nerang to Main Beach, and the start of a coastal highway. Though since outstripped by its surfside rivals, Southport remains the centre for Gold Coast City administration. Its commercial area extends along the inner shore of the Broadwater, behind a string of waterfront parks and an Olympic-size swimming pool.

Macintosh Island provides a tiny summary of

what has happened in this region since World War II. Not a trace survives of the sandy, scrub-covered patch that the early governors saw behind a fringe of mangroves. The Gold Coast Highway, rerouted to slash across it, feeds a constant rush of traffic to and from the ocean beaches. To the west, branching canals have transformed the island into a pair of stubby-fingered hands, to give every property buyer a waterfront site and a pleasure-boat mooring. Here even the island's name slips from memory, replaced by the real estate developer's preference—Paradise Waters. East of the highway, families can still picnic and children can play in a lavishly equipped reserve. But its landscape is man-made; its waterfalls, streams and lakes are all artificial. And the view is of the towering hotels, apartment buildings and construction cranes of Surfers Paradise.

East of Macintosh Island, the coastal strip squeezes through Narrow Neck to Main Beach. Just a short walk from the skyscrapers to the south, bungalows occupy sought-after beach-front land and a caravan park lies close to the patrolled surfing beach. High-rise development at Main Beach is a controversial issue, but in spite of opposition some building has gone ahead. Yachts and cabin cruisers line the Broadwater west of Seaworld Drive, which leads along the narrow tongue of the Spit. An air-sea rescue service, based next to the Southport Yacht Club's marina, operates two boats of its own and charters helicopters or float planes as needed. North of Southport the Australian Volunteer Coastguard monitors radio transmissions round the clock. Like the rescue service, it deals mainly with sailors in difficulty around the treacherous bar at the entrance to the Broadwater.

North of Main Beach the free-flight aviary at Bird Life Park attracts big crowds at feeding time. Other wildlife including reptiles and birds of prey is on display around an artificial lake, and Spanish-style performances by trained horses have recently been added. Farther north is the vast Seaworld complex of marine life displays and amusements. Beyond Seaworld, the remainder of the Spit is accessible only on foot. Some who make the effort to reach the lonely beach at Nerang Head claim the right to dress—or rather undress—as they please. But nudity is by no means officially sanctioned, and the police make occasional arrests to remind people of that.

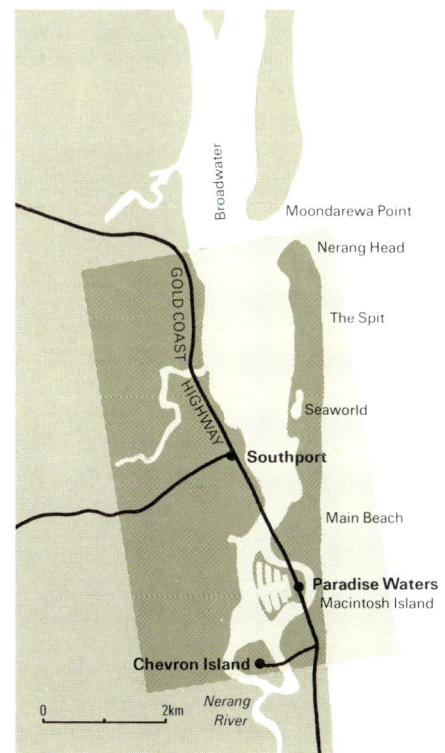

North of Macintosh Island and the Gold Coast Highway bridge the waters of the Nerang River become the Broadwater. This wide waterway has its exit to the sea just to the north of this photograph

Surfers Paradise

Garishly decorated takeaway food booths stand shoulder-to-shoulder with elegant restaurants. Fashion houses, boasting their links with Paris, New York and London, share arcades with cheap novelty shops and amusement parlours. Elderly foreign tourists, richly attired and bejewelled, jostle for pavement space among tanned and tousled youngsters undressed for the beach. Lumbering tour coaches vie with beach buggies in the narrow streets. Storefront displays and gaudy neon signs assault the eye in a silent clamour of urgings to spend. Rock and pop music blasts from shop doorways. And in block after block there are real estate agencies—not one, but two or three in each block.

Fringing the shopping zone, along the Pacific beachfront and back to the meandering confines of the Nerang River, are soaring apartment towers and massive hotels, the latter competing for custom with eye-catching offers of waterbeds, private saunas and films, tennis courts and pools. Topping it all are construction cranes, pulling the city ever higher. This is Surfers Paradise, the bustling, hustling hub of the Gold Coast.

For every holidaymaker who seeks a quiet spot away from it all, there is another who wants to be where the action is. And Surfers has it. Its funfair atmosphere is epitomised, beside a central mall devoted to outdoor dining, by a twisting, multiple-chute slippery dip four or five storeys high. Whooping, yelping sliders hurtle into a pool at the eye level of tourists heading for a snack, perhaps on their way to the waxworks museum or to sightseeing bus tours or river cruises. Behind are the light brown sands of an immense, straight beach with room for tens of thousands of sunbathers and surfers. But they may have trouble claiming their share of afternoon sun—long shadows from beachfront high-rises creep towards the water.

Gone now is the Surfers Paradise Hotel in the Cavill Avenue mall—the second one built by James Cavill, who came from Brisbane in 1923 and paid £40 for a site. He borrowed the hotel's

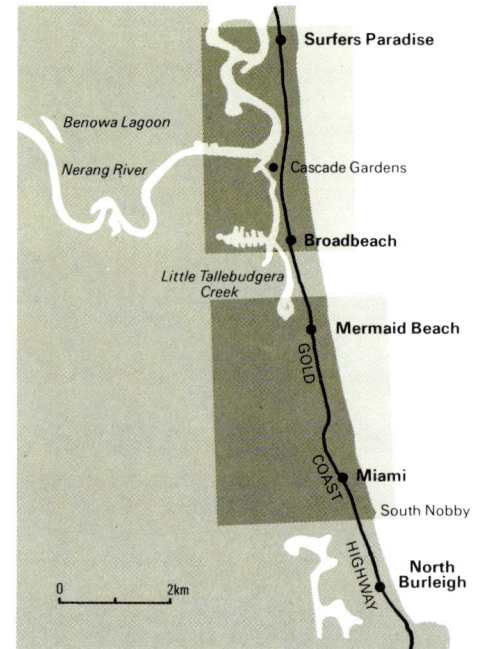

Between Surfers Paradise and Broadbeach, a maze of canals has been created at Cascade Gardens

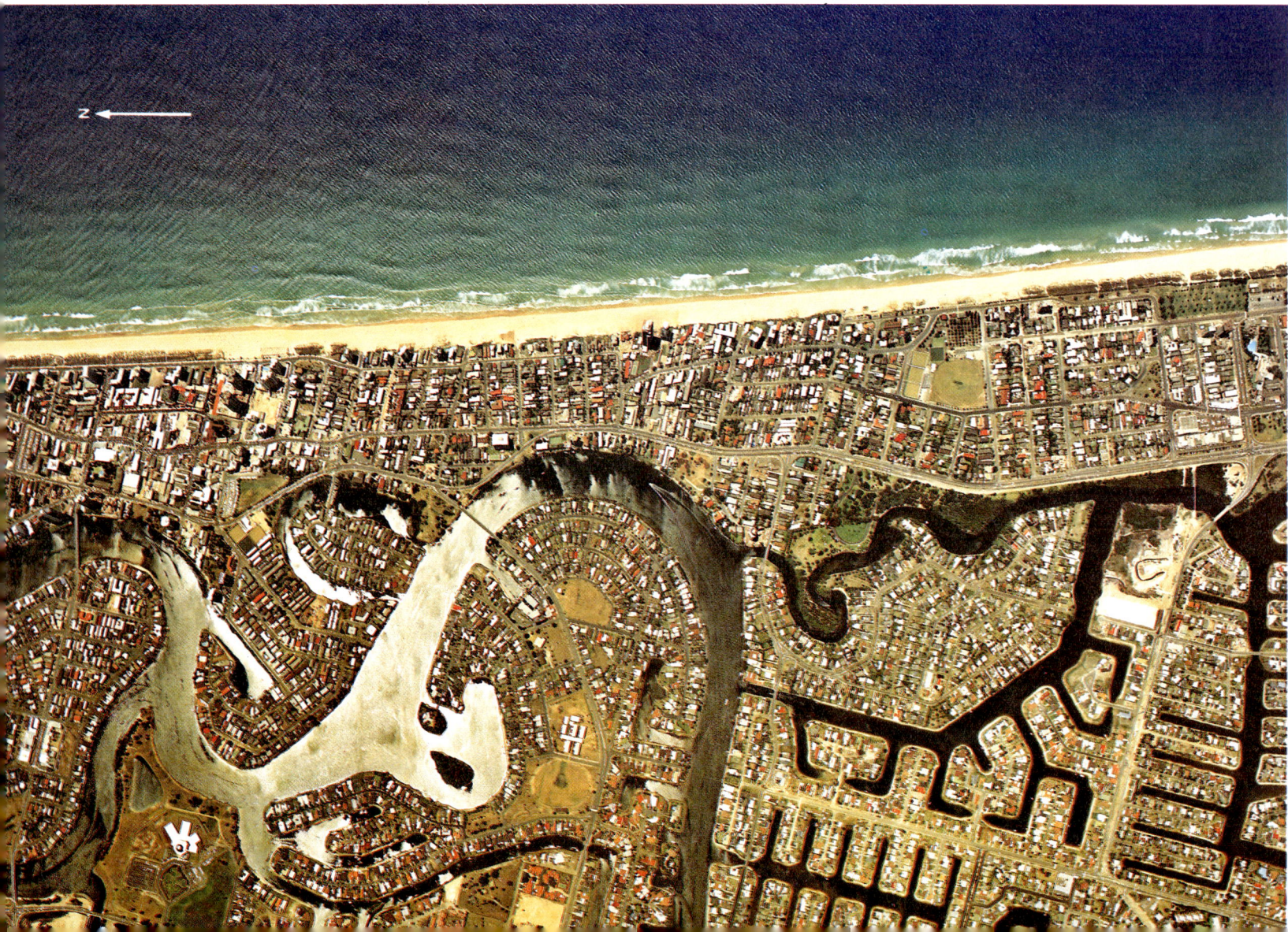

name from a claim in a real estate promoter's advertisement. But the locality was officially Elston. Aboriginal camps in the vicinity earlier had been known as Umbigumbi and Kurrungul. After 1925, when a bridge over the Nerang River replaced a horse-ferry crossing, and cars started to fill the roads, Brisbane people had easier access to the sandy ocean beaches and surf which they lacked around Moreton Bay. What had been a trickle of visitors—dedicated fishermen and early devotees of board-riding—turned into a stream of beach lovers. Cavill and other businessmen, considering how to attract holiday-makers to their district rather than to virtually identical spots elsewhere on the coast, wanted the name Elston changed. In 1933 they won a campaign to call it Surfers Paradise.

World War II stalled the progress of Surfers, and postwar building restrictions and material shortages impeded it until 1952. But land prices rocketed in anticipation of a boom. As early as 1950 a Brisbane journalist noted their extra-ordinary level and labelled the district—sarcas-tically—the Gold Coast. By the mid-1950s beachfront hotels and big apartment blocks were reaching skywards. The tourist stream be-came a flood, and residential and investment de-mand also soared. When the beach was built out, by the 1960s, developers turned to wetlands and dairy pastures behind the coastal strip. Canals were dredged in flood-prone land and the spoil was used to raise and consolidate what re-mained. As people of more and more affluence sought to indulge a passion for waterfront living and luxury boating, canal developments became less a means of preventing floods and more a way to make new sites exclusive and enhance their value. Damaging floods on the Nerang River in 1974, after a storm surge from the Pacific, showed that the canals had brought a change of tidal effects upriver. No more are permitted.

In spite of the pressures of rapid growth and intensive tourist activity, Surfers Paradise has pockets of surprising peace and charm. Rosser Environmental Park at Benowa Lagoon, a five-minute drive west of the city centre, is a sanct-uary for waterfowl nesting in an islet bamboo thicket. Barbecues are provided in a picnic area. To the south at Broadbeach, between the high-way and Little Tallebudgera Creek, are the Cas-cade Gardens. Short, easy nature walks lead through profuse and varied vegetation, and there is every facility for picnicking beside little waterfalls and streams.

Mermaid Beach and Miami continue the southward march of Gold Coast growth; tourists see no change

All the fun of the fair

ENTERTAINMENT on a grand scale is a Gold Coast specialty. Showmen vie for bigger and better attractions. Nightly extravaganzas in hotels, restaurants and clubs are accompanied by an ever-growing array of outdoor diversions to be enjoyed by day. As the area's tally of visitors mounts towards 2 million a year, it seems that their hosts will not rest until they have outdone California, Florida and Hawaii.

Sea World, on the Spit at Southport, is just one example. Already the biggest complex of marine displays in Australia, it has embarked on a three-year programme of expansion, remodelling and 're-theming' that will cost more than $20 million. Dreamworld, at Coomera, is another theme park that is bidding to rival Disneyland.

Jupiter's Casino, dominating the Broadbeach waterfront in company with a 600-bedroom hotel and a convention centre seating 2300, opened in late 1985 in a burst of razzmatazz publicity. Its gaming tables and slot machines are intended not only to satisfy the high-rolling urges of international guests, but also to stem the flow of Queensland gamblers over the border to Tweed Heads, which offers the lure of NSW's legal poker machines.

Amid a welter of slick, money-making enterprises, it is comforting to discover that some of the best entertainment to be had on the Gold Coast costs nothing. For admirers of the human form or students of human nature, the benches of Cavill Mall in Surfers Paradise are front-stalls seats to watch a fascinating parade of exhibitionists and eccentrics.

Show business takes to the streets, free of charge, for 'Tropicarnival', the annual festival. Concerts, displays, contests and feasts galore are crammed into 10 feverish days in October. The climax, an elaborately staged procession of marching bands, decorated floats, clowns and bathing beauties, brings Surfers to a rare standstill.

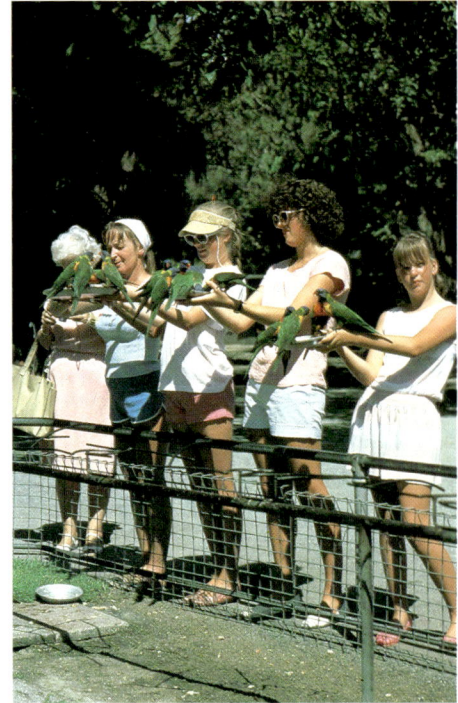

Feeding lorikeets, Currumbin Bird Sanctuary

A waterslide marks Cavill Mall (right) in Surfers Paradise

Dreamworld entertainment park, Coomera

Dreamworld's Puffing Billy

Seals perform at Sea World, on Southport Spit

Sea World's waterslides

Looping the loop on Dreamworld's roller coaster

Meter maid, Surfers Paradise

Burleigh Heads and Currumbin

After the ribbon of unrelenting, neon-lit commercial development that follows the Gold Coast Highway from Surfers Paradise, well inland through the almost indistinguishable districts of Broadbeach, Mermaid Beach and Miami, Burleigh Head rises refreshingly green and natural. The road at last gives a sight of the ocean, beside a long, tree-shaded reserve reaching back to South Nobby. Near a foreshore pool at the south end of Burleigh Beach, the route twists to avoid a climb over the headland, leaving untouched the forested heights of Burleigh Head National Park. Bush trails lead up into the 24-hectare park and over to Tallebudgera Creek. An easy 10-minute walk to the Tungum lookout pierces dense thickets of pandanus palms and breaks out on to an open clifftop before turning back to zigzag through eucalypts and patches of rainforest. Seats are provided along the path and picnic spots are plentiful.

At the Tallebudgera Creek mouth there are grassy picnic grounds on the south bank, just east of a sheltered beach below the highway bridge. The beach is suitable for family swimming except on the outgoing tide, when the current is so brisk that a weekend patrol of female lifesavers keeps watch for people, particularly children, who get into difficulties. From ramps west of the bridge, fishing boats head for a reef just offshore. Burleigh Head has a fringe of rock for anglers, as does South Nobby.

Palm Beach was severely affected by the storm damage which brought headaches to residents and businessmen along much of the Gold Coast in the 1970s. In 1980 its sand was so depleted that it was scarcely a beach at all: a bare rock revetment faced the sea as the only protection for waterfront flats and houses. The beach was recreated in 1981 with sand pumped from Currumbin Creek, and two stone groynes were built in an attempt to arrest its northward drift. Currumbin Creek has boat ramps on both banks, upstream from the highway bridge. A park and picnic ground adjoin the southern ramp, and to the east at the base of Currumbin Point there is another small reserve. Currumbin Bird Sanctuary, 1 km south of town at Flat Rock Creek, started by accident. In the late 1940s the land was used by a commercial flower grower, who kept bees to fertilise his blossoms. Lorikeets seeking nectar threatened to destroy the blooms, so to divert them he put out bread soaked in honey from his hives. Birds now flock in hundreds to be fed from tins held by tourists.

Tallebudgera Creek (left) has suffered the fate of many Gold Coast streams as developers try to meet an increasing demand for waterfront home sites

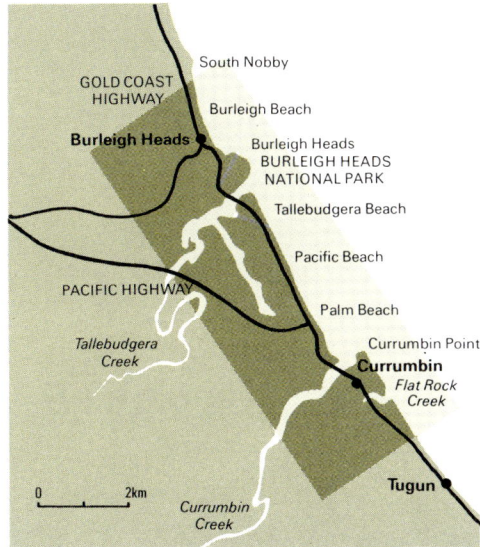

Women to the rescue

AUSTRALIA'S only self-governing, all-female life-saving club is based at Burleigh. Its members keep watch on the deceptively strong currents of Tallebudgera Creek. Their Neptune Ladies' Life-saving Club was formed in 1928 as a teaching body, under Royal Lifesaving Society auspices.

Since 1959, the Neptune Club has taken an active patrol and rescue role at the creek mouth. Adults who try to swim across, as well as children in difficulties, are plucked from the creek every summer, and the club is in radio contact with neighbouring surf clubs and air-sea rescue services in case anyone is swept out to sea.

Nearly all the 20-odd members come from Brisbane, but clubhouse living quarters enable them to mount patrols every weekend from October to April. The club intends to expand by recruiting among Gold Coast schoolgirls.

Cheerful smiles from the Neptune ladies in 1948

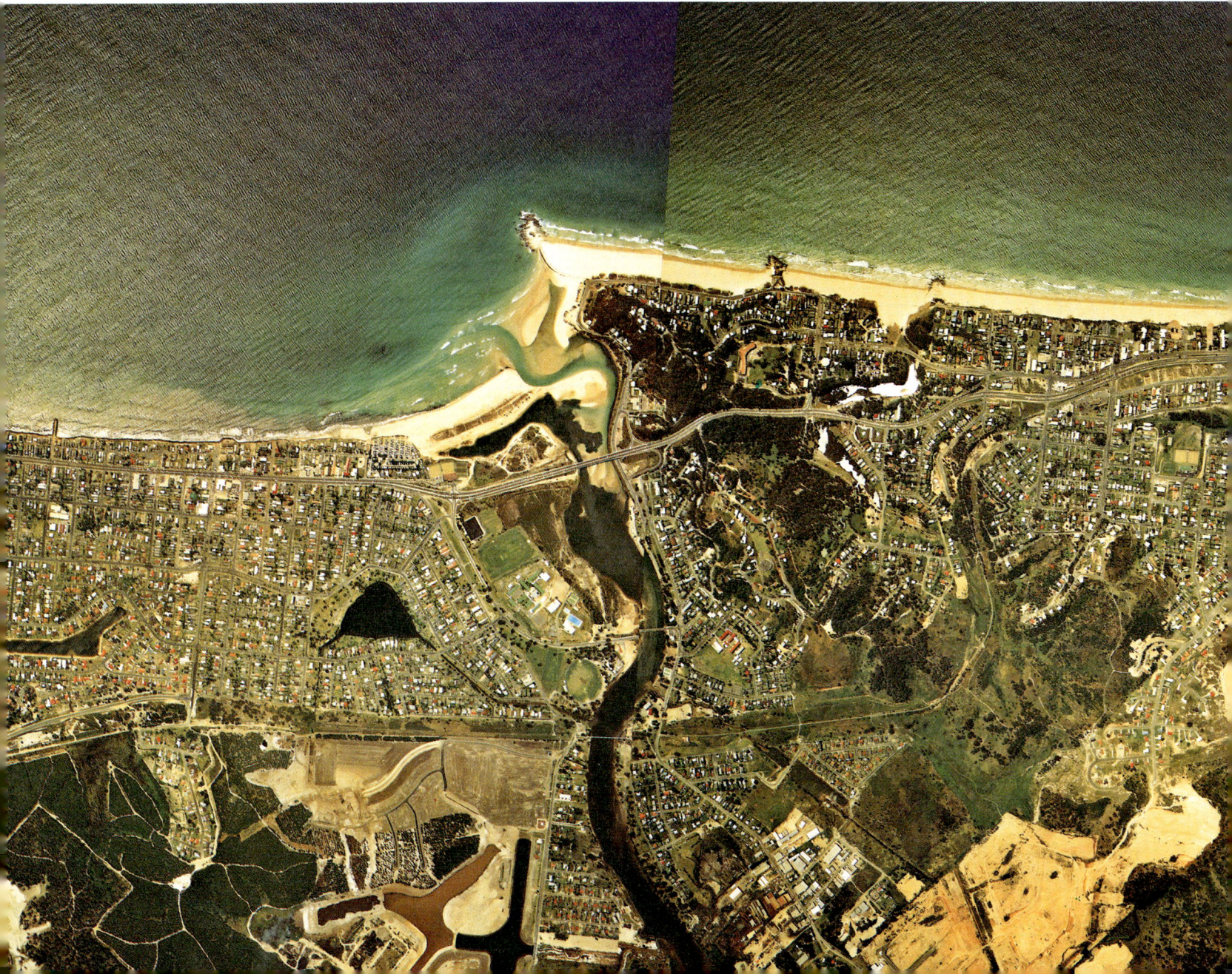

Coolangatta and Tweed Heads

Different building and gambling policies create a clear visual contrast between the cities sharing the Queensland-New South Wales border, though only a dog-leg line of streets divides them. Towering apartment buildings and hotels are permitted on the Coolangatta side, and older guesthouses fronting magnificent surf beaches are still being replaced by cliffs of concrete and glass. But Tweed Heads resisted high-rise development until the 1980s. Then a relaxation allowed for eight-storey and 16-storey buildings in strictly limited zones. So far the only evidence of the new dispensation is a pair of residential projects—Tweed Gardens, near the golf course, well south of the town centre, and Seascape. However the most dominant buildings in Tweed Heads are still its sprawling licensed clubs, surrounded by huge car and coach parks. Visitors—especially from Queensland—flock to them to play the poker machines allowed under NSW law.

The state border meets the coast at Point Danger, and is marked by an 18-metre-high memorial to Captain Cook. Iron ballast—recovered in Great Barrier Reef waters along with cannon jettisoned from the *Endeavour*—has been cast into a replica of the ship's capstan at the base of the monument. Cook named Point Danger—and Mount Warning, which dominates the coast from 40 km inland—because of reefs he

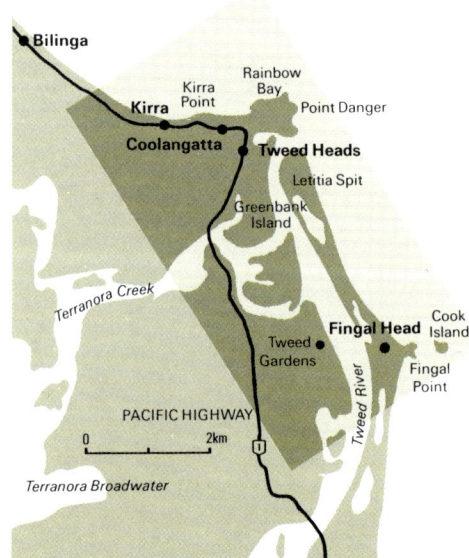

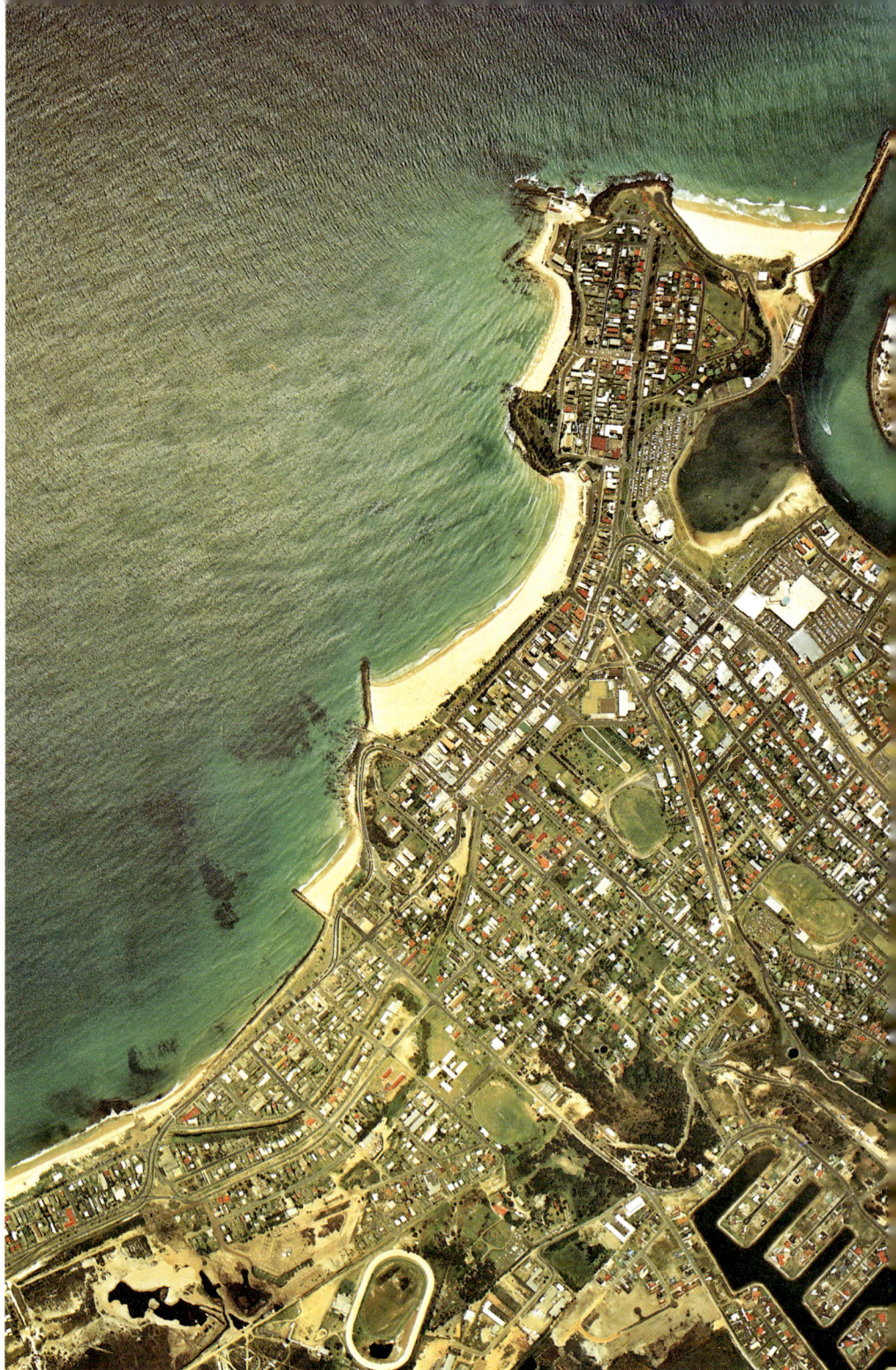

found to the south-east. The tower at the point was fitted in 1971 with Australia's first laser-beam light, but it proved unsatisfactory and was replaced by a conventional lamp.

Waves bending round Point Danger make Coolangatta's beaches the best on the Gold Coast for serious surfing, and in spite of a sand-drift problem they have ample room for tens of thousands of people who merely want to splash about or sunbathe. Bilinga Beach runs from the north in a continuous sweep that includes Kirra. At Kirra Point a lookout commands views back to Surfers Paradise and east to Point Danger. The rock groyne at Kirra holds a generous wedge of sand shared by the highly popular Coolangatta and Greenmount Beaches. The grassy, tree-shaded knob which gives Greenmount its name has another lookout and makes an agreeable picnic spot. Rainbow Bay is also popular for sea bathing, and has a pool at the eastern end in the shelter of Snapper Rocks.

Flagstaff or Duranbah Beach, the only surfing beach that Tweed Heads can call its own, is used only by board-riders and a few sunbathers seek-

ing seclusion. Tweed Heads is a river city, not a surfing resort. Its people cross to Coolangatta when they want to swim, or they head south to the quieter coast around the Kingscliff area. A bridge has long been proposed from the city to Letitia Spit, just inside the Tweed River mouth, but it is never likely to claim a high priority. The spit beach north of Fingal Head— nearly 15 km away by the existing bridges— remains little frequented. Fingal Point is famed, and especially popular with fishermen, for the Giants Causeway, a formation of basalt columns

descending like steps into the turbulent waves. A patrolled beach runs north from the point, past camping and picnic grounds. On the river side, the settlement has a small boat harbour, launching ramp and fuel supplies.

In Tweed Heads itself, a large residential and shopping area has been reclaimed by filling in much of the old boat basin and the sand and mangrove flats which used to separate Greenbank Island from the city. Provision was made for a smaller boat harbour to shelter the Tweed River fishing fleet. The main harbour and ramps for

A tree-lined street running the length of the small peninsula to the north of the Tweed River mouth marks the start of the NSW/Queensland border

private boats are not on the Tweed but beside its tributary, Terranora Creek. Upstream the shallow, mangrove-lined Terranora Broadwater is limited for boating, though popular with anglers. Out to sea through the river's breakwater entrance, fishermen make for grounds off Cook Island. On land, the breakwaters, rocks and beaches are popular casting spots.

Brisbane to Yeppoon

Tourists from the south who venture north of Brisbane frequently end up settling there permanently. Over the past 20 years some coastal towns have increased their populations by as much as 500 per cent. Apart from the climate, the area offers the unusual attraction of Fraser Island—the largest sand island in the world.

Supply run, Fraser Island

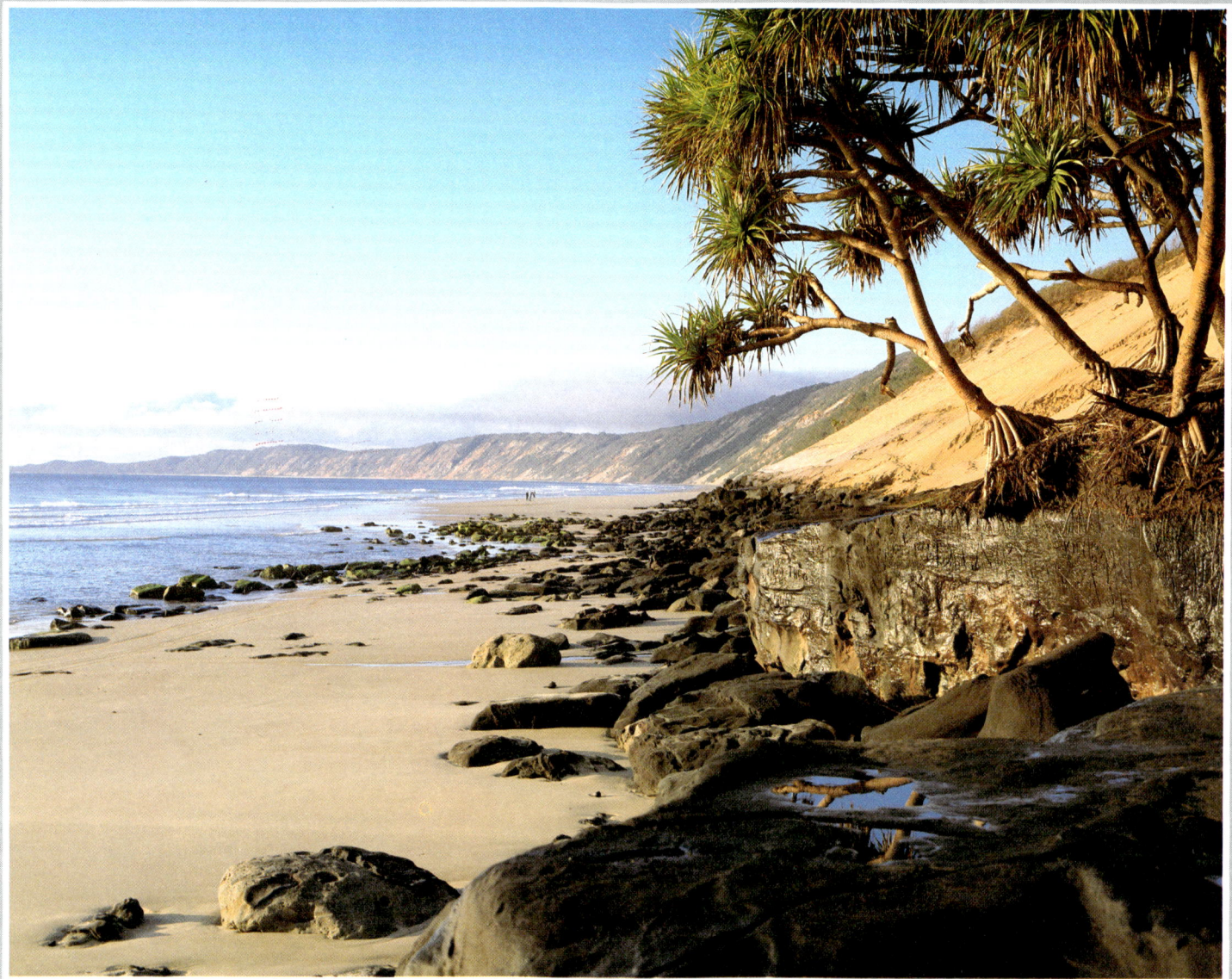

Cooloola National Park reaches south from Rainbow Beach

Beach business, Noosa

Lake Wabby, Fraser Island

QUEENSLAND

Yeppoon
Fitzroy River
Shoal Bay
Emu Park
Rockhampton
Keppel Sands
Great Keppel Island
CORAL SEA

Gladstone

GREAT BARRIER REEF

Burnett Heads
Bundaberg
Bargara
Burnett River
Elliott Heads
Hervey Bay
Waddy Point
Burrum Heads
Pialba
Fraser Island
Urangan
Maryborough
Mary River
SOUTH PACIFIC OCEAN

Tin Can Bay
Rainbow Beach

Noosa Heads

Coolum Beach

Maroochydore

Caloundra
Bribie Island

Brisbane

A rusting hull and rotting superstructure is all that remains of the Maheno, driven ashore on Fraser Island in 1953

Gentle change on a booming coast

A GERM of an idea, born on the Gold Coast, has caused an epidemic north of Brisbane. Each seaside district, competing for tourist and real estate dollars, adopts a catchy label—convenient in advertising but scarcely informative. Resorts from Caloundra to Noosa boast a Sunshine Coast, as if their suntanning hours exceeded those of neighbouring districts. Bundaberg offers a Sugar Coast, though Mackay grows far more cane and the industry is spread all the way from northern New South Wales to beyond Cairns. Yeppoon promotes a Capricornia Coast—all 35 km of it—while advocates of a breakaway Capricornia state have much more in mind.

If the Caloundra-Yeppoon strip has an established character, it is perhaps as a Pineapple Coast. Australia's only pineapple cannery, at Northgate in Brisbane, draws its supply from this region at an average rate of more than 100 000 tonnes a year. But since the early 1970s, a better description might have been the Growth Coast. Its phenomenal influx of people and capital in the past two decades matches what happened to the Gold Coast in the 1950s and 60s. District populations have variously increased threefold or even fivefold. Annual increases are still running at 10 per cent in some places, and school rolls are rising by 15 per cent. However, except for the transformation of Gladstone—to accommodate the world's greatest concentration of aluminium processing and shipment facilities, as well as coal exports on a prodigious scale—changes have been agreeably gentle. Nowhere in the region is there the beachfront building density of Surfers Paradise or Coolangatta or their degree of commercialism, though Noosa comes close to it.

Rather than crowd and wall off the seashore, new settlers have been content in many cases to leave it for holidaymakers. Instead they go to plateaux and easy slopes some way from the coast, and adapt to local ways of making a living. Many a former office worker or factory employee, raised in a harsher southern climate, now grows pineapples or dabbles in avocados and pawpaws. Some may belong to the growers' co-operative supplying Australia's only ginger-processing factory, at Buderim, to the west of Maroochydore. Cottage industries abound, particularly in the nearby Blackall Range. Its winding scenic roads are studded with the potteries, craft shops and art galleries of newcomers to the district.

Nature presents an ancient and awesome face in the hinterland: the volcanic cores of the Glasshouse Mountains jut from the southern downlands, and high, forested ranges and stark granite escarpments loom farther north. The Bruce Highway runs well inland, obliging seaside tourists to sidetrack but enabling them to visit imposing old cities that grew on wool, beef and minerals. Maryborough and Rockhampton are of major historical interest. The sleepy hill town of Gympie served goldmines that kept Queensland solvent in the depression of the 1880s and 90s.

A coast generously endowed with open beaches is overwhelmingly dominated by the enormous sand mass of Fraser Island. Multi-coloured sand cliffs on the mainland to the south mark an arm of Cooloola National Park—perhaps Queensland's most beautiful and certainly its most varied. Well developed for visitors yet preserving wide expanses of virgin wilderness, the park embraces lonely beaches and heaths, mangrove creeks, a vast treeless plain and a chain of river-linked lakes amid forests abounding in wildlife.

Temperatures in the region are mild to warm, and from Hervey Bay north they vary little with the seasons. Summer humidity is high, under the influence of tropical weather systems, and about two-thirds of a moderate annual rainfall occurs from December to May.

Hoop pines and melaleucas fringe placid AB Lake on Fraser Island. Dense forest covers much of the 120 km-long sand island

Living fossil was eaten as salmon

QUEENSLAND's central coast has the world's most exclusive freshwater fish. It originated in just two rivers—the Burnett and the Mary—which flow into each end of Hervey Bay. And its only near relatives have been dead for 200 million years. Even its classification as a fish is arguable, for it has many of the characteristics of an amphibian.

Fossil studies in the 1830s showed that a large aquatic creature, with an air-breathing lung as well as gills, developed about 250 million years ago. It reached worldwide abundance during the next 50 million years, then disappeared. It had crushing teeth formed like a rooster's comb, big overlapping scales, tiny eyes, leaf-shaped fins and a blunt tail. Scientists gave it the name *Ceratodus*—'horn-tooth'.

Just such a creature was discovered in the Burnett River in 1870. Settlers knew it—and ate its pink flesh—as 'Burnett salmon'. Soon it was found also in the Mary River, and in the 1890s it was introduced to streams and rivers nearer Brisbane. It so closely matched the fossil evidence that it too was called *Ceratodus*. Later knowledge revealed minor variations justifying a special classification of *Epiceradotus forsteri*, commonly known as the Queensland lungfish.

Tropical Africa and South America have their own lungfish, of distinctly different types. They can live without water, surviving droughts in cocoons that they secrete. But the Queensland

A Queensland lungfish, Epiceradotus forsteri

lungfish relies on a wet habitat. Its air-breathing ability is used only to augment the oxygen content of evaporating or fouled water. Kept in an aerated tank, it need not come up for air at all.

Queensland lungfish spawn in the manner of frogs, coating their eggs in a jelly, and the development of the embryo is like that of an amphibian until fins are formed in four to five months. The growth of the fish goes on for decades—the biggest specimens found, nearly 2 metres long and weighing more than 40 kg, are thought to be as much as 100 years old. Lungfish in Australia are totally protected.

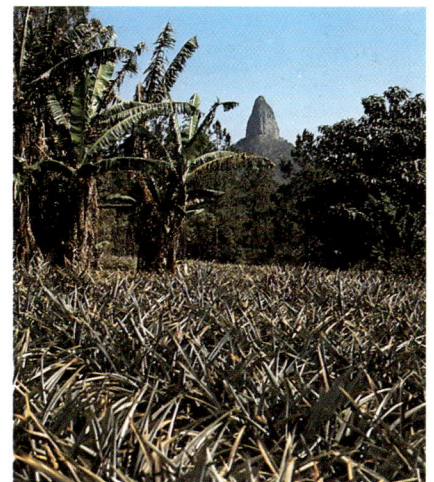

An eroded volcanic peak, one of the Glasshouse Mountains, towers over plantations to the north of Brisbane

The artificial island (left) created in the mouth of the Noosa River shows the tip of the residential development called Noosa Sound. The area is enjoying a building boom as southerners move north in search of the sun

Caloundra to Maroochydore

A high, commanding site distinguishes Caloundra from rival Sunshine Coast and Gold Coast resorts. Hilly streets are set on a headland up to 80 metres above a semi-circle of small, varied beaches. Buildings appear at uneven heights, avoiding the wall-like effect that would occur if the city had been flat. Visitors can stroll in a superbly appointed commercial area and still catch good views of the sea.

At Kings Beach, less than 500 metres from the post office, surf boils onto a rock platform around a saltwater pool. Dunes behind the level white beach are protected by a row of trees. Past a recreation reserve on Deepwater Point, Bulcock Beach has still water suitable for young children. A launching ramp leads into a green channel encircling the broad sand bar between the mainland and the northern tip of Bribie Island. Scenic cruises to the foot of the island, along

Pumice Stone Channel, leave from a jetty beside the ramp. Golden Beach, to the south, is lined with dinghies for hire.

Moffat Beach, the closest on the northern side of Caloundra, has dangerous currents and swimming is discouraged. Dickey Beach, beyond Tooway Creek, is patrolled and highly popular. Just north of the smaller Bunbubah Creek mouth is the rusted, century-old iron spine of the wrecked steamship *Dickey*, which gave the beach its name. Across Currimindi Creek is Currimindi Lake Environmental Park, a 44-hectare expanse of heath richly decked with wildflowers in late winter. A little-used ocean beach can be reached on foot through the park. Beyond it is Queensland's biggest maze of canals, cut for a recent real estate development, Kawana Waters.

At Mooloolaba Beach, long breakers wash towards a grassy, casuarina-shaded park in front

of the shopping centre. Across the peninsula, just inside the Mooloolah River, anglers drop their lines among trim yachts and squat cabin cruisers, and by mid-afternoon the harbour is jammed with commercial trawlers. It is also the base for pilot boats on the northern approach to Moreton Bay and Brisbane, though they are controlled from Caloundra. To the east around Point Cartwright, steps lead down to Buddina Beach, its northern end capped by a rock platform.

From Cotton Tree Park at the Maroochy River mouth, Maroochydore's buildings gleam behind a screen of casuarinas and old cotton trees. Construction cranes dominate the skyline of a fast-developing city. A rocky headland forms a boundary between a generous breadth of good surfing beach and the river mouth cluttered with fishing dinghies. Paddle boats and canoes are for hire next to the Esplanade swimming pool, and

Bribie Island points its northernmost finger at the lively tourist town of Caloundra, ringed by a variety of surfing and still-water beaches

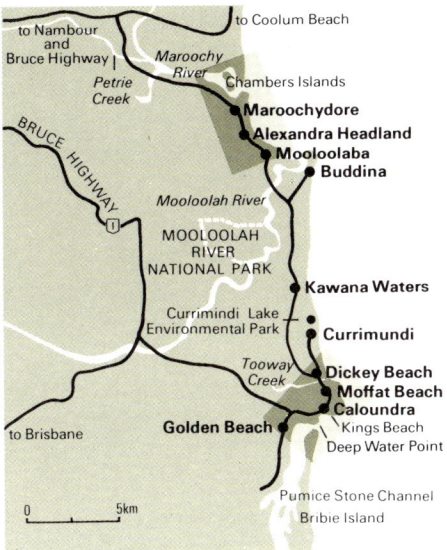

rowing boats at a multitude of sheds upriver. Cruises lasting four to five hours run to Dunethin Rock, which visitors can climb to gain impressive views of the inland ranges and canefields, and the Glasshouse Mountains. Shorter cruises are available to islands in the river's lower reaches, or up Petrie Creek towards Nambour. Most islands can be reached only by boat, but there is a causeway footpath to Chambers Island, 2 km upriver from the post office.

CALOUNDRA (pop. 16 758) east of Bruce Highway 85 km north of Brisbane (turn off 9 km north of Landsborough).

TRANSPORT: trains Brisbane-Landsborough with connecting buses daily; buses Brisbane-Caloundra daily; flights Brisbane-Caloundra and Sydney-Maroochydore daily.

SURF CLUB PATROLS: Kings Beach and Dickey Beach October-April, Saturday 08.00-17.00, Sunday and public holidays 07.00-16.00.

MAROOCHYDORE-ALEXANDRA HEADLAND-MOOLOOLABA (pop. 17 457) east of Bruce Highway 106 km north of Brisbane (turn off 16 km north of Landsborough northbound, at Nambour southbound).

TRANSPORT: trains Brisbane-Nambour daily with connecting buses most days; buses Brisbane-Maroochydore daily; flights Brisbane-Maroochydore and Sydney-Maroochydore daily.

SURF CLUB PATROLS: Maroochydore, Alexandra Headland and Mooloolaba Beaches October-April, weekends and public holidays 07.30-16.30.

YOUTH HOSTEL: open year-round.

CALOUNDRA												
	Jan	Feb	Mar	Apr	May	Jun	Jul	Aug	Sep	Oct	Nov	Dec
Maximum C°	28	27	27	25	23	20	20	21	23	25	26	27
Minimum C°	21	21	20	17	15	12	11	12	14	17	18	20
Rainfall mm	186	217	222	149	150	102	89	58	57	90	101	148
Humidity %	76	82	74	69	60	60	55	59	58	63	73	78
Rain days	11	13	14	11	10	7	8	7	6	8	9	9
Sunshine hrs	Summer 6 +			Autumn 7 +			Winter 8 +			Spring 9 +		

Residential and tourist development is continuous from Maroochydore to Mooloolaba

Mudjimba to Coolum

Mount Coolum, its rock faces climbing almost vertically to a blunt, folded summit 208 metres high, dominates the central section of the Sunshine Coast. In one Aboriginal legend the truncated mound is associated with Mudjimba Island, which is said to have been its head. But Mudjimba is also called Old Woman—in another legend the island represents the body of a mother who dived from Dunethin Rock, in the Maroochy River, in a vain attempt to save her daughter.

Mudjimba Beach reaches to the river mouth, opposite Maroochydore, but travellers from the south must make a long inland detour almost to Bli Bli before they come to a bridge. Turning back to the coast on the far side of the river, the route passes Suncoast Pioneer Village, where an extensive collection of old vehicles and other equipment is displayed in a bushland setting, 09.00-17.00 daily. Beyond is the increasingly busy Maroochy airport. Its operations frequently shatter the peace at Mudjimba Beach and four-wheel-drive tracks scar the sand. A gravel road leads south past fenced dunes and mangroves to popular angling spots at the river mouth.

At Marcoola, a rough track through a screen of trees north of the lifesaving clubhouse opens out onto a huge expanse of cream-honey sand—if the tide is out. When it is in and seas are heavy, the swash of the surf eats at the backshore sandhills. In a determined effort to resist erosion, the dunes are planted with grasses, fenced and bound with barbed wire. But black smudges along the back of the beach show where the sea has exposed soft sedimentary rock, not fully consolidated and containing organic material. Oily black streaks mark the sand, and with each storm more rock is washed away.

In Birrahl Park at Yaroombah, musk and rainbow lorikeets in the banksia trees override the roar of the ocean with their shrieking. A creek cuts a steep channel to the beach beyond a sheltered picnic area and playground. Board-riders wait for green rollers to mount, 60 metres out. To the north at Point Arkwright, the sea foams onto a long rock platform, near another park with wide views from Mooloolaba to Noosa Heads. Past the point, in contrast to the straight expanse of Yaroombah Beach, are secluded little beaches enclosed by rocky bluffs, easily reached by sand tracks from the coastal highway.

Coolum's public picnic area on Point Perry stands high over the sea, just south of the surf beach and the towering pines of Tickle Park, which includes a camping ground. Beyond, exposed layers of black rock line the backshore in

Mount Coolum casts a deep shadow towards Yaroombah golf course, south of Point Arkwright

front of grass-bound dunes studded with casuarinas. The beach is broken at Stumers Creek, which forms a reed-lined lagoon beside another picnic and camping ground. To the north, light brown sands run straight to Noosa, past the expanding resorts of Peregian, Marcus and Sunshine Beaches. Just south of Peregian, between the highway and the sandhills, 93 hectares of heathland have been preserved as an environmental park. Vividly coloured with wildflowers in winter and spring, the park represents the type of country which before European settlement occupied almost all of the Sunshine Coast.

MUDJIMBA-MARCOOLA east of Bruce Highway 123 km from Brisbane (turn off at Nambour).
TRANSPORT: as for Maroochydore, previous page.
SURF CLUB PATROL: Marcoola October-April, weekends and public holidays 07.30-16.30.

YAROOMBA-COOLUM BEACH (pop. 2954) east of Bruce Highway 129 km from Brisbane (turn off at Yandina).
TRANSPORT: as for Maroochydore, previous page, or Noosa, following page.
SURF CLUB PATROL: Coolum October-April, Saturday 08.00-17.00, Sunday and public holidays 09.00-16.00.

COOLUM												
	Jan	Feb	Mar	Apr	May	Jun	Jul	Aug	Sep	Oct	Nov	Dec
Maximum C°	29	28	28	27	24	22	21	23	24	26	27	29
Minimum C°	20	21	19	15	13	8	7	8	9	13	16	19
Rainfall mm	240	361	166	131	102	54	178	64	45	166	162	207
Rain days	16	24	16	16	14	11	11	10	9	12	12	12
Sunshine hrs	Summer 7 +			Autumn 7 +			Winter 7 +			Spring 8 +		

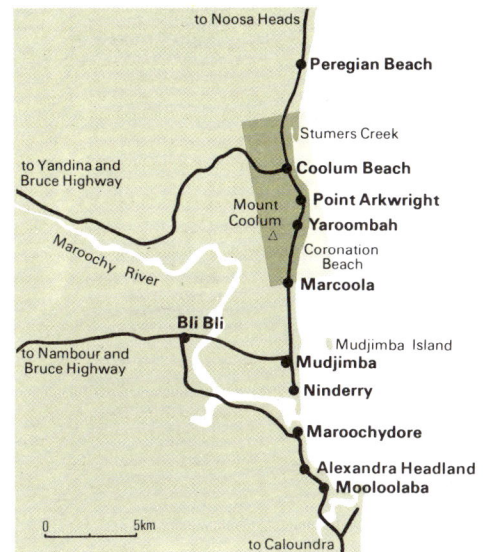

Something for everybody

PROMOTERS of the tourist trade took a liberty in naming the strip from Caloundra to Rainbow Beach the Sunshine Coast. Its annual hours of sunshine are often exceeded in districts farther north. But the waters that lap those bright shores are mostly sluggish—shielded by the sand mass of Fraser Island or by the coral ramparts of the Great Barrier Reef. The real advantage of the Sunshine Coast is that it is the warmest place where the full power of Pacific Ocean waves can be enjoyed.

Surfers need no wetsuits, even in winter. In fact the winter months are preferred by many beachgoers because humidity is at its lowest and rainy days are least likely. Board-riding champions give high ratings to many of the breaks along this coast—especially at places like Alexandra Headland at Mooloolaba.

But there is much more than golden beaches and big breakers to bring delight to holidaymakers. Enchanting scenery can be found in the hills of the back country and among the Glasshouse Mountains. Commercial amusements abound, though they seldom compete for attention with the brash clamour of similar enterprises on the Gold Coast. And utter peace and quiet await on the district's natural inland waterways—particularly the Noosa River and the spacious lakes that it links in Cooloola National Park.

The park's hinterland is a bird-breeding paradise of forested hills, heathlands and reedy swamps—Americanised by cruise companies as 'the Everglades'. Its focus is salty Lake Cootharaba. Tour boats and hired craft tie up at a pylon-mounted headquarters beside Kinaba Island, at the head of the lake. An easy nature trail includes a boardwalk straddling dense mangroves, and a hide for watching waterfowl. Tougher bushwalks can be taken in the area, and others from an upriver landing place known as Harry's Hut.

Cooloola's coastal side offers a complete contrast. A straight, lonely beach reaching to Double Island Point is backed, beyond Teewah, by multi-coloured sand cliffs. The beach can be safely negotiated only with four-wheel drive. Companies at Noosaville and Tewantin operate bus tours that incorporate river ferry rides.

Rainbow Beach – end of the line on the Cooloola coast. Fraser Island lies beyond

Spiky pandanus palms and melaleucas fringe Coolum Beach

Kinaba Island, Lake Cootharaba, in Cooloola National Park

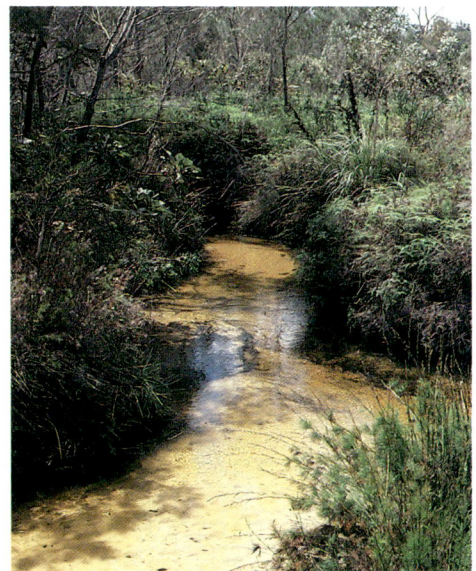

Seary's Creek, near Rainbow Beach

Caloundra's Kings Beach faces the northern tip of Bribie Island

Sunset over the waterways of Noosa

Setting sail from Noosa Heads

Hell's Gate in Noosa National Park, which has a 3 km coastal walking track

Noosa Heads and River

Tangled waterways and islands, a forested headland and a ring of surfing beaches and rock platforms give Noosa the most varied concentration of leisure possibilities on Queensland's southern and central coasts. Commercial development in the adjoining town centres of Noosa Heads and Noosaville, extending almost continuously east and west to Sunshine Beach and Tewantin, is geared to a year-round swarm of visitors from the south. Prices in an imposing array of shops and restaurants are also scaled to the free-spending habits of holidaymakers. But the best things in Noosa are free, or nearly so.

Conservation of the headland forest and heaths has been the saving grace of a town area which might otherwise have been overloaded with tourist development. Noosa National Park (382 hectares) has well-equipped picnic grounds at its entrance from Park Road, and visitors can take an easy 3 km walk from the car park to Alex-andria Bay, along a rugged coast broken by small beaches. Rock terraces and pools are exposed at low tide. Four other tracks of up to 4 km loop inland: Tanglewood, Palm Grove and Pine Circle lead through sandy rainforest, while the Noosa Hill track goes through more open stands of eucalypt and banksia.

Expansive Sunshine Beach draws championship surfers. Patrolled swimming and surfing for the less expert is at the town beach fronting the

Hastings Street shopping centre—a beach which has been doubled in size by ambitious engineering. The Noosa River used to curl through sand bars to an unreliable entrance near the camping ground. In 1978 a new entrance was dredged and a groyne built out to protect it. The dredged sand was pumped along the shore to the east to form a 700-metre frontal dune which was grassed with spinifex and planted with casuarinas. Behind it is a 16-hectare expanse of sheltered sand, planted with more varied vegetation. The amount of foreshore sand on the surfing beach is still subject to winds and currents in Laguna Bay, but the river entrance is stable and the permanence of the man-made dune wall has permitted the safe development of residential canal systems in the inlet backwaters towards Noosaville.

Upstream from Noosaville post office, all the emphasis turns to river activities. Boat-hire sheds, launching ramps, public and private jetties and cruise bases line the bank all the way to

Noosa's forested headland park guarantees ample breathing space in a district of rapid development

Tewantin. Doonella Lake, south of the Tewantin bridge, is a playground for canoeists and youngsters learning to sail or windsurf. Water-skiers head upriver to high-speed courses between Tewantin and Lake Cooroibah. Anglers bob in dinghies or wade in the shallows of the river and its tributary creeks.

The Noosa River is navigable almost to its headwaters near Tin Can Bay. It leads through the swamps and forests of Noosa River National Park (469 hectares), which has no facilities for visitors, to the extensive sandy heaths and rainforests of Cooloola National Park (23 000 hectares). Camping permits are obtainable at Kinaba control station and information centre, at the northern end of Lake Cootharaba, where walking tracks are being developed in a special nature conservation area. The park's coastal arm runs to Rainbow Beach and includes the remarkable coloured sand cliffs north of Teewah. More than 70 colours, caused by the oxidation of minerals and the decay of organic material, have been discerned in these formations. They can be seen on coastal tours from Noosaville or Tewantin.

NOOSA HEADS-NOOSAVILLE-TEWANTIN (pop. 9965) east of Bruce Highway 155 km from Brisbane (turn off at Cooroy).
TRANSPORT: trains Brisbane-Cooroy with connecting buses daily; buses Brisbane-Noosa daily; flights Sydney-Maroochydore, Brisbane-Noosa daily.
SURF CLUB PATROL: October-May, Saturday 08.00-16.00, Sunday 07.00-17.00, public holidays 07.00-16.00.
YOUTH HOSTEL: at Sunshine Beach, open year-round.

TEWANTIN	Jan	Feb	Mar	Apr	May	Jun	Jul	Aug	Sep	Oct	Nov	Dec
Maximum C°	29	28	28	26	23	21	21	22	24	26	28	28
Minimum C°	21	21	20	18	14	12	10	11	13	16	18	20
Rainfall mm	232	233	241	171	143	118	86	53	69	95	111	157
Humidity %	67	69	65	61	59	59	56	56	56	62	60	67
Rain days	12	13	15	11	11	9	8	7	8	8	9	10
Sunshine hrs	Summer 6 +			Autumn 7 +			Winter 7 +			Spring 8 +		

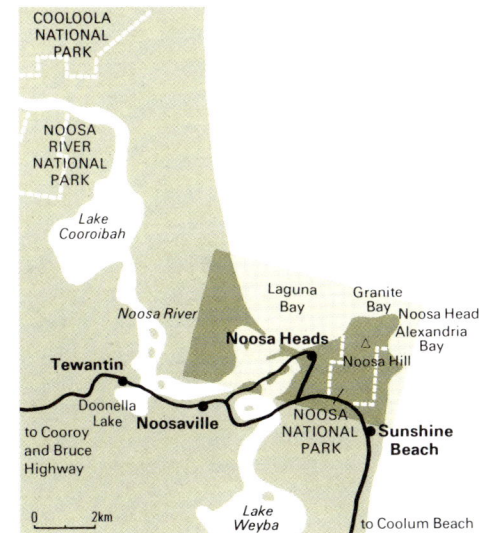

Tin Can Bay and Rainbow Beach

Boating is everything in the sheltered reaches of Tin Can Inlet, south of Wide Bay Harbour. At Tin Can Bay township, a huge car park reclamation on Norman Point adjoins a ramp capable of launching three craft at once. Throughout winter and spring camper vans, four-wheel-drives, utilities, cars and trailers fill the park. Snapper Creek is lined with commercial fishing berths, private jetties and boat-hire sheds, and leads to a newly extended public marina. Some of the spoil gained by dredging the marina went into the car park development, which includes

a swimming pool fed tidally by pipes from the creek. South towards the head of the inlet, Toolara holiday village has cabins, a caravan park and its own store. A launching ramp gives access to Crab Creek and the main inlet waters. They are mostly shallow and flat-bottomed, so the tidal effect is extensive: where there are sandbars the waterline may retreat hundreds of metres in three or four hours. Anglers make good catches, but must take careful note of the tides.

Rainbow Beach, on the open coast of Wide Bay, is only 8 km east of Tin Can Bay but travel-

lers must make long detours to get there—looping north around Inskip Point by boat or south around the inlet by car. They reach a popular surfing beach backed by multi-hued sand cliffs, and a well-appointed township which sprang up in the early 1970s to support Fraser Island sand mining activities. A sealed road leads on to Inskip Point, where barge services to Fraser Island are based.

A branch road 5 km south of Rainbow Beach enters the coastal section of Cooloola National Park. Picnic facilities and short walking trails

Norman Point, with a new boat marina cut into its base and a car park reclamation blunting its tip, spears into the popular fishing waters of Tin Can Inlet

through varied forest are provided at several spots along this road, which leads to a fully developed campsite at Freshwater Creek, 100 metres from the beach running south to Noosa. Wedged in the sand 5 km north towards Double Island Point is the wreck of the 1600-tonne ship *Cherry Venture*, driven ashore by a cyclone in 1973. There is another campsite on Wide Bay just across the narrow isthmus of the point, and bush camping is allowed in some parts of the park. Permits can be obtained at Gympie or Maryborough, or from rangers permanently stationed at Freshwater Creek.

TIN CAN BAY (pop. 683) east of Bruce Highway 228 km from Brisbane (turn off at Gympie northbound, Maryborough southbound).
TRANSPORT: train Brisbane-Gympie daily (4 hrs); bus Gympie-Tin Can Bay most days.

RAINBOW BEACH (pop. 726) 40 km east of Tin Can Bay by road.
TRANSPORT: train Brisbane-Gympie daily (4 hrs); bus Gympie-Rainbow Beach most days.

DOUBLE ISLAND POINT												
	Jan	Feb	Mar	Apr	May	Jun	Jul	Aug	Sep	Oct	Nov	Dec
Maximum C°	27	27	26	25	22	20	19	20	22	24	26	27
Minimum C°	22	22	21	20	17	15	14	14	16	19	20	21
Rainfall mm	180	175	174	134	140	125	92	61	56	73	83	135
Humidity %	74	77	75	72	68	67	64	64	65	68	71	72
Rain days	13	14	17	14	15	12	11	9	9	9	9	11
Sunshine hrs	Summer 6 +			Autumn 8 +			Winter 7 +			Spring 8 +		

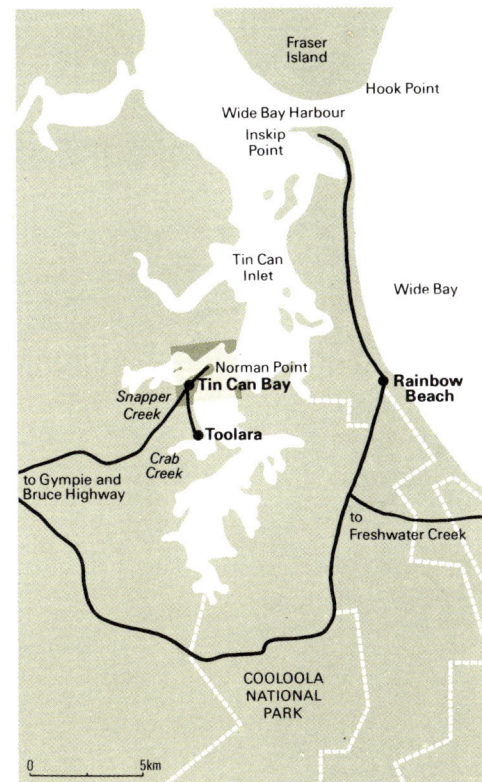

The saltwater crocodile, big and dangerous, has a short, broad snout

Tigers of the waterways

GIANT saltwater crocodiles range well beyond Queensland's tropical zone—at least as far south as Tin Can Inlet. In 1982, so many were seen in the nearby Mary River estuary that the townsfolk of Maryborough demanded an organised shoot.

The saltwater species, *Crocodylus porosus*, is normally about 5 metres long but can grow to 7 metres. It mainly frequents estuaries and tidal swamps, but can travel far inland up rivers and between flood-plain waterholes. And it voyages in the open ocean—in the Arafura Sea, for example, and according to some reports into New South Wales waters.

Crocodiles seek food mostly between sunset and dawn. They wait motionless, with only their eyes and nostrils out of the water, at spots where animals lower their heads to drink. Seizing their prey by the nose, they spin in the water to throw it off its feet. In this way a big saltwater crocodile can render even a horse or a bull helpless, and drown it. By day, crocodiles may be seen basking on riverbanks. If disturbed they scuttle into the water, lashing their tails at anything in their way. Many people have died from a single blow of the tail after coming on a basking saltwater crocodile unexpectedly.

Hungry *porosus* crocodiles on rare occasions may also leap out of the water—snatching people or animals from riverbanks or jetties or even lunging into fishing dinghies. Late in 1981 a policeman on the shore near Bamaga, Cape York, narrowly escaped the snapping jaws of a 6-metre crocodile. It attacked again and took his dog.

A freshwater species, *Crocodylus johnstoni*, may be found as far south as the Bundaberg district. It is seldom more than 3 metres long and not normally dangerous, though it may bite if it is cornered and can inflict a serious wound.

The relatively harmless freshwater crocodile's snout is long and narrow

(Map labels)
Fraser Island
Hook Point
Wide Bay Harbour
Inskip Point
Tin Can Inlet
Wide Bay
Norman Point
Tin Can Bay
Snapper Creek
Rainbow Beach
Toolara
to Gympie and Bruce Highway
Crab Creek
to Freshwater Creek
COOLOOLA NATIONAL PARK
0   5km

Fraser Island

People struggling with beach erosion in New South Wales, and wondering where all their sand gets to, need only look at Fraser Island. This is the terminus for a vast system of sand transport that has been virtually continuous for perhaps 2 million years. Powerful, wave-induced currents have pulled enough sediments from as far south as Sydney to build Moreton, Bribie and the Stradbroke Islands off Brisbane, the high sand cliffs north of Noosa, and Fraser—the biggest sand island in the world.

Fraser Island is 120 km long and up to 22 km wide, with Breaksea Spit extending underwater for a further 45 km to the north-east. Three small outcrops of volcanic rock are clustered near Orchid Beach, and there is one other halfway along the west coast. The rest of the island is formed of fine sand, piled more than 200 metres above sea level in some places and reaching more than 60 metres below it to the ocean floor.

To the surprise of newcomers, however, much of Fraser Island is richly vegetated. Sea spray gave it a coating of nutrient salts, permitting the germination of seeds and spores carried by birds or the wind. Decayed plant matter formed a thick mat of humus in which tall forests developed, to the delight of the timber-getters who first came in 1863. For four decades they floated huge log rafts of sought-after softwoods—hoop pine, kauri and white beech—to Maryborough for milling. When accessible stands were exhausted, they turned to hardwoods such as tallow and blackbutt, using steam tramways to speed their output. Felling was brought under control between 1908 and 1923, when the forests were reserved by the state. Today almost two-thirds of the island is state forest, although less than half of that area is logged. Birds are prolific and wildflowers bloom profusely, especially around August.

Pockets of rainforest with a luxuriant growth of palms and ferns occur in the shelter of high dunes, which run in parallel ridges south-east to north-west. Often the rainforest patches are fringed by towering stands of satinay, *Syncarpia hillii*, which is almost unknown except on Fraser Island. Satinay, one of a group inaccurately called 'turpentine' trees, is exceptionally resistant to marine borer: its long, straight trunks were used to line the Suez Canal and London's Tilbury Docks. Blackbutt, now the main species for commercial harvesting, is also found near the rainforest zones. Coast cypress grows on the western side of the island, in a belt behind skirting mangroves. Scribbly gum and bloodwood predominate on semi-arid soil inland and to the north.

Fresh water is plentiful except in the north. Rain soaking into the sand is held near sea level in a lens-shaped water table. Where this reservoir pierces the island's surface, pure water gushes in streams to the coasts or fills 'window' lakes whose level rises or falls with that of the water table. But Fraser Island also has the world's greatest concentration of 'perched' lakes, far above the natural water level. These are formed when plant matter and minerals cement the bottom of a depression between dunes, creating a saucer-shaped rain trap. Boemingen, covering about 200 hectares, is the biggest such lake in the world; the Boomerangs, 130 metres above sea level, are the highest.

Tourist cabins at Happy Valley have been

Waddy Point is formed by a tiny rock outcrop—one of only four in a huge island of sand

Sandy Cape

Rooney Point

Hervey Bay

Ocean Lake
● **Orchid Beach**
Waddy Point
GREAT SANDY ISLAND NATIONAL PARK
Middle Rock

Boomerang Lakes Cathedrals

Moon Point

Pialba ●━━● Urangan
Fraser Island ● Maheno Wreck
Happy Valley
● Rainbow Gorge
Seventy-Five Mile Beach

Woongoolbver Creek

Ungowa ●
Maryborough ● **Eurong**
Lake Boemingen

Great Sandy Strait
● 'Dilli Village'

Hook Point Inskip Point Wide Bay
0 10km
to Inskip Point

Thick scrub behind Seventy-Five Mile Beach is swamped at intervals by 'blows' of bare, wind-driven sand

patronised since the 1950s. More ambitious resorts at Eurong and Orchid Beach have promoted a regular traffic of visitors since the 1960s. But sand mining companies were interested, too. Rutile and zircon extraction from the south-eastern coastal strip began in earnest in 1971. A subsidiary of the international Dillingham Corporation joined in, on leases extending to the high dunes. A rutile export contract was approved at the end of 1974—almost on the eve of the proclamation of federal environmental protection laws—and large-scale mining started in mid-1975. It provoked Australia's greatest legal confrontation between mining companies and conservationists, and culminated in a prohibition of Fraser Island mineral exports after 1976. The island was the first National Estate item listed by the National Heritage Commission. Dillingham's field centre became 'Dilli Village', a National Fitness Council camp.

Visitors wanting a holiday off the beaten track flock to Fraser Island in their tens of thousands and their numbers look likely to soar far higher. Inevitably, vehicles are needed if tourists are to reach the resorts and to see the most celebrated sights—the astonishing 'blows' of wind-driven sand, the wild horses descended from cavalry mounts and sawyers' draughthorses, Rainbow Gorge and Woongoolbver Creek, the Cathedrals sand cliffs, the *Maheno* shipwreck. Four-wheel-drives and trail bikes make a day-long din on the east coast strip and some of the inland forestry tracks. Seventy-Five Mile Beach is constantly scarred by tyres—except after a storm, when it may be soft and not passable at all.

The people who gain most enjoyment from Fraser Island, once having seen what it has to offer, are those prepared to strike out on foot over its abundant trails, away from the tourist-thronged surf beach. Trails leading north-west between dune ridges are not unduly strenuous. A direct crossing of the island, however, must follow an up-and-down course made more difficult by soft sand, so it calls for extreme fitness. State Forest traversing and camping permits are obtainable in Brisbane or Maryborough. The northern third of the island is occupied except along the east coast strip by the desolate woodlands, heaths and swamps of Great Sandy Island National Park (49 400 hectares). Creeks are few and lakes are difficult to reach, so bush walkers must carry plenty of water. Park headquarters are just north of the Cathedrals.

FRASER ISLAND north of Wide Bay 261 km from Brisbane via Inskip Point, 325 km via Urangan.
TRANSPORT: frequent vehicular barges Inskip Point-Hook Point and Urangan-Ungowa daily; launches Urangan-Ungowa most days; flights Urangan, Maryborough, Maroochydore or Brisbane to Orchid Beach most days.

🛏 🏠 ⚓ 🚻 ⚙ 🍴 🍽 🛶 🥾 ⛴

NOTE: facilities are scattered; motoring four-wheel-drive only.

SANDY CAPE												
	Jan	Feb	Mar	Apr	May	Jun	Jul	Aug	Sep	Oct	Nov	Dec
Maximum C°	29	29	28	26	24	22	21	22	24	26	27	28
Minimum C°	22	22	21	20	17	15	14	15	17	19	20	21
Rainfall mm	172	167	160	119	113	109	91	64	55	55	66	102
Humidity %	67	70	67	66	65	65	62	60	61	63	66	67
Rain days	14	15	17	16	14	13	12	10	8	8	9	10
Sunshine hrs	Summer 6 +			Autumn 7 +			Winter 7 +			Spring 8 +		

Eliza Fraser

The tall tale of Eliza Fraser

FRASER ISLAND owes its name to showmanship. A week after the brig *Stirling Castle* was wrecked off Mackay in 1836, survivors reached Waddy Point in the ship's pinnace. Eliza Fraser, the captain's wife, was among them. Five men, including Eliza's husband, died during the two months they waited for rescue. The others were looked after by Aborigines, but made to hunt, fish and perform menial tasks.

Of the Aborigines, one survivor stated: 'I cannot call them a cruel people.' Yet Eliza—hastily and secretly remarried—turned up in England with a claim that she had been speared and tortured, and her husband murdered. She told of the ship's mate roasted alive over a slow fire, and hinted at unspeakable indignities to herself. Her account, more and more embellished, became a money-spinning entertainment for uninformed Britons who would believe any tale of savagery in the Antipodes. And Eliza's fame became so great that the formal name, Great Sandy Island, was superseded by Fraser Island.

Eliza Fraser's fictions could be laughed at now, but for the influence they must have had on the attitudes of the British who later settled Hervey Bay. The district was the territory of the Butchalla Aboriginal tribe, 2000-3000 of whom used to occupy Fraser Island seasonally. In 1860 the island was proclaimed as a reserve for the whole tribe, and any not wanted as labourers or servants were banished from the mainland. The reserve provision was ignored soon after, when the wealth in the island's forests was discovered. The Butchallas were herded into a mission settlement and timber-getters took over.

When the Gympie gold-rush started in 1867, Fraser Island was made an immigration and quarantine station. Sailors and miners flooded in, bringing alcoholic liquor, opium and alien diseases which together took an appalling toll of the overcrowded Aborigines. Fewer than 200 remained when the settlement was closed in 1904, and they were dispersed to missions as far away as Cairns. Deportation of Aborigines from the Hervey Bay district, simply because they were unemployed, continued into the 1930s.

Hervey Bay and Burrum Heads

Maryborough people had Hervey Bay virtually to themselves as late as the 1960s. Bulk sugar terminals elsewhere had rendered the railhead at Urangan obsolete, and its long wharf was little used. Seaside settlements to the west were scarcely known to outsiders. But population around the bay shore multiplied fivefold in the 1970s. Along with this rapid residential growth came a surge in holiday interest. Now a string of villages has merged into a continuous band of development, though the district preserves a relaxed and simple style. So far it has little of the commercial glitter and building pressure associated with Gold Coast and Sunshine Coast resorts. Flat waters offer nothing for surfers, but plenty for boat enthusiasts, anglers and water-skiers. Camping grounds and caravan parks abound—in

fact Hervey Bay's publicists proudly claim for it the title of 'Caravan Capital of Australia'.

Along the Esplanade from Torquay to Urangan, signs advertise reef fishing and Fraser Island cruises. At Neptune's Coral Cove on Dayman Point, living coral from local reefs decorates aquarium tanks stocked with a wide variety of colourful fish. A monstrously ugly stonefish, with venomous spines that can kill humans, shares a tank with a similarly deadly sea snake. The aquarium is open daily 09.00-16.00. Around the long jetty pointing north, brown sand attracts anglers pumping for shellfish bait. From a park and picnic area by the aquarium, the beach running south towards the boat harbour is so flat that the water is only ankle-deep 50 metres from the shore. Tall mooring posts within the grey

stone harbour walls obscure the hulls of cruising yachts and launches. Behind them loom the blue outline of Fraser Island and the closer, dark green profile of Woody Island. The harbour car park has room for more than 100 vehicles, and the ramp can launch four boats at once.

Vera's World at Torquay has an unusually comprehensive collection of sea shells, amassed from nearly every maritime country in the world, open 09.00-17.00 daily. Boat-hire and public launching facilities are concentrated nearby, next to the sailing club. Pioneer buildings and relics are on display at the museum complex at Scarness, open 13.00-17.00 Friday to Sunday and daily during school holidays. At Point Vernon, grassy picnic grounds lead to a thin strip of beach sand ringed by a low shelf of rocks, sprinkled with

puddles after high tide. Gatakers Bay has its own cluster of boating and angling facilities. The shallows, though little more than a mass of oozing sand, smell fresh and sweet and the trees teem with birds. They flock to Parraweena Bird Sanctuary to be fed at 07.30 and 16.00 daily.

Burrum Heads, isolated on the north-western reach of Hervey Bay towards Bundaberg, is favoured by anglers and families seeking a quiet time on an increasingly busy coast. The township stands at the entrance to a wide estuary formed by the confluence of the Burrum, Isis and Gregory Rivers. Extensive sandbanks clog the estuary and the bay offshore, but channels are marked and the Burrum is navigable some distance upstream by boats of shallow draught. Banks of smooth sand, cut by two concrete boat ramps, run in front of a caravan park shaded by jacarandas, mango trees and palms.

PIALBA-URANGAN (pop. 13 569) north-east of Bruce Highway 293 km from Brisbane (turn off at Maryborough northbound, Howard southbound).
TRANSPORT: train Brisbane-Maryborough daily (6 hrs); bus Maryborough-Hervey Bay most days; flights Brisbane-Maryborough daily.
YOUTH HOSTEL: at Torquay, open year-round.

BURRUM HEADS (pop. 895) north of Bruce Highway 300 km from Brisbane (turn off at Howard).
TRANSPORT: coach Brisbane-Torbanlea daily (6 hrs); none beyond Torbanlea, 14 km away.

Urangan's long industrial jetty and railway terminal are rarely used, but fishing boats crowd the artificial harbour to the south; at Point Vernon (left) sand flats clog the shores except in Gatakers Bay

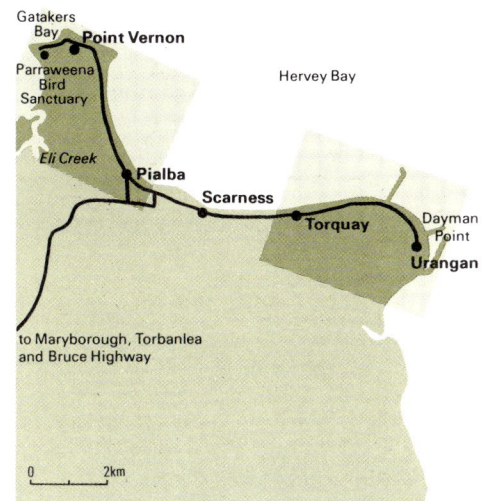

Empire of the corals

AMONG the tens of thousands of structures making up the Great Barrier Reef system, no two places are the same. Some 400 kinds of coral grow here—far more than anywhere else in the world. Other life forms are even more diverse. And the geographical range is vast. Sites where public visiting is encouraged span nearly 2000 km, from subtropical Lady Elliott Island (really a cay of coral debris) off Bundaberg to Lizard Island, situated beyond Cooktown.

Seen by day, corals are colourful but stonily inert. Most of the reef-builders are at their best when spotlit, on a night dive. Then they are feeding, their feathery tentacles out and waving gently in search of microscopic plankton drifting by. The corals' tentacles—like those of their cousins, the jellyfish—are armed with barbed stinging cells that paralyse the prey.

But an array of corals is only one delight of a reef. It is a breeding and feeding ground for myriad animals, visible at any time. Along with about 1500 fish species frequenting various parts of the reef region are thousands of different molluscs and crustaceans, sponges, anemones and sea stars, marine worms, sea urchins and cucumbers, in forms and hues that often test a diver's credulity. Reef flats and sandy cays attract well over 200 bird species.

All of this teeming animal life is supported by marine plants. Seaweeds, seagrasses and algae, using dwindling sunlight to produce organic matter, start a complicated food chain that reaches from plankton to giant groper. Some minuscule algae live in the flesh of corals, supplying much of their nutrition and energy. Other algae encrust the reefs and in fact help to build them with limy deposits that bind together coral skeletons, shell fragments and sand.

Feather star on corals

Heron Island is really a cay of coral debris, occupying a tiny part of a vast reef platform

Corals of Bird Reef

Nudibranch 'sea slug' – a mollusc that has no shell

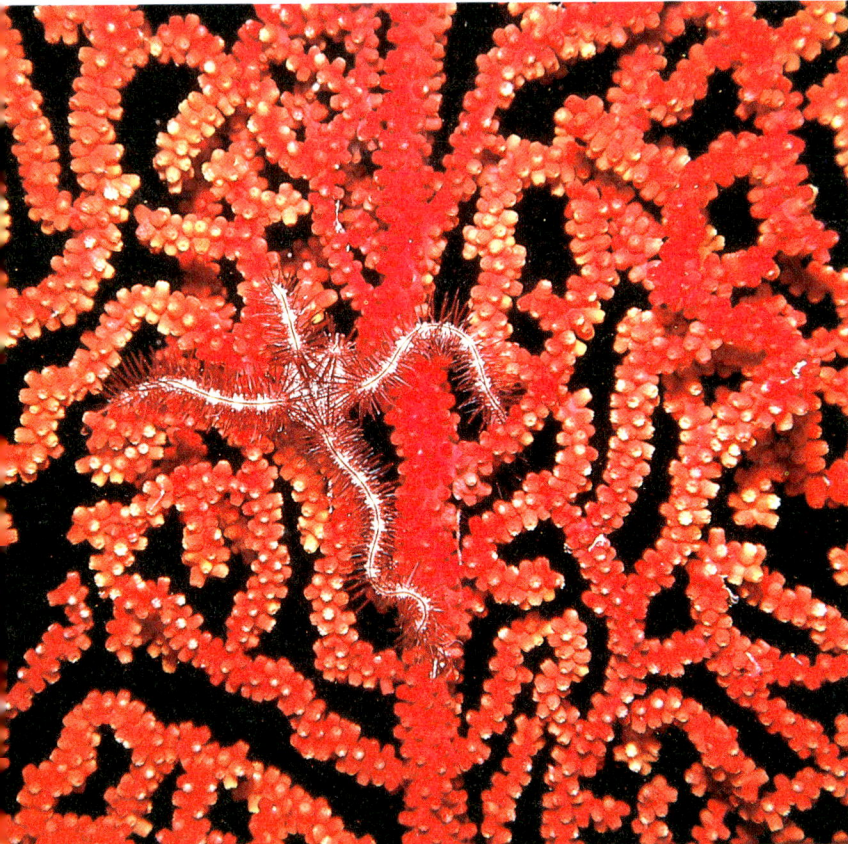
Brittle star on a soft whip coral

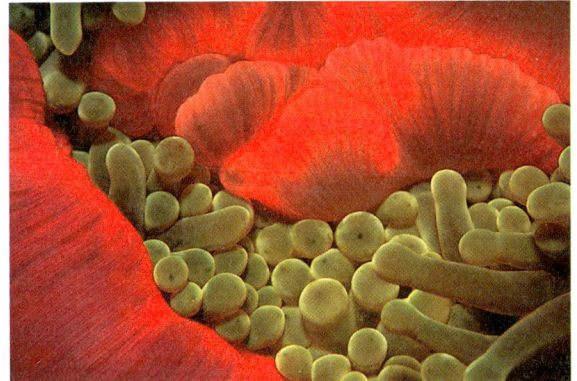
Fan corals and anemone tentacles

Soft sponge

High tide covers staghorn corals

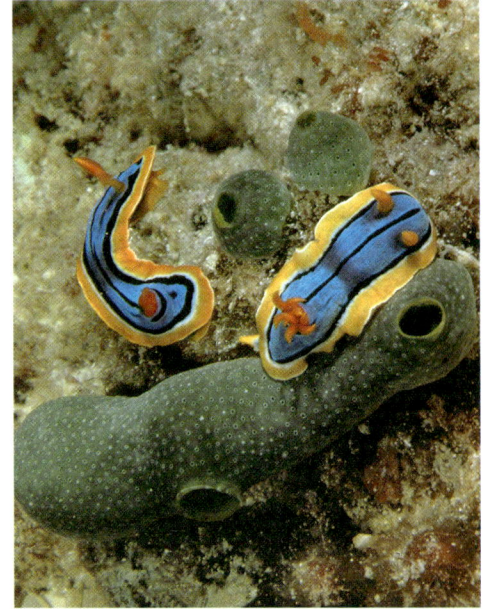

Nudibranchs feeding on sea squirts

Feather stars – sometimes called sea lilies – can crawl and some of them can swim

Hypsicomus tube worm

Anemone fish, one of the damselfish family

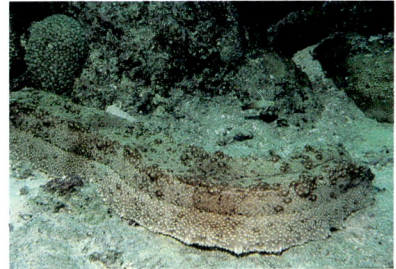

Sea cucumber

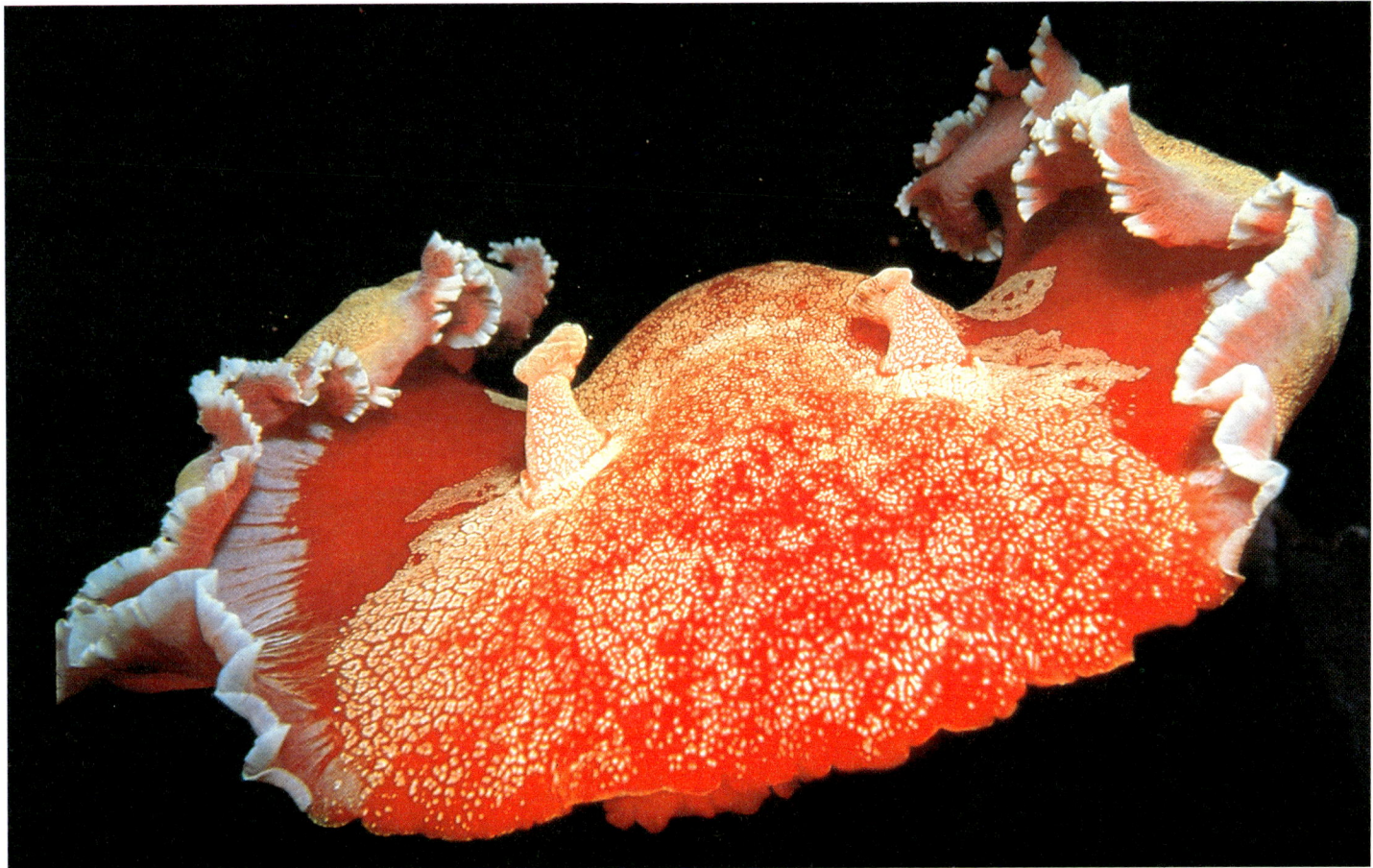

A Spanish dancer nudibranch flutters through the water with a grace and agility that belies the term 'sea slug'

Canefields reach from the scattered settlement of Burnett Heads to Bundaberg's sugar terminal

Bundaberg beaches

Beach roads fan like the fingers of a hand from the handsome riverside city of Bundaberg. Visitors can choose from four major seaside resort areas, or if they have cars they can make their base in town and try a variety of beaches, all within 20 minutes' drive. Buss Park, beside the Burnett River in the city centre, has fine gardens and playgrounds overlooking the moorings of the trawler fleet, with excellent freshwater baths nearby. Bundaberg, surrounded by canefields, is the only place in Australia where the entire activity of the sugar industry is on view. At other centres, sugar processing is taken only to a stage of raw crystallisation. But the Millaquin company has its own refinery, producing about 30 000 tonnes a year of table sugar along with golden syrup and treacle. And its distillery turns out more than 2 million litres of Bundaberg rum and 4 million litres of industrial alcohol a year. Guided tours at 13.00 on weekdays include the crushing mill during the July-December harvesting season, and the refinery and distillery

year-round except January. The bulk sugar loading terminal near the river mouth can also be inspected, at 15.15 on weekdays.

From the river mouth to Elliott Heads, ribbons of black rock interrupt a flat coastline and contrast vividly with its short stretches of pale, sandy surfing beach. The rock is solidified lava from an ancient volcano which has its remnants in the Hummock—at 97 metres the district's only significant hill. The beach in front of the lifesaving clubhouse at Elliott Heads is man-made, created by shifting the rocks to form groynes. Inside the river mouth a grassy park runs behind rocks lining the north bank. Beyond are sandy river beaches favoured by elderly people and families with young children. Riverview, farther upstream, has a fully equipped picnic area with a kiosk and playground. Boats are available for hire and private craft can be launched from a ramp near the picnic ground.

Bargara Beach and Kellys Beach lie each side of the well-appointed township of Bargara.

Behind the surf at the northern end of Kellys, a ring of rocks encloses the Basin, a shallow, sandy pool ideal for young children. Christsen Park beside it has picnic tables and swings. The town foreshore is rocky, but a sandy gap has been cleared to launch boats. Bargara Beach is pleasantly shaded by tall palms and drooping casuarinas, but disco music intrudes from the roller skating rink of the nearby Neilson Park caravan ground. Mon Repos Beach, 1 km west, can be reached on foot from Bargara although its road access from Bundaberg is by a different route. Mon Repos is the most accessible turtle nesting ground in Australia and attracts nightly audiences of tourists from late November to late March. For the first two months of the season females of three large species, loggerhead, flatback and green turtles, come ashore for one night. Each lays scores of eggs in scooped-out sand nests above the high-water mark. Hatchlings swarm to the sea in February or March.

Burnett Heads is a quiet little settlement behind a short sandy break in the coast's rocky rim. Bundaberg Harbour, to the north-west around South Head, is a dredged basin for shallow-draught craft behind the southern

ELLIOTT HEADS (pop. 462) east of Bruce Highway 390 km from Brisbane, 18 km from Bundaberg.
TRANSPORT: train Brisbane-Bundaberg daily (7½ hrs); flights Brisbane-Bundaberg daily; bus Bundaberg-Elliott Heads most days.
SURF CLUB PATROL: October-April, Saturday 14.00-16.30, Sunday and public holidays 09.00-16.30.

BARGARA (pop. 1718) east of Bruce Highway 385 km from Brisbane, 13 km from Bundaberg.
TRANSPORT: Bundaberg services as for Elliott Heads; bus Bundaberg-Bargara most days.
SURF CLUB PATROLS: Bargara and Kellys Beaches October-April, Saturday 13.30-16.30, Sunday and public holidays 09.00-17.00.

BURNETT HEADS (pop. 1037) east of Bruce Highway 387 km from Brisbane, 15 km from Bundaberg.
TRANSPORT: Bundaberg services as for Elliott Heads; bus Bundaberg-Burnett Heads most days.

Elliott Heads has a tiny surf beach just north of the river mouth, and quiet boating waters upstream

Breaks in Bargara's shoreline rim of volcanic rock leave sandy pockets for pleasant bathing; a thin cut by the town centre is man-made, to launch boats

breakwater of the river entrance. Beside the harbour channel the tide moves more than 200 metres over muddy sand. The harbour seems neglected in comparison with the busy sugar terminal and fuel wharves around the first bend of the river, and the thriving city upstream. Shores on the far side of the river mouth are swampy and undeveloped, but a fine sweep of patrolled surfing beach starts at Moore Park, 20 km from Bundaberg. An immense camping and caravan park there has its own shopping centre.

BUNDABERG												
	Jan	Feb	Mar	Apr	May	Jun	Jul	Aug	Sep	Oct	Nov	Dec
Maximum C°	30	30	29	27	25	22	22	23	25	27	28	29
Minimum C°	21	21	20	18	14	12	10	11	14	17	19	21
Rainfall mm	221	183	141	84	66	69	54	32	37	60	79	133
Humidity %	60	61	60	57	53	52	48	46	48	53	57	60
Rain days	12	12	12	8	7	6	5	4	5	6	7	10
Sunshine hrs	Summer 6 +			Autumn 8 +			Winter 7 +			Spring 8 +		

Reclamations have transformed the city waterfront, and will result in a world-class yachting marina

Gladstone

A grassy park high on Auckland Point, ornamented by jacarandas and palms, gives nature a tiny foothold among the emphatic marks of industry that have transformed Gladstone beyond recognition in less than two decades. From a hilltop lookout, sightseers gaze east past the squat silver tanks of fuel oil installations to a chain of bulk carrier wharves and black mountains of coal awaiting shipment. Beyond are red dunes of bauxite waste, and the grey towers and tangled pipes of a vast alumina plant. To the south-west, coal smoke billowing from Queensland's biggest power station smudges the horizon for kilometres. Nearer at hand to the west, embankments spearing into shallow water mark an area that was first intended to be reclaimed entirely by filling it with power station waste. But rapid population growth and affluence has brought a surge in boat ownership. In 1982 a third of the enclosed area began being dredged to make a harbour for small craft. It is now being developed as a marina. But the twin lines of pile berths reaching nearly 2 km up Auckland Inlet remain in demand, as do the launching ramps and commercial wharves strung along the southern bank. The first bend of the inlet is increasingly busy as the base for tourist cruises to fishing grounds and nearby islands.

Gladstone was favoured—or cursed, depending on whether the viewpoint is economic or environmental—with intensive industrial development mainly because of its nearness to the rich Bowen Basin coal measures inland, and to de-

renowned Heron Island, either by helicopter or by launch. Charter fishing trips and harbour cruises are available. Facing Island is privately leased and has no visitor facilities. Curtis Island, mostly a cattle-grazing property, has a little settlement at Southend, visited by barges and launches from the city. The district's best mainland beach, at Tannum Sands, has been surrounded since 1980 by housing developments to accommodate the workforce of the Boyne Island smelter. Attractive picnic spots remain at Wild Cattle Creek and the Boyne River mouth, and upriver near the entrance to South Trees Inlet.

GLADSTONE (pop. 22 080) north of Bruce Highway 558 km from Brisbane (turn off at Benaraby northbound, Calliope southbound).
TRANSPORT: train Brisbane-Gladstone daily (11½ hrs); flights Brisbane-Gladstone daily.

TANNUM SANDS (pop. 5000) north of Bruce Highway 526 km from Brisbane (turn off 5 km north of Rodds Bay).
TRANSPORT: bus Gladstone-Tannum Sands most days.
SURF CLUB PATROL: October-April, weekends and public holidays.

GLADSTONE												
	Jan	Feb	Mar	Apr	May	Jun	Jul	Aug	Sep	Oct	Nov	Dec
Maximum C°	31	31	30	29	26	23	23	24	26	29	30	31
Minimum C°	22	22	21	19	16	14	13	14	16	19	20	22
Rainfall mm	190	153	90	35	50	40	37	33	21	63	82	150
Humidity %	63	63	61	59	57	55	51	53	55	58	61	62
Rain days	20	15	10	7	5	6	7	7	5	6	11	9
Sunshine hrs	Summer 7 +			Autumn 8 +			Winter 7 +			Spring 9 +		

posits of limestone needed in alumina refining. Its rivers offered abundant fresh water for cooling or steaming, and a sheltered port was already well established for grain and beef exports. Gladstone's days as a quiet little provincial town were numbered when its old meatworks were demolished and Queensland Alumina Ltd, an international consortium led by Comalco, started building a plant to refine alumina from bauxite mined at Weipa, on the Gulf of Carpentaria. Opened in 1967, the refinery is approaching a capacity of 2.7 million tonnes a year—the world's biggest. Meanwhile Gladstone Aluminium Ltd, also with Comalco as the major participant, has been set up to convert alumina into aluminium. The Boyne Island plant is one of the most advanced aluminium smelters in the world and produces 25 percent of all Australia's primary Aluminium. Gladstone's coal exports, which started on a massive scale in 1969, and the movement of bauxite, alumina or aluminium in and out have made it Queensland's leading port in tonnage handled.

Sited at the bottom of the Great Barrier Reef, Gladstone offers day trips to the coral cays. By modern catamaran the trip to Mast Head Island, named by Captain Cook, takes only 1½ hours. Gladstone is also the take-off point for the world-

Keppel Sands and Emu Park

Emu Park is so well endowed with beaches that the fine stretches to the north and south are deserted

Keppel Sands, the first coastal settlement north of the Tropic of Capricorn, makes no claim to any other eminence. No coconut palms wave for tourists, and the little township does nothing to exploit its position commercially. Like the waters of Keppel Bay, it is quiet and slow-moving. Its residents are happy to yield the lime-light to Emu Park and Yeppoon, which between them share what travellers are told is the 'Capricornia Coast'. The few outsiders who come to Keppel Sands are principally fishing and boating enthusiasts who appreciate its peaceful character. South of the wide, shallow estuary

formed by Cawarral and Coorooman Creeks, a shell-littered beach has scarcely any perceptible slope: tides advance and retreat about 100 metres across rippled brown sand. Boats can be launched across the sand in front of a caravan park just inside the estuary, but only on fuller tides—otherwise the blue centre channel is cut off by extensive mudflats. The same limitation applies to the launching ramp at the mouth of Pumpkin Creek, reached by a single-lane road.

Emu Park has the most imaginative of all the monuments to Captain Cook that dot the east coast of Australia. In the Singing Ship—a stylised,

12-metre-high representation of a mast, sail and rigging—hollow pipes are pierced to produce harmonised musical tones when the wind blows. Now and then, random fluctuations of wind pressure produce a flute-like melody. The soaring memorial, a photographer's delight, stands in an attractive headland park on Emu Point. To the south a wide, shelly beach runs to Rocky Point. Behind the lifesaving clubhouse is a shady park crammed with tables, swings and see-saws. A lookout at Rocky Point gives a fine view of the islands of Keppel Bay, and of marshes and grass-lands stretching inland towards the Ross Range.

EMU PARK (pop. 1429) east of Bruce Highway 691 km from Brisbane (turn off at Rockhampton).
TRANSPORT: train Brisbane-Rockhampton daily (13½ hrs); flights Brisbane-Rockhampton daily; bus Rockhampton-Emu Park-Mulambin daily.
SURF CLUB PATROL: October-April, Saturday 14.00-16.30, Sunday and public holidays 09.00-16.30.

KEPPEL SANDS east of Bruce Highway 683 km from Brisbane, 35 km from Rockhampton (turn off Emu Park road 5 km north of Coolcorra).
TRANSPORT: none beyond Rockhampton.

Keppel Sands, remote from the main tourist routes, slumbers beside the quiet waters of Keppel Bay

The sparsely settled district can be explored by sealed or gravel roads, amusingly unpredictable in their directions and connections.

North of Emu Park there is another well-equipped picnic ground at Bell Park, where the beach starts a deep curve towards Tanby Point. The closest road takes a course well inland, but tracks give access farther up the quiet, scrub-bordered beach. The northern end at Tanby Point can be reached by a gravel road—not signposted—branching at right angles from the main road about 2 km north of Emu Park. A rough track, unsuitable for highway vehicles but manageable on foot, leads 200 metres to a high headland on the point. The hilltop commands views back to Emu Park, or north over a further beach which is largely inaccessible and deserted.

N
Yeppoon
to Bruce Highway
and Rockhampton
Rosslyn
Bay
Statue
Bay
Double Head
Kemp
Beach
Bluff Point
Mulambin Beach
Causeway
Lake
Shoal
Bay
Kinka
Beach
0
2km
to Emu Park

South of Rosslyn Bay tourist launch terminal, empty beaches run to water-sport resorts at Causeway Lake

From Great Keppel's busy resort and airstrip, walkers can find their way to forested heights and a variety of quiet beaches and fishing spots

Shoal Bay and Great Keppel Island

Causeway Lake, a tidal inlet spanned at its Shoal Bay entrance by a rock-wall roadway, is a favourite playground of Rockhampton's water-skiers and windsurfers. Visitors can try its waters in all kinds of small craft for hire at Lakeside Park. Children play on sandy shores, and anglers fish the quieter reaches. An easy walk north at Mulambin Beach, camping grounds and a caravan park run behind grassy dunes sprinkled with sunflowers, and a flat beach stretches more than

100 metres to the waterline at low tide. Kinka Beach, starting south of the causeway, has a further cluster of tourist facilities at the far end.

Bluff Point forms the major part of a small national park which also includes Double Head. Both have walking tracks, and Bluff Point has a fully developed picnic area with fine views. At Rosslyn Bay, to the north around Double Head, a long, drive-on breakwater topped by twin lines of concrete blocks protects a modern boat harbour. The little bay and its westward neighbour, Statue Bay, offer nowhere for travellers to stay and little to do: most come only because the harbour is the launch base for holidays on Great Keppel Island or day cruises in the Keppel group.

Great Keppel, a continental island covering 1400 hectares and rising to 165 metres, has the quiet and calm that comes with freedom from motor vehicles. Visitors can walk its bush tracks for minutes or hours, or simply loll on its beaches. Behind protectively fenced dunes at Fisherman Beach, just north of TAA's resort buildings, is Wapparaburra Haven, a tranquil camping ground. Short and easy walks lead to Putney Beach, where there are sailboards and motorskis for hire, and to extensive swimming areas at Long Beach and Leekes Beach. An hour's climb

inland, past a lookout with impressive views, is a homestead surviving from the 19th century, when the island was a cattle station. The track carries on, rough and rocky, to a fork where one route leads to Butterfly Beach and the other to Bald Rock Point. Breaks in the bush lining the Bald Rock track give glimpses of handsome Wreck Bay. After a few minutes a sea vista opens to the south and two islands with glaring sand beaches draw the eye: the green mound of Halfway Island, and beyond it Humpy Island, a national park with a well and picnic grounds. Visitors planning a boat trip across must beware of reef shallows and rocks.

MULAMBIN east of Bruce Highway 699 km from Brisbane, 10 km south of Yeppoon (turn off 8 km north of Rockhampton).
TRANSPORT: as for Emu Park, previous page.

GREAT KEPPEL ISLAND 16 km east of Rosslyn Bay, 704 km from Brisbane.
TRANSPORT: frequent launch and hydrofoil services from Rosslyn Bay daily (20-60 mins); flights from Rockhampton daily.
YOUTH HOSTEL: at Fisherman Beach, open year-round.

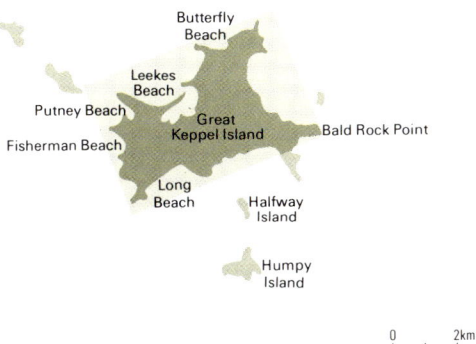

Yeppoon and Lammermoor Beach

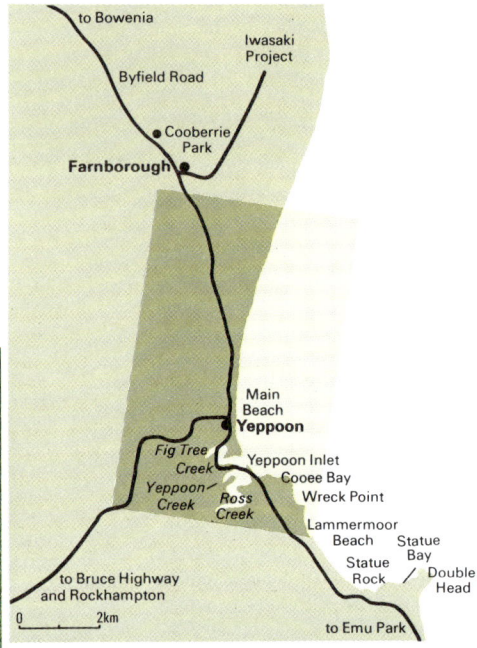

From Beak Bridge at low tide, Yeppoon's boat mooring area at the junction of Ross and Fig Tree Creeks looks like a disaster area. Broad sand flats are littered with trawlers, yachts and dinghies—high and dry. The creeks' outflow is a mere braid of shallow runnels, and the sea is nowhere to be seen. Some catastrophe seems to have doomed the boats never to sail again. But in two or three hours they are bobbing at their moorings, buoyed by a tide that can rise as much as 4 metres from low to high. Its ebb and flood along Yeppoon Inlet and in the two creeks spans hundreds of metres. Main Beach, stretching north from the inlet mouth, is so wide and flat that the retreating tide leaves big salt lakes on the sand at the northern end, to the delight of small children.

Rocks line the shore east of the inlet and run almost continuously to the green mound of Wreck Point. At tiny Cooee Bay the rocks recede beyond the high-water mark, so that young children can play and paddle on a sheltered patch of sand. Beyond a line of white posts marking the rim of the Wreck Point hill is a lookout affording splendid views of the town and south-

east to Double Head. Lammermoor Beach forms a wide, flat sweep running almost straight to Statue Rock. A sand track, negotiable by car, runs close behind the beach.

Past Cooberrie Park fauna and flora sanctuary, the Byfield road north of Yeppoon leads 30 km to Bowenia State Forest. The forest is named after a plant, *Bowenia serrulata*, which occurs only in this district and is commonly called the Byfield fern. In fact it is not a fern but a member of the more primitive order of cycads. Fronds up to 1 metre tall, springing from an underground trunk, are so glossy that when used in floral displays they are easily mistaken for plastic.

Bowenia plants cannot be taken from the forest, but seeds may be obtained through Queensland forestry service offices.

Back towards Yeppoon, in an 8500-hectare coastal wedge between Corio Bay and Farnborough, the Iwasaki Sangyo company hopes to finish its bitterly contested international holiday complex of five hotels by 1994. A decade of controversy over the passing of such a large area to Japanese control culminated in 1980 in a damaging bomb blast. Iwasaki's devel-

Yeppoon Inlet leads to a maze of snaking tidal creeks at the southern end of the main beach

opment rights oblige it to make four-fifths of the land available to the public as bushland reserve, and the whole length of the beach is to remain accessible to all comers.

YEPPOON (pop. 6447) east of Bruce Highway 689 km from Brisbane (turn off 8 km north of Rockhampton).
TRANSPORT: train Brisbane-Rockhampton daily (13½ hrs); flights Brisbane-Rockhampton daily; bus Rockhampton-Yeppoon daily.
SURF CLUB PATROL: Main Beach October-April, Saturday 14.00-16.30, Sunday and public holidays 09.00-16.30.

YEPPOON												
	Jan	Feb	Mar	Apr	May	Jun	Jul	Aug	Sep	Oct	Nov	Dec
Maximum C°	30	29	28	26	24	22	21	23	24	27	29	29
Minimum C°	23	23	22	19	15	12	11	12	15	19	21	22
Rainfall mm	265	244	186	104	78	80	47	30	36	65	73	145
Humidity %	68	72	72	70	69	65	68	67	61	68	66	67
Rain days	11	10	11	8	6	5	4	4	4	5	6	8
Sunshine hrs	Summer 7 +			Autumn 8 +			Winter 7 +			Spring 9 +		

The long fight for a Capricornia state

REGIONS north of Moreton Bay were barely explored, let alone settled, when Queensland was granted separate colonial status in 1859. But soon the right of 'southerners' in Brisbane to tax and govern the north was challenged. Calls for self-rule started as early as 1864, with Rockhampton favoured as a capital. By the 1880s the Capricornia separatists' argument was impressive. They could well have won—if they had not been joined by the angry sugar planters of Mackay. The Mackay men were chafing at regulations which made the employment of Pacific Islanders difficult and expensive. They demanded the right to import labourers from India, as British and Australian planters were doing in Fiji. Failing that, they wanted a northern government, more sympathetic to the problems of industry in the tropics.

This was at a time when public indignation was at its height over unscrupulous methods of recruiting Kanakas from the Islands. The traffic was despised in the south, sometimes on genuinely humanitarian grounds but more often because of White Australia racism. By encouraging talk that the northerners wanted to set up a slave state, the Brisbane regime was easily able to discredit the separatists—even though many of them had nothing to do with Islands labour.

After Federation in 1901, northern representation in the Australian parliament and the abolition of intercolonial customs duties took much of the heat from the separatist argument. It was sparked again by economic stresses in the 1930s, however, and flared after World War II—fuelled by resentment of the apparent readiness of southern leaders to abandon the north to invaders. A vigorous Capricornia New State movement in Rockhampton was still going strong in the early 1980s.

Mackay to Cape York

Queensland's tropical coast has one unique attraction—the Great Barrier Reef. Romantic images of lush, green islands set in a turquoise sea are an irresistible magnet that draws thousands of travellers north every year. The adventurous, equipped with their own four-wheel drive vehicles, take the punishing road to Cape York.

Cape Bedford, north of Cooktown

Floodplains near Kuranda, Gulf of Carpentaria

Coral sands, Port Douglas

TORRES STRAIT

Thursday Island

Cape York

Bamaga •

Weipa •

GULF OF
CARPENTARIA

Endeavour River   • Cooktown

QUEENSLAND

Mossman •• Port Douglas

Ellis Beach •
Yorkeys Knob •   Green Island
Cairns •

SOUTH PACIFIC OCEAN

Innisfail •
• Mourilyan
Bingil Bay •   • Kurrimine Beach
Mission Beach •   • Dunk Island

Herbert River   Cardwell •   • Hinchinbrook Island   GREAT
                                                        BARRIER
                      • Lucinda   REEF

Magnetic Island

Townsville •

Burdekin River

Bowen •
Airlie •   Whitsunday
Shute Harbour •   Group

Seaforth •   Cape Hillsborough
Bucasia •   • Eimeo
Mackay •

Admiralty Island, Trinity Inlet, Cairns

Coral cays—such as Michaelmas Cay on the Barrier Reef—offer a safe haven for many bird species

The entire island of Hinchinbrook—separated from the mainland by Hinchinbrook Channel—is a park

Steamy shores and enticing islands

PEOPLE in the tourist industry like to call tropical Queensland 'the winterless north'. Year-round warmth justifies the term, on the coast and islands at least. But the north does have its seasons, with an important bearing on comfort and activity. They are seasons of low or high—often phenomenally high—rainfall and of benign or violent winds. North of Cooktown, this division of wet and dry seasons is complete. From December to April, Cape York Peninsula is dominated by the drenching storms of the north-west monsoon. For the rest of the year, the south-east trade winds blow steadily. Although they are moist winds, almost no rain falls.

Around Cairns, skies are nearly always sunny during winter and spring. Temperatures reach 26-30° by day and fall pleasantly at night. Summer daytime temperatures are not much higher: the average maximum is about 32°, and Cairns never suffers the heatwaves of many southern cities. But there is persistent rain, and summer nights stay hot. Under leaden, dripping skies, the heat and humidity can be intolerable.

South of Cairns, local climate is dictated by geography. Lofty ranges crowd the rich sugar-growing strip from Gordonvale to Ingham, catching Australia's highest rainfalls. Readings of more than 3000 mm a year are common, and Tully averages 4300 mm—about six times the rainfall of Melbourne and four times that of Sydney. Even in the driest months, during spring, Tully and Innisfail are soaked one day out of every three or four.

Immediately south of Ingham, coastal lowlands as far as Bowen have substantial summer rains, but so little at other times that canefields give way to fruit orchards. This stretch is aligned unlike the rest of Queensland. It runs sharply north-west to south-east, so the prevailing south-easterlies flow along it rather than across it.

Farther south, from Proserpine to Mackay, rainfall increases again. It is markedly heavier in summer, but enough moisture is distributed year-round to make this the leading sugar-producing region in Australia, and to sustain luxuriant vegetation on the nearby Whit-

sunday and Cumberland Islands. However, anywhere in the north, summer is wetter than winter. Summer humidity makes the tropical heat more oppressive, and many tourist activities are less enjoyable. The period from December to January or March also carries the greatest probability of floods cutting roads, and of cyclones developing in the Coral Sea. Actual cyclone risk is slim, but interference with transport and communications can wreck holiday plans.

Offshore resorts, generally drier and sunnier than the mainland coast, have become Queensland's most powerful tourist magnets. Living coral and vivid reef fish are an irresistible attraction, and the extent of coral formation in the Great Barrier Reef has no equal in the world. Many a mainland port that was built on mining or agriculture in the hinterland has taken a new lease on life through its proximity to a popular resort island or to game fishing grounds. Coastal settlement is still sparse, however, and ports are scarce. By nature the shore is widely inhospitable because a reef-shielded sea, tepid and sluggish, fosters a profuse growth of mangroves and the formation of swamps and mudflats. Even where there are sandy beaches, the sea at low tide commonly recedes kilometres away from the shade provided by backshore trees. And surf is almost non-existent. The main purpose of 'surf clubs' here is to render first aid to victims of box jellyfish and other warm-water menaces—another reason why winter and spring are better for visiting the north. In any case the summertime sea is seldom noticeably colder than the air and offers little refreshment. Local swimmers favour hilly country with cool, fast-flowing freshwater streams.

In all its 745 km north from Mackay, the 'coastal' Bruce Highway runs close by the sea only at Townsville, Cardwell and Cairns. The railway follows a similar inland path to avoid flood plains and swamps. So travellers eager to experience the special quality of tropical shores must allow ample time for side trips. In the opportunity it affords to see a profusion of characteristic vegetation and wildlife, the extra effort is rewarding.

Making the most of a coral reef

THE FIRST SIGHT of an exposed coral reef may not live up to expectations. It is likely to be drab and lacking in variety. Few coral species grow on the top surface, and if they are not regularly immersed in the sea they die and lose brilliance and colour. Those garish specimens displayed in some souvenir shops are dyed.

Living corals, in their amazing diversity of form and delicacy of shading, are best appreciated under water. Then the richness of accompanying marine life can also be seen. If it is not possible to dive with mask or goggles, or to use a glass-bottom boat, then a reef walk at the lowest tide—just after full moon or new moon—offers most possibilities. But several precautions should be taken:

- Follow the tide out, and turn back before it does. Tides have a big range in the Great Barrier Reef region and flood rapidly, creating currents in channels and over shallows.

- Wear strong-soled footwear with ankle protection, and socks and long trousers. Coral can cause easily infected cuts and grazes. And stonefish with dangerously poisonous spines may lie, perfectly camouflaged, in shallow pools and crevices.

- Wear a hat and shirt—light reflected from the sea can burn harshly, even in overcast conditions. Polarising sunglasses not only cut out glare but also assist in spotting near-transparent jellyfish and other stingers.

- Wear gloves if turning over rocks or picking up shells. Some species of cone shellfish and small octopus are extremely venomous.

- Avoid breaking fragile forms of coral, replace rocks that are moved, and obey any restrictions on collecting. Let the reef go on living.

- Do **not** take a boat over or near coral without local knowledge. Water depths vary sharply, and vigorous eddies and tide races occur.

As the reef is exposed at low tide, Heron Island has great appeal for reef walkers

Many houses, such as this one in Townsville, are built high above the ground on stilts—the traditional way to cope with not only the climate, but also the profuse vegetation and the wildlife of the north

Characteristic of the far north are mangrove forests and mudflats, seen here at Portland Roads

Mackay

Cane fires smear the horizon with smoke and light up night skies around Mackay from June to December. Sugar farmers stage their plantings so that the crop comes to maturity at different times through the season. Firing, to remove unwanted foliage before the mechanical harvesters move in, must be finely judged or else unripe cane is burnt. Wind direction is all-important, and a farmer at harvesting time is never far from a radio to pick up special cane-firing forecasts. Sugar-cane—a giant grass species originally imported from the West Indies—is grown commercially from Grafton, NSW, to Mossman, north of Cairns. But nearly a third of the national crop, about 7 million tonnes, comes from the Mackay district, off an area only a quarter that of Sydney. The cut cane is taken by miniature railways to one of seven mills, where it is crushed and the sugar juice processed to a raw crystalline stage. It is shipped through the world's biggest sugar terminal at Port Mackay, where up to 667 000 tonnes can be stored. Conducted tours are available at 10.15 and 15.15 on weekdays throughout the year. Pleystowe mill has tours at 15.00 on weekdays during the harvest season.

In front of the Mackay Sailing Club, a launching ramp runs into the harbour behind a crowd of pleasure craft and commercial fishing trawlers. The boats are tied to mooring poles which tower above them at low water, allowing for the tidal range of up to 6.5 metres. Launches based at the port operate day trips through the Whitsunday Passage and longer trips to outer reefs. Before the building of Port Mackay, the Pioneer River was the city's harbour. Boat owners still find it navigable as far as the Forgan Bridge when the tide is in. Much of the river drains during extreme low tide, so keelers may have to find one of the deep pools left in the river bed or lie alongside a wharf to remain upright.

Within a stone's throw of the busy port, surfboard riders take advantage of occasional small waves at Harbour Beach below its lifesaving club, shady picnic park and playground. Far Beach, the popular swimming spot in south Mackay, is so flat that the tidal range can cause the water to recede more than 2 km, leaving shallow swimming holes suitable for children, but a long walk for others. At Slade Point, Lamberts Lookout has a panoramic view over the

steep, pandanus-lined face of the point, Lamberts Beach to the south and the Cumberland Islands. The shores of Slade Bay are blocked by mangroves and houses as far as the mouth of McCreadys Creek, a tidal stream that is normally not navigable.

Visitors entering Mackay on the Bruce Highway from Rockhampton are greeted at the edge of the city by a Chinese junk set in concrete on the roadside. The *Shin Hsun Yuan No 3*, from Taiwan, was captured with a load of giant clams taken illegally from the Great Barrier Reef. After a court ordered its confiscation, the junk was turned into a tourist information office.

Mackay's artificial port—built to serve the world's biggest sugar-loading terminal—replaced a harbour on the Pioneer River, which drains at low tide

MACKAY (pop. 35 356) on Bruce Highway 1019 km from Brisbane.

TRANSPORT: train Brisbane-Mackay most days (21 hrs); coach daily (17½ hrs); flights daily.

SURF CLUB PATROL: at Harbour Beach October-April, Saturday 13.30-17.00, Sunday and public holidays 09.00-17.00.

MACKAY												
	Jan	Feb	Mar	Apr	May	Jun	Jul	Aug	Sep	Oct	Nov	Dec
Maximum C°	31	30	29	28	25	24	23	25	27	29	31	31
Minimum C°	22	22	21	18	15	12	10	12	13	17	19	21
Rainfall mm	368	343	291	136	84	60	37	27	28	46	73	179
Humidity %	64	70	67	64	62	58	54	55	52	55	55	60
Rain days	15	16	15	13	10	7	5	4	5	6	8	11
Sunshine hrs	Summer 7 +			Autumn 8 +			Winter 7 +			Spring 9 +		

Eimeo and Bucasia

Eimeo's headland commands impressive views of the sweeping crescent of Sunset Bay and the distant, purplish mounds of the Cumberland Islands. Below, at the entrance to the mangrove flats of Eimeo Creek, a boat ramp leads into a clear channel marked with buoys and flags, and a sign warns of shark nets laid off the creek entrance. Launches lie moored between mangroves and narrow planked jetties immediately upstream of the ramp. A grassy park with a playground runs behind the beach to the east. Signs along the beach warn that the deadly box jellyfish is found in these waters in summer months and indicate the nearby sources of anti-venom.

At the popular holiday spot of Blacks Beach, just south of Eimeo, scrub-covered dunes stretch towards Slade Point. There are no shops but the area is crowded with holiday units, caravan parks, camping grounds, beach homes and a youth centre. Catamarans, sailboards and surf skis are available for hire. A grassy park shaded

Canefields backing the holiday cottages of Shoal Point and Bucasia give way to mangroves beside the snaking shallows of Eimeo Creek

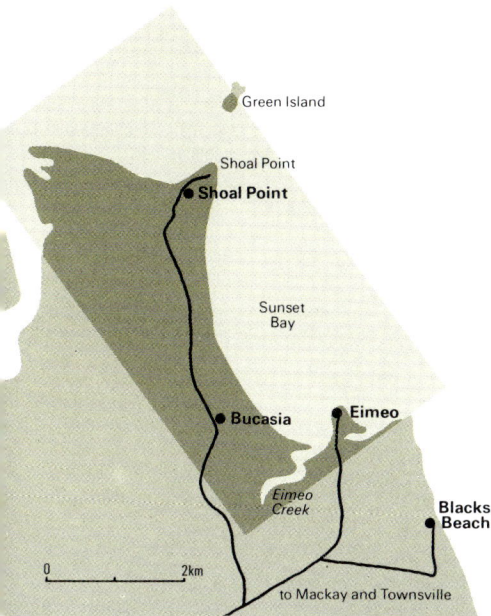

by casuarinas, gums and coconut palms—alive with screeching parrots—runs from the caravan park on Eimeo Creek to the northern end of the settlement at Bucasia. Protection against box jellyfish is afforded swimmers by a netted enclosure which residents combine to renew every year before the stingers' summer onslaught.

On Sunset Bay's northern end a cluster of holiday homes at Shoal Point is surrounded by green reserves. Four-wheel-drive vehicles launch boats over the rock and sand foreshore. The point looks out over Green Island, one of the few free-hold islands off the Queensland coast. The island remains undeveloped by its owners, though several dilapidated buildings testify to a history of casual occupation, which included an attempt at citrus-growing.

EIMEO-BUCASIA (pop. 1729) north of Bruce Highway 20 km from Mackay, 1039 km north of Brisbane (turn off at North Mackay).
TRANSPORT: as for Mackay (previous page); buses Mackay-Eimeo-Bucasia weekdays.

The deadliest menace of tropical waters

THE BOX JELLYFISH—*Chironex fleckeri*, also called the sea wasp—kills more humans in Australian tropical waters than do sharks, crocodiles, stonefish and all other harmful marine creatures put together. Scores of people have died of their stings this century, including 20 Aboriginal children around Melville Island, near Darwin.

These deadly, darting swimmers are almost transparent. They show faintly blue in clear water but move below the surface, so the first sign of their presence may be a shadow on a sandy seabed. They may be encountered anywhere north of the Tropic of Capricorn, but not usually over coral or weed beds. Their season is limited to summer and early autumn except in extreme northern waters, where they may appear at any time.

Hot days with an overcast sky and a calm sea are the most dangerous, especially just after local rain. Then box jellyfish move into shallow water—particularly near river and creek outlets—for prawns, their natural prey. Before drawing them into their body cavities for digestion, they sting and paralyse them. Each adult carries enough paralysing venom to deal with myriads of prawns—or to kill three or four people. Even a young one only 80 mm wide can kill a child.

The box-shaped 'bell' or body may be as big as a salad bowl, with 60 or more tentacles streaming from it in four bunches. The tentacles extend up to 3 metres and are covered by millions of capsules, some loaded with venom and some with a sticky substance. They cling when touched—even if they are broken—and the venom capsules discharge through threadlike stingers.

Box jellyfish venom has three different effects on humans. The most potent ingredient may stop the heartbeat and breathing mechanisms, causing death within three minutes if the victim is not aided. A second component destroys red cells in the blood, and a third damages skin tissue.

A victim invariably screams with intense pain, and may collapse in the water or soon after running from it. Long purple or dark brown welts appear like whip marks—the more of them there are, the more serious the case. Swelling and redness occur within five minutes and blistering may follow.

ANTI-VENOM Supplies of a serum to counter box jellyfish stings are distributed to hospitals, doctors, ambulance depots and lifesaving clubs on tropical coasts. At more remote beaches, anti-venom ready for injection may be held at shops or even in private homes, identified by signposts.

PRECAUTIONS Learn resuscitation techniques—they save lives in many kinds of emergency. Seek local advice on the day's weather and water conditions. Note the location of the nearest first aid service and anti-venom supply. Have vinegar on hand. Wear a T-shirt while swimming. And do **not** enter the water without a companion nearby.

TREATMENT Call for trained assistance and anti-venom. Stay with the victim if possible and be ready to use resuscitation techniques if breathing or heartbeat stop. Do **not** try to wash or wipe off clinging tentacles—more venom will be discharged. Pour vinegar—**not** alcoholic liquor or methylated spirit—on the welts to deactivate any undischarged venom cells. Unless under professional direction, do **not** move the victim until his or her breathing has been normal for 10 minutes.

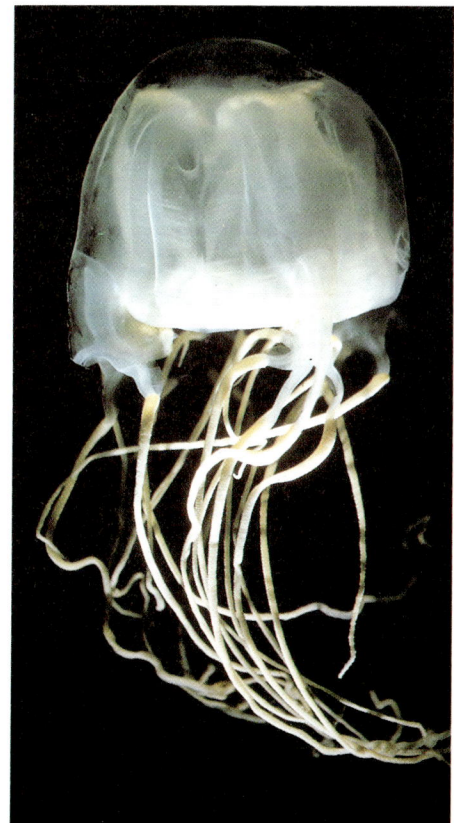

The extendable tentacles of an adult box jellyfish may trail up to 3 metres from its body

Cape Hillsborough to Seaforth

Wallabies evading the tropical sun doze serenely under the trees that shelter the Cape Hillsborough holiday resort, 12 km east of the main settlement at Seaforth. Black brush turkeys with vivid red heads and yellow collars strut with equal tameness in the picnic grounds. The resort, which has cabins, a caravan park and a camping area, straddles an isthmus between two sections of Cape Hillsborough National Park. Mangroves choke the shore on the western side, but a generous scoop of beach faces north.

The park has about 7 km of walking tracks. They take in Wedge Island—reached at low tide by a rocky causeway—a freshwater swimming hole at Cascade Creek, and rainforest at Hidden

Valley. There are eight lookout points, and on the shore east of Hidden Valley can be seen the remains of a stone fish trap built by the cape's earlier residents, Aborigines of the Jiupera tribe. A more strenuous walk, taking about six hours, leads over the rugged central hills of the cape to Smalleys Beach. It is not a cleared trail but a 'tag track' marked by plastic numbers fixed to tree trunks. The beach can also be reached by an unsealed road from the south-west. Wide mud-flats occupy the western shore of Ball Bay, but beyond, at tiny Hallidays Bay, both sand and water are clear and clean. The beach has a wire-mesh enclosure, to protect swimmers from summertime encounters with box jellyfish, below the

camping ground at the northern end. Casuarinas, palms and eucalypts, filled with shrieking lorikeets, line the bay.

At Seaforth, mud causeways at low tide connect the two Redcliff Islands to the northern mainland at Finlaysons Point. The islands are popular with walkers and fishermen. A gravel road runs around Finlaysons Point through head-high grass, dense paperbarks and tangled mangroves. Short tracks lead to shaded picnic spots at the edge of a wide mangrove flat. A sealed road running west from Seaforth takes boat owners to a wide launching ramp on Victor Creek. The creek leads out to fishing grounds around larger offshore islands. They are national parks, but

Free of the mudflats clogging Ball Bay, national park beaches between Cape Hillsborough and Wedge Island slope to good swimming waters

camping permits can be obtained from the park ranger in Seaforth. Rabbit and Outer Newry Islands, both within 10 km of Victor Creek, have water supplies and camping grounds with lavatories and picnic facilities.

SEAFORTH (pop. 366) north-east of Bruce Highway 1082 km from Brisbane (turn off northbound at Yakapari, southbound at Mt Ossa).
TRANSPORT: train Brisbane-Mt Ossa most days (22½ hrs); none beyond Mt Ossa, 12 km away.

🏠 ⛱ ▲ 🛖 🚻 ⛲ 🔥 ⚓

CAPE HILLSBOROUGH 12 km east of Seaforth.

🏠 ⛱ ▲ 🚻 🔦 ⚓ ≈

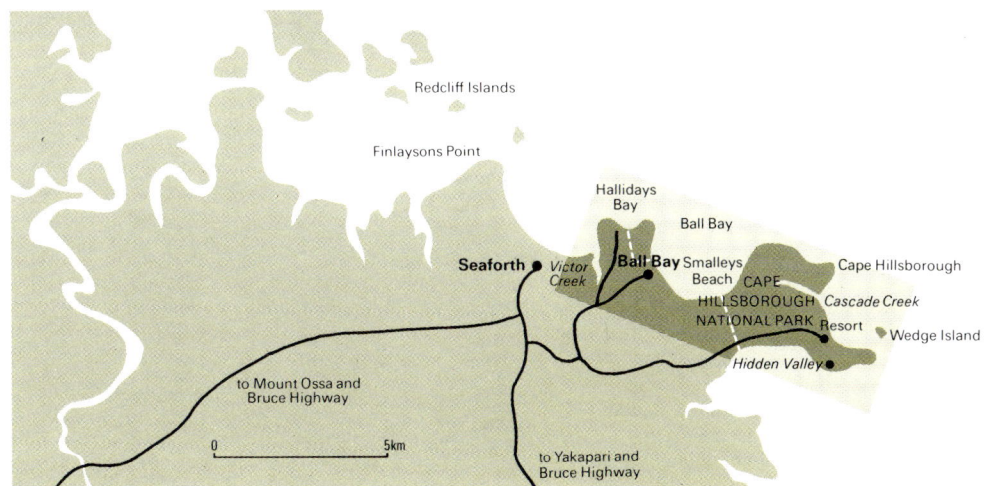

Redcliff Islands
Finlaysons Point
Hallidays Bay
Ball Bay
Seaforth ● *Victor Creek* **Ball Bay** ● Smalleys Beach
CAPE HILLSBOROUGH Cape Hillsborough
HILLSBOROUGH *Cascade Creek*
NATIONAL PARK Resort ● ● Wedge Island
Hidden Valley ●
to Mount Ossa and Bruce Highway
0 —— 5km
to Yakapari and Bruce Highway

Brampton and Lindeman Islands

Aircraft landing at Lindeman Island can taxi all the way to the resort on Home Bay, flanked by a golf links

The thickly wooded slopes of Brampton Island National Park rise from the holiday resort at Sandy Point, its pool and lodges scattered among coconut palms behind the beach. The palm grove was established by the island's first settlers, the Busuttin family, who raised sheep on two other Cumberland Islands, St Bees and Keswick, and arrived on Brampton in 1916 to breed horses for the British Army in India.

Brampton became a tourist resort in 1933, in company with Lindeman Island, which started taking guests earlier. They were resort-farms,

maintaining their herds of sheep, cattle and goats while accommodating a trickle of visitors. Since World War II the livestock has gone and both resorts have grown to cope with more than 200 people at a time. Pools, bars and restaurants are well patronised and active guests can go diving, water-skiing, sailing and ocean swimming as well as play tennis or golf.

A coral reef joins Brampton to hilly, undeveloped Carlisle Island across a narrow channel, and there are fringing reefs on many of Lindeman's beaches. At low tide visitors can

wade across the reefs, snorkel, or view the coral in a more leisurely manner from glass-bottom boats. Camping is not permitted in the national parks of Brampton or Lindeman, but there are many beaches where people are free to pull a boat ashore and follow walking trails to the beaches, or to the island peaks. Wharf mooring can be arranged in advance with the resort managements. They welcome casual visitors but do not specifically cater for them.

There are 75 other national park islands, uninhabited, in the Cumberland group. Many are

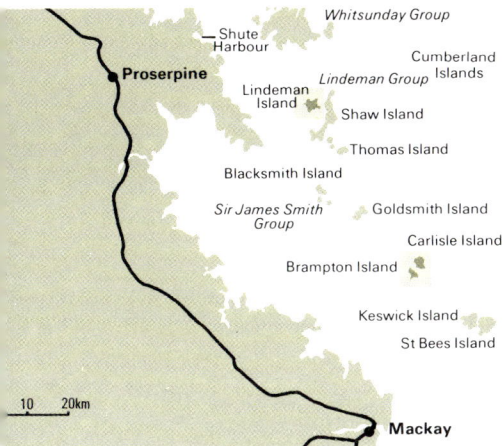

Whitsunday Group
Shute Harbour
Proserpine
Cumberland Islands
Lindeman Group
Lindeman Island
Shaw Island
Thomas Island
Blacksmith Island
Sir James Smith Group
Goldsmith Island
Carlisle Island
Brampton Island
Keswick Island
St Bees Island
Mackay
10   20km

easily accessible and have established camping grounds. People without their own boats can arrange transport on the sailing boats and cruisers based at Shute Harbour. Campers may be alone on these islands throughout their stay. There is no communication, so they should be equipped with a good first-aid kit. They should also check on the availability of fresh water. Visitors to most islands need to take their own, allowing 4 litres a day for each person, including three days' extra as a precaution against bad weather delaying departures or pick-ups. Camping permits are necessary for all islands and can be obtained from national parks offices in Mackay, Shute Harbour or Seaforth. Rangers also supply information on camping sites, water supplies and the best places to beach a boat.

BRAMPTON ISLAND 32 km north-east of Mackay. **TRANSPORT:** as for Mackay (page 348); launch and regular flights from Mackay most days.

LINDEMAN ISLAND 67 km north of Mackay. **TRANSPORT:** regular launch from Shute Harbour (next page); flights from Mackay daily, Proserpine most days.

Brampton Island's palm-shaded resort and airstrip face Carlisle Island across a narrow channel, blocked to the south by a coral reef which guests can explore on foot when the tide is out

Whitsunday fun

ENJOYMENT and informality are the bywords of the Whitsundays. This is a holiday world, pure and simple. Without tourism, Airlie would scarcely have reason to exist. Shute Harbour, which is a near-chaotic collecting point for buses, cruising craft and charter boats every morning and night, would be a quiet and sleepy fishermen's backwater.

Resort managements and boat proprietors run sophisticated, competitive operations. Guests at the seven island resorts, or at countless more that have mushroomed on the mainland side of Whitsunday Passage, can try every conceivable water sport and sample all the delights of high, forested islands, coral cays and superb reef formations. They can cruise in big motor-catamarans, reclining in airliner-style seats, or they can look lively hauling sail on a maxi-yacht.

'Bareboating' offers the best deal for people with an urge for discovery and a moderate competence in sailing. Several Shute Harbour companies specialise in chartering small boats, fully provisioned, that holidaymakers can take where they please among dozens of islands and safe, secluded havens.

The Whitsunday Village Fun Race, contested every October from Airlie Beach through the Whitsunday Islands, is a fine excuse for a good time. They call it the biggest yacht race in the Southern Hemisphere. With annual entries approaching 300, and a hundred other boats following to give encouragement, it very likely is. Yet no one cares much who wins—or how. The only prizes are a few bottles of rum. Rules are minimal. Ingenious cheating and sabotage are much admired. Ashore at Airlie and the island resorts, the race weekend is one long party. Since contending skippers took to adorning their bowsprits with female friends—bare-breasted in line with nautical tradition—the highlight of festivities has become the crowning of 'Miss Figurehead'.

Palms shade picnic grounds at Airlie Beach, on the mainland side of Whitsunday Passage

Shute Harbour is the principal terminal for Whitsunday Islands cruising

Catamarans off Hamilton Island

Daydream Island resort, West Molle

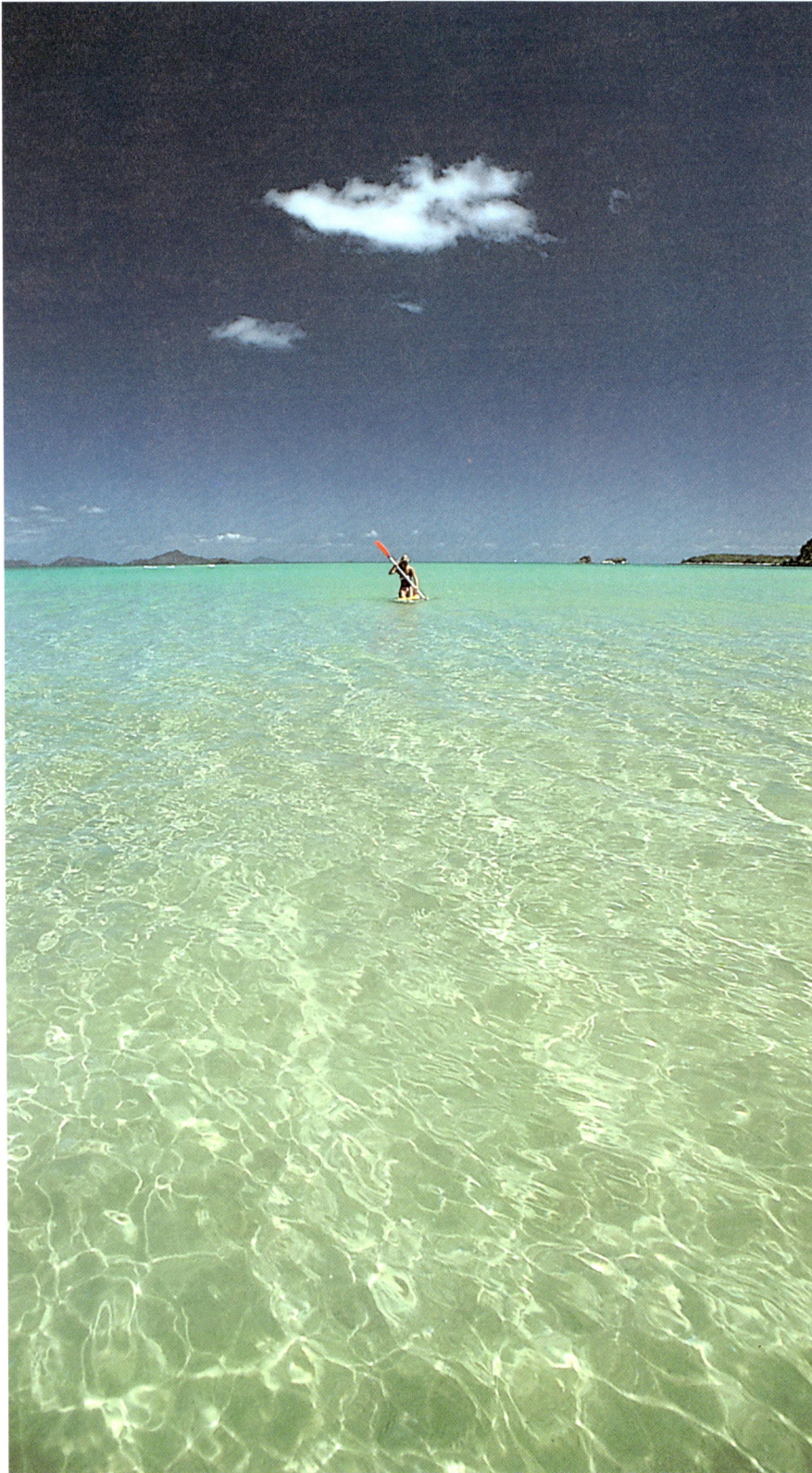

Paddling to the coral reef off Brampton Island

Starting a yachting holiday

Boom-netting – cooling and exhilarating

Lindeman Island, seen here from Shaw Island, is a national park with one small resort (far left)

Wilderness surrounds Shute Harbour in Conway National Park

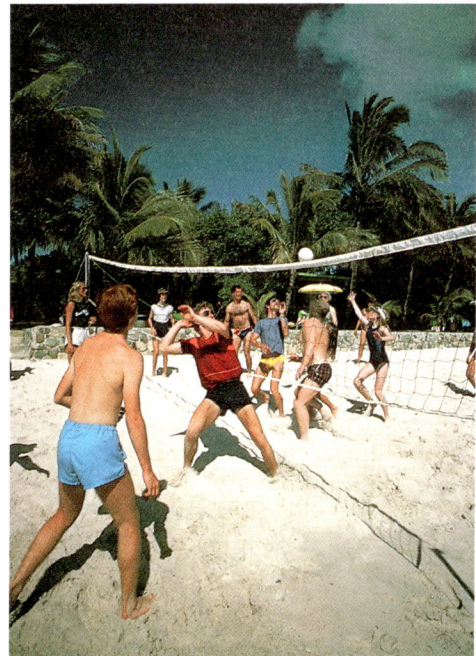

Hot competition at South Molle resort

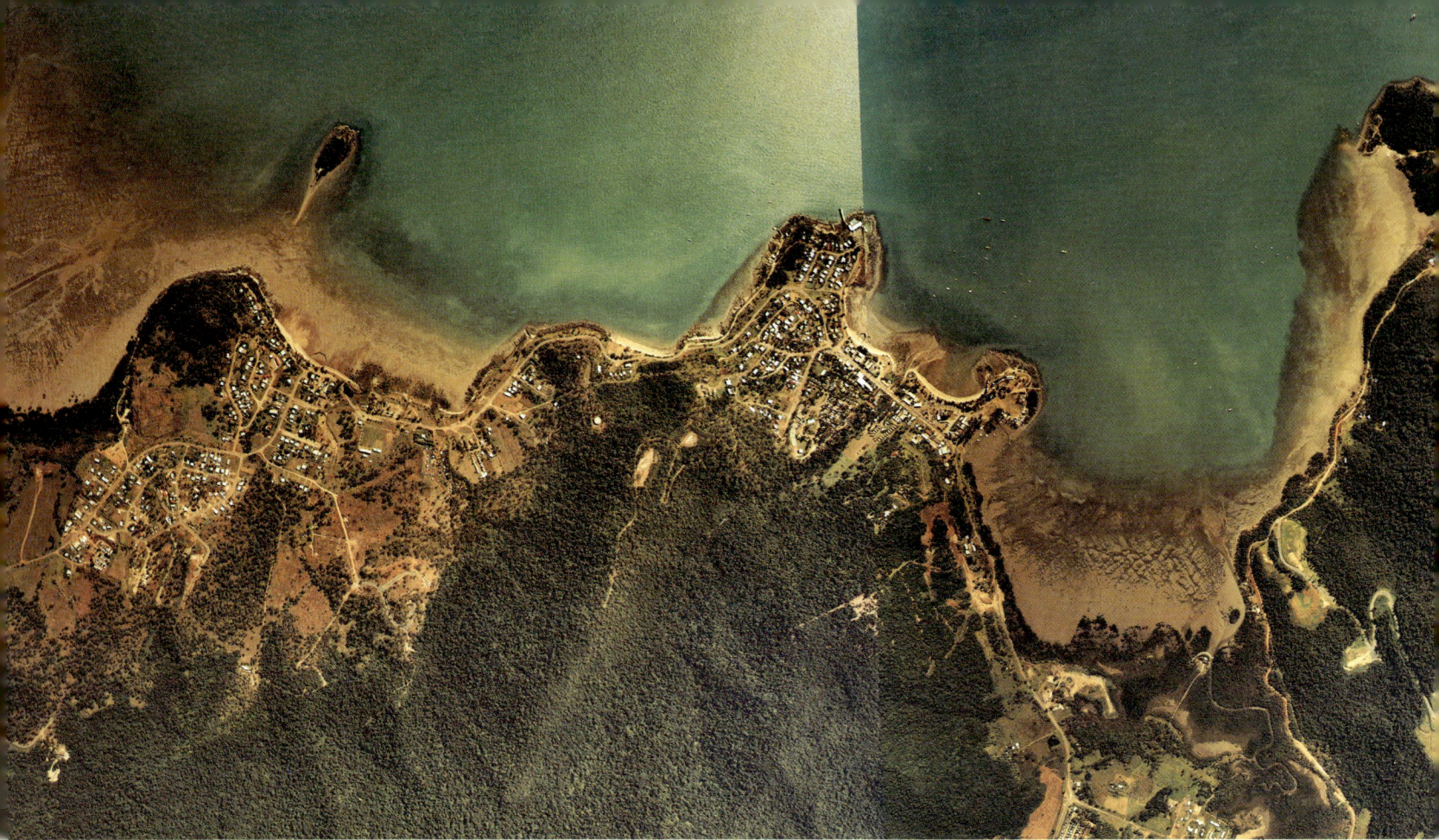

Expansion of tourist accommodation has almost linked Cannonvale and Airlie as one town, hugging the shores of Pioneer Bay and hemmed by dense bush; Airlie's role as a base for public cruises among the Whitsunday Islands has passed to Shute Harbour, but it remains a busy boating centre

Shute Harbour and Airlie

Shute Harbour's jetty is a hive of activity each morning as cruising yachts, launches and hired sailing boats make for the holiday resorts and uninhabited national park islands of Whitsunday Passage. The islands rise from the waters of the continental shelf, sheltered by outer coral formations of the Great Barrier Reef, and often have their own fringing reefs with small bays and deserted beaches.

The cruising yachts, including a Sydney-Hobart winner, *Solo*, and Australia's first America's Cup contender, *Gretel*, set their daily courses according to winds and tides. More reliable timetables to scheduled destinations are offered by motor cruisers. A water-taxi is available for short trips around the closer islands, or to transport campers to any of the islands and pick them up on a pre-arranged date. Amphibious planes and some of the launches operate trips to outlying reefs. Cruise costs range from around $25 for a one-day trip to hundreds of dollars for the cabins and full meal service provided on the longer excursions. The shortest coral viewing trip is in a glass-bottom boat which cruises over the reefs fringing the small islands in Shute Harbour, and the outcrops along the harbour shores backed by Conway Range National Park. The tall eucalypts and dense rainforest of the park's mountains and gorges are untouched except for a well-equipped camping ground along the road to Shute Harbour, and walking tracks branching out through the surrounding forest to a nearby mountain lookout. Those intending to camp on the offshore islands can obtain permits from the ranger at the camping ground.

At Airlie and Cannonvale, on the road into Shute Harbour, caravan parks and resorts accommodate many visitors planning trips to the islands as well as those who base their holidays in the area. The Whitsunday Aquarium and Animal Park has displays of shells and coral with live tropical fish, kangaroos, emus and crocodiles. At the Mandalay Coral Gardens, reef fish swim in pools of living coral. The Flame Tree Grove has rainforest walks, a bird sanctuary and a plant nursery. Cruises and fishing charter boats also operate from Airlie.

Unwanted guests eat more than their share

'THEY'RE OFF!' The ringmaster whips away a plastic bucket and the shouts go up for Hotlips, Princess Di, Premier Joh and the rest of an ungainly and unlovely bunch. It's toad-racing time at the Airlie hotel. For a $2 sweepstake entry, tourists can enjoy some light-hearted sport. But poultry farmers and bee-keepers curse the day that toads were brought to the canefields of North Queensland.

The cane toad or giant toad, *Bufo marinus*, grows up to 200 mm in length and has an appetite to match its ponderous bulk. Its diet is insects, and it was brought from Hawaii in 1935 because it was successful there in combating a sugar-cane beetle. It was soon discovered that Australia's small native frogs did a better job. But the multiplication and spread of the voracious imports could not be stopped. Now they breed wherever there is water throughout Queensland and northern NSW, raiding beehives and upsetting the natural balance of insect life. They even endanger large birds and snakes, because they can puff themselves up to choke anything that tries to swallow them. And they can poison creatures—including domestic pets and fowls—that bite or peck at them around the head.

Cane toads have grossly enlarged salivary glands, between the eyes and the back of the neck, which secrete a fairly potent toxin. Although it can kill a hen or a small animal it is unlikely to be harmful to humans. At worst, poison carried from the hands to the eyes could cause severe irritation, which is why the racing toads of Airlie are held inside paper bags or handled with gloves.

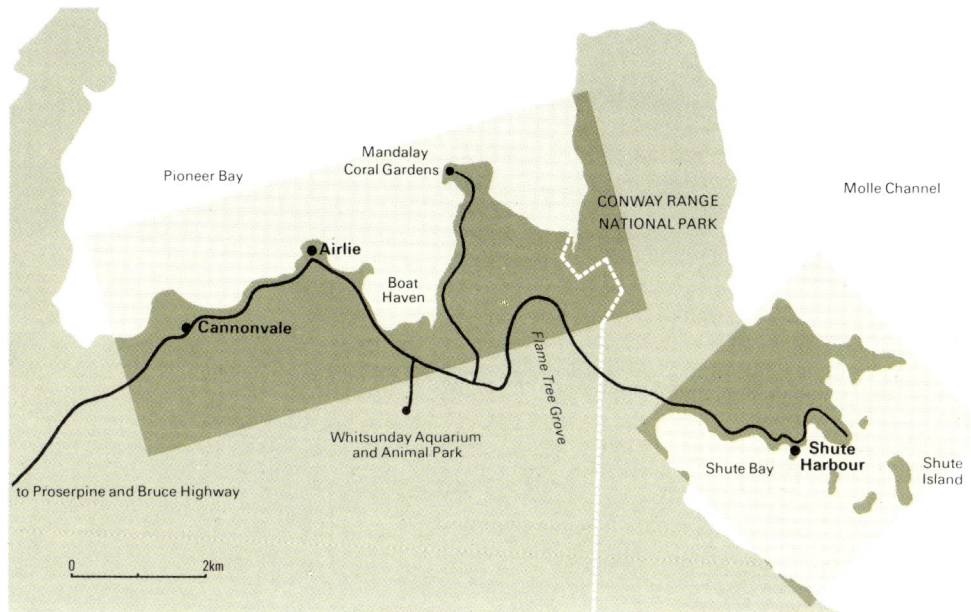

Forested ranges and islands shelter Shute Harbour, the main terminal for island cruise boats

CANNONVALE (pop. 1209) north-east of Bruce Highway 1165 km from Brisbane (turn off at Proserpine).
TRANSPORT: train Brisbane-Proserpine most days (24 hrs); coach daily (19 hrs); flights daily; bus Proserpine-Cannonvale-Airlie-Shute Harbour daily.

AIRLIE (pop. 1704) 3 km east of Cannonvale.
TRANSPORT: as for Cannonvale.

SHUTE HARBOUR 13 km south-east of Cannonvale.
TRANSPORT: as for Cannonvale.

West Molle (top left) is densely forested, but much of South Molle is yet to recover from over-grazing

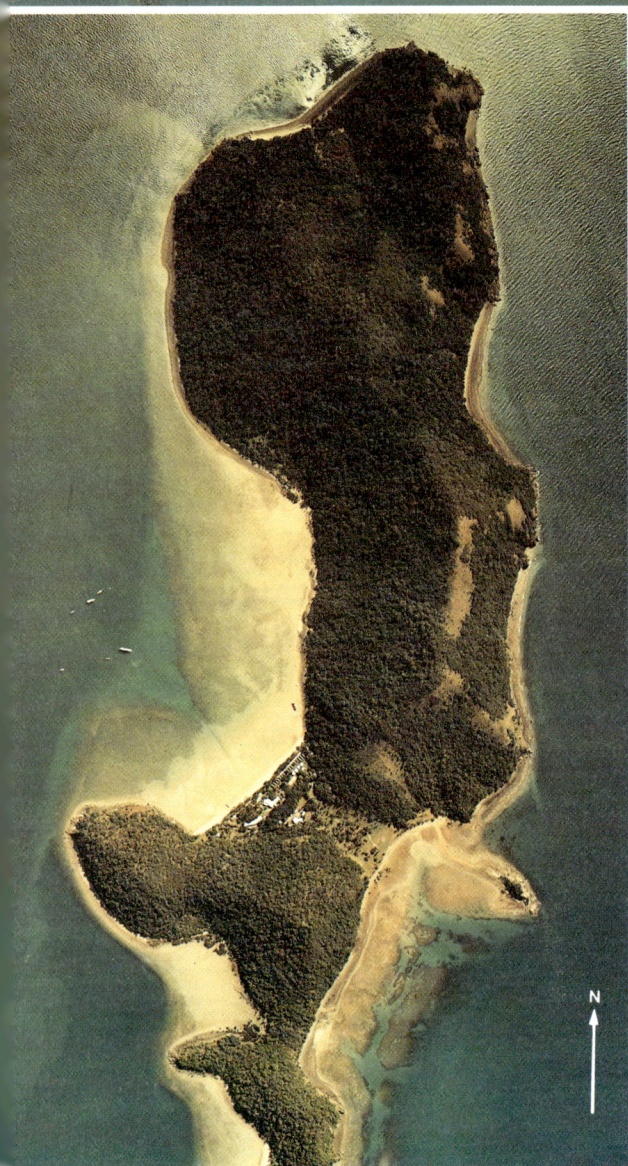

Happy Bay resort occupies a narrow neck near the tip of Long Island, the closest to the mainland

Whitsunday Islands

Islands rising from sparkling blue-green waters surround cruise passengers sailing through Whitsunday Passage, as James Cook did in 1770 on Whit Sunday, the seventh after Easter. Above ribbons of sandy beaches, scrubland and grassy slopes are overlooked by precipitous cliffs and forested peaks rising above 300 metres. The narrow shipping lane is criss-crossed daily by a small armada of tourist craft and private boats wending their way among the islands on fishing charters, resort tours and trips to the outer coral reefs.

Approached from the sea, the island resorts present similar faces. Beachfront cabins are scattered between avenues of coconut palms below heavily wooded slopes. Behind the palms, however, resort life can differ greatly.

Visitors arriving at Happy Bay, on Long Island, transfer from their launch to a barge which carries them over the coral to the beach shallows. There a truck waits to take them ashore. An easy 20-minute walk along a path through thick bush leads to a cluster of nine

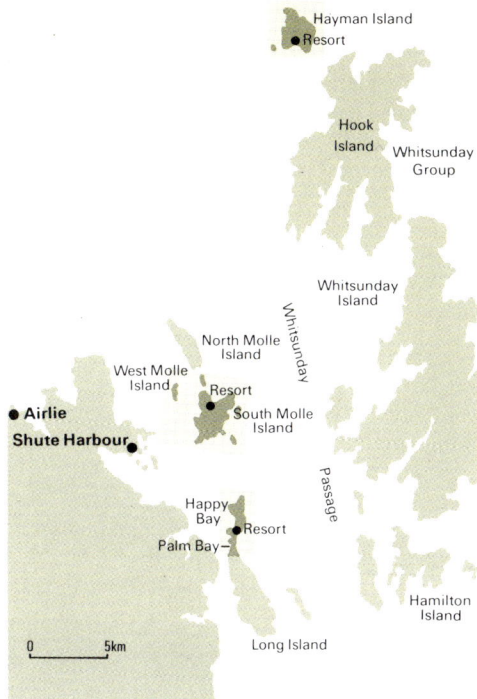

cabins on Palm Bay. Here guests do their own cooking, share a communal shower and lavatory block and organise their own entertainment, sports and bush walks. Apart from the resort grounds, the island is a national park.

At Hayman Island, giant helicopters deliver passengers directly from mainland airports to a landing pad within 200 metres of the first beachfront cabins. More than 350 guests are accommodated in rows of cabins and long two-storey hotel blocks where about 200 resort staff run bars, restaurants and a nightclub, and conduct organised daytime activities.

South Molle's resort management believes people should keep moving to have fun. It has designed a tight daily schedule of sports, outings and entertainment, aided by a public address system which alerts guests to the next activity. The pace at West Molle—called Daydream Island in tourist publicity—is less strenuous. But this smallest of the settled islands offers the usual range of diversions—water-skiing, scuba diving, snorkelling, fishing trips and coral viewing. Centred on an 80-metre saltwater swimming pool, with a bar on an island in the middle, Day-dream attracts a clientele mostly under 30.

At Hamilton Island, tucked in close to the south-western shore of Whitsunday Island, the most ambitious complex of all is taking shape. The resort already accommodates 1000 guests in 120 hotel suites, 50 Polynesian 'bures' and 200 self-contained apartments. The waterfront offers a full range of restaurant, sports, shopping and charter facilities. The marina will ultimately take 400 boats. An 80-hectare fauna park has deer, kangaroos and emus, plus a koala village. The airstrip is unique to the Whitsundays in giving direct access to and from Australia's capital cities. Two further resorts are planned.

HAYMAN ISLAND 28 km north-east of Shute Harbour (previous page).
TRANSPORT: launch from Shute Harbour daily; regular helicopter flights from Proserpine.

HAPPY BAY 8 km east of Shute Harbour.
TRANSPORT: launch from Shute Harbour daily; helicopter from Proserpine most days.

SOUTH MOLLE 8 km north-east of Shute Harbour.
TRANSPORT: launch from Shute Harbour daily; helicopter from Proserpine most days.

Holiday lodges and a luxurious hotel crowd the only flat land among Hayman Island's high ridges; a long jetty reaches to the edge of its broad fringing reef

	HAYMAN ISLAND											
	Jan	Feb	Mar	Apr	May	Jun	Jul	Aug	Sep	Oct	Nov	Dec
Maximum C°	31	30	29	28	26	24	23	25	26	28	31	31
Minimum C°	25	25	24	22	20	17	17	18	19	21	23	24
Rainfall mm	368	364	256	196	109	93	61	14	13	59	56	63
Humidity %	68	74	70	72	71	72	70	67	58	61	60	67
Rain days	15	14	19	15	12	7	6	3	5	6	6	6
Sunshine hrs	Summer 7 +		Autumn 7 +			Winter 8 +			Spring 9 +			

Bowen and Queens Beach

Fishing boats, luxury launches and cruising yachts crowd Bowen's bustling small-craft harbour, at the northern end of Port Denison between the town centre and Flagstaff Hill. A distinctly different waterfront lies to the south, where clanking railway wagons relay coal from Collinsville, 85 km inland, to twin jetties reaching into deep water beyond the mudflats. Freighters of up to 25 000 tonnes load shipments here for the steel mills of Japan. But Bowen is soon to lose the coal trade: in the mid-1980s a specially constructed port at Abbot Point, 25 km north, will become operational.

Port Denison, now facing a doubtful future, played a crucial role in the early development of the north as a region for raising beef cattle. Settlement was so hindered by a scarcity of harbours in the 1850s that the New South Wales government offered a £200 prize for a suitable discovery. Four adventurers from Rockhampton took up the challenge in a tiny ketch. They succeeded by accident, finding Port Edgecumbe

and then Port Denison while taking shelter in the lee of Gloucester Island. But by then it was 1859, and the separate colony of Queensland had been created. The Sydney reward was withdrawn—but all four men were compensated by appointment to government posts when the port of Bowen was established in 1861.

Gloucester Island remains much as they saw it. Except for a camping ground and picnic areas, barbecues and lavatories, the rocky, mountainous island is covered in open eucalypt woodland. Now a national park, it has beaches suitable for swimming and skindiving, and a boat can be pulled ashore at North-West Beach on any tide. Permission for overnight camping can be obtained from the Queensland National Parks and Wildlife Service in Bowen. Several other camping sites and picnic grounds are situated along Queens Bay and in the small bays of Cape Edgecumbe. Horseshoe Bay, on the eastern shores of the cape, is a secluded cove shaded by palms and weeping casuarinas and sheltered at

each end by smooth boulders. The bay is a cool change from the streets of Bowen, and the oozing mangrove swamps along the access road. At Murray Bay, a steep, narrow gravel track leads to a caravan park behind a striking stone headland surrounded by delicately balanced boulders with pandanus trees sprouting from their cracks. A short, marked walk through thick bush leads to the beach.

Behind Queens Beach, Mount Nutt Reservoir overlooks the tomato gardens, mango orchards and salt-evaporation ponds which surround Bowen. Westward the hinterland is dotted with sites where fossickers pick away at dusty rocks searching for semi-precious stones such as opalised wood, petrified palm, jasper, agate and amethyst. Most of the outcrops are approached off the road from Bowen through Collinsville to Mount Gordon, 211 km inland. The Bowen-Collinsville Lapidary Club has mounted a display in Bowen and welcomes inquiries on where and how to find interesting stones.

Vegetable plots and orchards back Queens Beach, beside the Don River. Beaches east of Cape Edgecumbe are less developed but highly popular

BOWEN (pop. 7660) on Bruce Highway 1025 km from Brisbane.

TRANSPORT: train Brisbane-Bowen most days (25½ hrs); coach daily (21 hrs); flights Brisbane-Proserpine with connecting bus daily.

	BOWEN											
	Jan	Feb	Mar	Apr	May	Jun	Jul	Aug	Sep	Oct	Nov	Dec
Maximum C°	31	31	30	29	26	25	24	26	27	29	30	31
Minimum C°	25	24	24	21	18	17	15	17	18	21	23	24
Rainfall mm	253	247	157	69	36	39	24	18	16	22	34	106
Humidity %	65	70	66	63	61	60	58	59	56	58	61	64
Rain days	12	12	10	6	5	5	3	2	2	2	4	8
Sunshine hrs	Summer 7 +			Autumn 7 +			Winter 8 +			Spring 9 +		

Coal trains run to twin jetties jutting from the Bowen waterfront, south of a sheltered small-boat basin

Townsville and Pallarenda

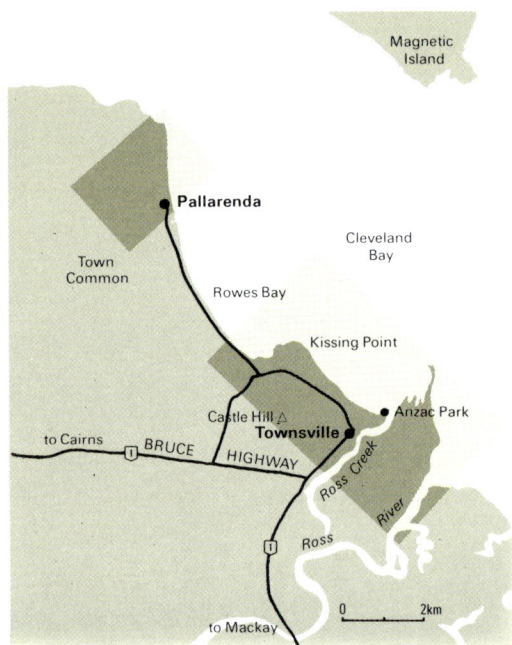

Bare, rust-red granite slopes rise steeply behind Townsville's busy shopping and hotel area. A narrow road winds to the 286-metre summit of Castle Hill, where a lookout, car park, restaurant and kiosk have panoramic views. The Town Common stretches away to the north-west, the city spreads out east and south-west, and mountainous Magnetic Island lies 7 km offshore.

Townsville is a major shipping centre for beef from the inland plains, the ores extracted at Mount Isa's mines, and sugar from the Burdekin River irrigation area. The city grew from its port, which was established at the mouth of Ross Creek in 1864 as a private depot for a Sydney businessman, Robert Towns. He took up extensive pastoral leases inland, but only once visited the settlement named for him. Upstream from the modern port, the Ross Creek boat harbour is crowded with commercial fishing boats, pleasure craft and tourist cruisers. Regular ferry services operate to Magnetic Island, and cruise boats ply to outer reefs. Fishing trips of one to

Pallarenda (left) is backed by the marshes and heaths of Townsville Town Common; the red granite hump of Castle Hill towers over the city (right)

five days' duration combine bottom fishing, snorkelling and some heavy-tackle angling for game fish. More specialised trips concentrate on scuba diving around reefs, under the supervision of a licensed instructor.

Netted enclosures at Kissing Point, Rowes Bay and at Anzac Park, near an Olympic-size pool, provide safe swimming spots during the summer months, when box jellyfish infest tropical waters. During the stinger-free winter months the stretch of beach from Kissing Point to Pallarenda provides uncrowded swimming with picnic grounds and playgrounds dotted along the beachfront park, and there is chopped wood on hand for barbecues.

Relief from the heat of the coast is found in Mount Elliot National Park, 32 km south. Camping sites and picnic grounds are serviced with water and lavatories. Established walking tracks branch out along the heavily wooded slopes to creeks, rock pools and waterfalls.

Crystal Creek-Mount Spec National Park is a longer drive from Townsville—67 km—but an ideal resting place for travellers going north to Ingham. It, too, has well-developed camping and picnic grounds and walking tracks.

TOWNSVILLE (pop. 86 106) on Bruce Highway 1408 km from Brisbane.
TRANSPORT: train Brisbane-Townsville most days (29½ hrs); coach daily (23½ hrs); Brisbane and interstate flights daily.

PALLARENDA (pop. 926) 7 km north-west of Townsville.
TRANSPORT: buses to Townsville-Pallarenda daily.

TOWNSVILLE	Jan	Feb	Mar	Apr	May	Jun	Jul	Aug	Sep	Oct	Nov	Dec
Maximum C°	31	31	30	29	27	26	25	26	28	29	31	31
Minimum C°	24	24	22	20	17	15	13	15	17	21	23	24
Rainfall mm	307	330	236	61	29	25	15	11	8	19	50	113
Humidity %	62	66	63	57	54	52	47	51	51	52	56	58
Rain days	16	17	15	8	6	5	2	3	2	4	7	10
Sunshine hrs	Summer 7 +			Autumn 7 +			Winter 8 +			Spring 9 +		

Billabong ballet on the Common

DANCING brolgas, normally a sight seen only in the outback, delight winter visitors to the Town Common on Townsville's north-western outskirts. At the height of the dry season as many as 3000 brolgas, along with up to 180 other species of bird, flock to the common's salt-marsh lagoons and waterholes.

The brolga, *Grus rubicundus*, is famed for its graceful group-courtship dance. Elements of this complicated display form part of the Aboriginal corroboree dance, and the bird's colours are used in make-up. Some people still call the brolga by its old name—the native companion.

Dancing in unison, pairs of birds strut towards each other and then retire, shaking half-opened wings, bowing, and bobbing their bright red heads. Occasionally they leap in the air and parachute down on outstretched wings, or throw back their heads to trumpet loudly.

Brolgas courting on the Town Common

Making up for lost time

TOWNSVILLE, by far the biggest and most solidly established city of tropical Australia, is a latecomer to the modern tourist scene. Only in 1984, for example, did sportsmen discover that the waters off Cape Bowling Green—just minutes from a city mooring—were prime grounds for light-tackle game fishing. Rich sponsorship has gone into promoting an annual tournament in the hope of winning a world reputation to rival that of Cairns.

The 1980s have seen—along with the airport's upgrading to international status—the private investment of hundreds of millions of dollars in projects aimed at accommodating and amusing visitors. Luxury hotels have mushroomed, one of them including North Queensland's only casino. Jostling for custom in a remodelled downtown precinct are boutiques and restaurants with themes and names that would have staggered the district's pioneering cattlemen.

Where a ferry ride to Magnetic Island was once the height of adventure, surface and aerial tours out to the Barrier Reef are heavily patronised. Soon the reef is to be brought to Townsville in the lavish construction of Barrier Reef Wonderland, where tunnelled walkways will take visitors among living coral structures surrounded by tropical fish.

In the grace of its old buildings and ornamental trees, parts of Townsville retain a Victorian dignity and charm that set the city apart from any other tourist base. And in spite of the dizzying pace of recent development, the district has generous tracts of wilderness that hold unusual interest to nature-lovers, as close as the Town Common or the heights of Magnetic Island. Bowling Green Bay National Park is among the world's most remarkable in the variety of its landforms and vegetation which range from bird-breeding mangrove flats to upland rainforests, an area that many locals still refer to as Mt Elliot National Park.

Central Townsville, seen from a Castle Hill lookout, straddles the Ross River. Magnetic Island rises in the background

Open-air chess at the Post Office

Elegant tropical architecture

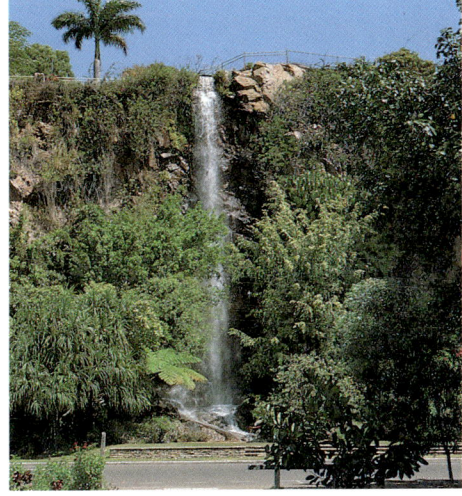

A touch of nature along the Strand

Handsome old buildings surround the Anzac Memorial Fountain

Granite sands at Radical Bay, Magnetic Island, are lightened by coral fragments from the island's many fringing reefs

Australian Institute of Marine Science, Cape Ferguson

The Institute's launch takes scientists to the Barrier Reef

Mangroves colonise mudflats at Bowling Green Bay, which is slowly filling with Burdekin river silts

Alligator Creek, near Mount Elliot

Hoop pines among granite boulders, Magnetic Island

Map labels:

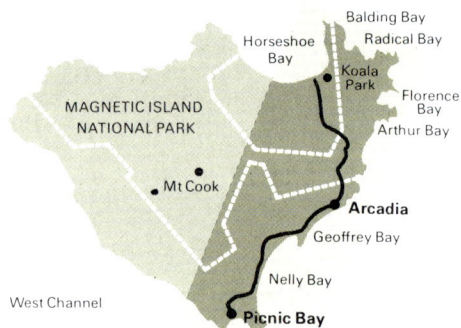

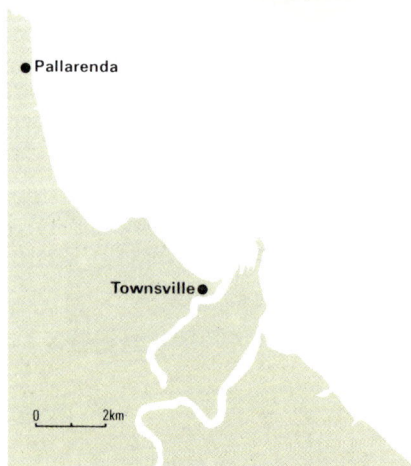

MAGNETIC ISLAND NATIONAL PARK

Horseshoe Bay
Balding Bay
Radical Bay
Koala Park
Florence Bay
Arthur Bay
Arcadia
Geoffrey Bay
Nelly Bay
Picnic Bay
Mt Cook
West Channel

Pallarenda

Townsville

0   2km

Magnetic Island

A 40-minute ferry trip from Townsville connects the city with its island suburb. At Picnic Bay, Magnetic Island's main settlement, the shores are lined with wide, shady Moreton Bay fig trees below a lively shopping centre and a residential community which even supports a surf lifesaving club. But board riders will find few if any waves: the club is there to deal with box jellyfish stings in summer. A wooden enclosure gives further protection to swimmers. Taxis and open-air buses ply the 24 km of sealed road linking the bays and sandy beaches between rugged headlands on the island's eastern shores. Cars can be taken to the island by booking on a regular vehicle ferry, and there are bicycles, motor-skis, power boats and more than 100 Mini Mokes for hire. The Shark World aquarium at Nelly Bay shows dangerous reef sharks cruising among turtles. Few sharks of this species are more than 1 metre long, but they are savage feeders. Smaller tanks at the aquarium hold a varied collection of brilliantly coloured tropical fish from the Great Barrier Reef. At Geoffrey Bay tall paperbarks, coconut palms and casuarinas crowd the shore between huge boulders, typical of the rugged coast which impressed James Cook in 1770. He named the island 'Magnetic' because the *Endeavour's* compasses behaved oddly near

Settlements strung around the eastern bays of Magnetic Island are officially part of Townsville, and comprise Australia's most uncharacteristic suburbs

it. Cook surmised—wrongly—that the island contained iron. Scientists now know that a magnetic anomaly in the structure of the sea bed caused the unusual readings he recorded. At the eastern end of the bay, concrete walls hold back sand from a cool creek. A shaded, grassy park fills half of the backshore, sharing the bay with the Alma resort. At Radical Bay, black boulders lie scattered through densely forested slopes rising steeply from another small resort. A 100-metre buffer zone between the beach and the resort maintains the bay's peace, even when the resort is crowded with visitors for lunch. Horseshoe Bay, the largest inlet, is a popular mooring spot for visiting boats and shelters the island's small fleet of trawlers. Koala Park has a permanent dis-

play of wallabies, kangaroos, brolgas, peacocks, cockatoos and koalas, and operates a hospital for birds and animals found injured or sick.

Much of Magnetic Island is a national park, left in its rugged natural state. Away from the popular beaches, resorts and sealed roads, 22 km of walking tracks lead to isolated bays and high vantage points. Several walks of 3-5 km criss-cross the gullies and ridges of eucalypt forest at the north-eastern end of the island. Cleared tracks link Arthur, Florence, Radical, Balding and Horseshoe Bays, all of which are suitable for swimming, or snorkelling over patches of fringing coral reef. An 8 km trail to West Point heads out along the south-western shores, normally taking about two hours. It crosses four freshwater

creeks and skirts mangrove flats and salt swamps where wetland wildlife can often be seen at low tide. Mount Cook (506 metres) can be climbed from a branch off the Arcadia-Nelly Bay track. There is no marked trail, so a compass and a talk with the park ranger at Picnic Bay are recommended. Sturdy boots are needed, and the hike up and down takes most of a day.

MAGNETIC ISLAND (pop. included in Townsville) 8 km east of Townsville.
TRANSPORT: frequent daily launches and vehicular ferries from Townsville connecting with island buses.
SURF CLUB PATROL: at Picnic Bay October-April, Saturday 14.00-16.30, Sunday and public holidays 09.00-16.30.

Lucinda, Cardwell and Hinchinbrook Island

Where harbours cannot be found in North Queensland's mangrove-choked shallows, sometimes one has to be made—whatever the cost. At Lucinda the price was high. Creation of a deepwater port to handle expanded production from the Herbert River canefields required not only a pier reaching nearly 6 km over the mudflats but also a 3 km causeway to span mangroves on the inland side of the terminal. The pier, completed in 1979, can take bulk sugar carriers of up to 40 000 tonnes. An earlier jetty, still used when small freighters load molasses, is a popular spot for handline fishing.

Lucinda Beach, south of the port, is suitable for swimming except in summer, when box jellyfish are about. Most visitors come not to swim but to launch boats. Dungeness, at the entrance to Enterprise Channel, has a jetty and wide ramp reached by a second causeway west of Lucinda. The Herbert River is navigable on a full tide to Halifax and beyond. Ocean-going craft head out for fishing or scenic cruising around Hinchinbrook or the Palm Islands.

Cardwell, facing the other end of Hinchinbrook Island, has a beach on Bruce Highway—the only such beach between Townsville and Cairns. The sea is often muddy, but the honey-coloured sand with the town strung out behind it offers invitingly shaded spots to rest and picnic. Almost opposite the town jetty there are modern freshwater pools for children and adults. Beachfront sites are reserved for caravans and camping. Cardwell was settled in 1864 as the first port north of Bowen, but was quickly eclipsed by Townsville with its easier access to cattle country inland. Cardwell struggled along on fishing and timber milling, and as a wayside station for travellers. Now it is increasingly popular as a base for island holidays or pleasure cruising. A sealed forestry road climbing inland from Kennedy, 13 km north, leads to the Kirrama Range with remarkable views of the islands offshore, from Great Palm to Dunk.

On Hinchinbrook Island, many streams and forested ridges have not been named, let alone frequented by anyone but the most dedicated bushwalkers. At 39 350 hectares this is the world's biggest all-island national park; most of it is wilderness. The only dwellings are a scattering of resort lodges at Cape Richards, the tip of the island's north-eastern arm. The resort welcomes day visitors. Moorings are available near the resort jetty in Orchid Bay, or small boats can be pulled up on the beach. Camping sites have been developed at Macushla Point, 3 km south of the resort, and at the Haven (Scraggy Point), opposite the mainland just south of Cardwell. National park camping permits can be obtained at Cardwell. Easy walking tracks of 1-2 km

branch out from Cape Richards and Macushla Point to the shady shores of North Beach on Shepherd Bay, and between the twin-humped Kirkville Hills to South Beach. Mangroves, extending up to 5 km into Missionary Bay, can be negotiated by boat. The second-last creek at the south of the bay leads to a boardwalk laid over 100 metres of tangled mangrove roots and mud. At the end, backed by a narrow spit of sand dunes, Ramsay Bay faces the Coral Sea.

CARDWELL												
	Jan	Feb	Mar	Apr	May	Jun	Jul	Aug	Sep	Oct	Nov	Dec
Maximum C°	32	32	31	29	27	26	25	27	28	30	31	32
Minimum C°	23	23	22	20	18	15	13	15	16	19	21	22
Rainfall mm	452	461	421	205	91	51	32	29	35	51	105	194
Humidity %	68	71	68	67	65	64	59	58	58	59	62	65
Rain days	16	16	17	14	11	7	6	5	5	6	8	11
Sunshine hrs	Summer 6 +			Autumn 7 +			Winter 7 +			Spring 9 +		

High tide brings the waters of Hinchinbrook Channel almost to the Bruce Highway at Cardwell, affording motorists the only seaside stop in 350 km

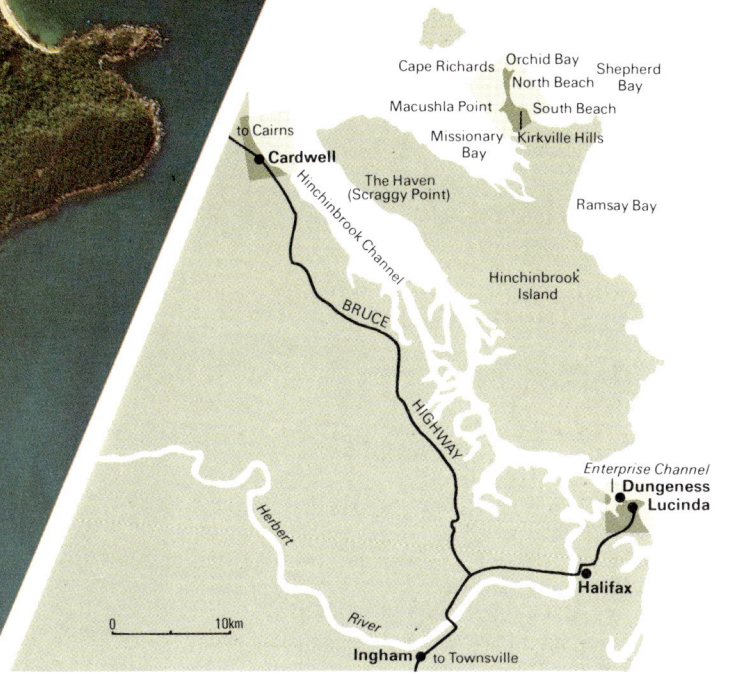

Mangroves choke the Herbert River delta at Lucinda

Map labels: Cape Richards, Orchid Bay, North Beach, Shepherd Bay, Macushla Point, South Beach, to Cairns, **Cardwell**, Missionary Bay, Kirkville Hills, The Haven (Scraggy Point), Hinchinbrook Channel, Ramsay Bay, Hinchinbrook Island, BRUCE HIGHWAY, Enterprise Channel, **Dungeness**, **Lucinda**, Herbert River, **Halifax**, 0 10km, **Ingham** to Townsville, to Townsville

Hinchinbrook Island's tiny tourist resort perches on the northernmost tip, at Orchid Bay (above)

LUCINDA (pop. 663) east of Bruce Highway 1548 km from Brisbane (turn off at Ingham).
TRANSPORT: train Brisbane-Ingham most days (32½ hrs); coach daily (26 hrs); none beyond Ingham, 27 km away.

CARDWELL (pop. 1249) on Bruce Highway 1573 km from Brisbane.
TRANSPORT: train Brisbane-Cardwell most days (33½ hrs); coach daily (26½ hrs).

Mission Beach and Dunk Island

On the road from Tully to Mission Beach, through rich tropical rainforest and head-high grass, a sign warns of cassowaries crossing. The beach is a smooth strip of honey-coloured sand, as flat as glass. A boat ramp falls more than 60 metres short of the sea at low tide, but the firm sand can take a highway vehicle. Behind the beach is a profusion of trees nourished by red volcanic soil and high rainfall—mangoes, pawpaws, bananas, mauve and red bougainvilleas, and palms heavy with coconuts. Pupils at the state school, on the slope across Porter Promenade, have some of their lessons outside in the shade of pines and jacarandas. On the slopes towards Clump Point, the red leaves of java fig trees show out against deep jungle greens. At Clump Point, rocks are scattered along the beach on either side of the jetty below the high tide mark; the morning water is an opaque jade green. Wylie Creek emerges from a tangle of vines to cut a sharp-edged channel across the sand. The waxy oval leaves of a giant touriga (*Calophyllum*) tree shelter two kiosks where tourists buy tickets for Dunk Island trips or reef cruises.

Dunk was immortalised as a South Seas paradise by a turn-of-the-century writer who settled there. In *The Confessions of a Beachcomber* and three other books, E. J. Banfield created an idyllic image of what he called 'the Isle of Dreams'. In the hilly part of Dunk, preserved as a national park, there is still the natural beauty which inspired Banfield. Lower-lying areas, however, have undergone great changes. Land has been cleared for grazing and an airstrip, and TAA's resort hotel at Brammo Bay accommodates up to 200 people. Day visitors are welcome there, but sporting facilities are for the use of guests only.

In a patch of rainforest beyond the resort's dairy farm is a small colony of artists and craftsmen, founded by Bruce Arthur, a weaver and former professional wrestler. Its members live simply, and scoff at the tourist hotel and its luxury trappings as 'the Last Resort'. But relations are amicable: resort guests on island walks are welcome callers at 'Arthur's'. Other walks, from the resort and nearby national park camping grounds, cover 19 km of graded tracks along the southern shores of the island and into

Lowlands of Dunk Island, cleared for grazing and now the site of a big resort, contrast sharply with its forested hills, protected as a national park

the ranges behind. One trail leads to a swinging rope-and-plank bridge over a deep, vine-choked gully. The most strenuous leads to the 271-metre summit of Mount Kootaloo. Many small, coral-fringed islands of the Family group are suitable for day trips. Wheeler and Coombe Islands have picnic facilities. Bedarra Island—officially called Richards Island—is shared by three freehold owners, one of whom is a tourist launch operator and runs a small resort. Little Timana (Thorpe) Island is occupied by a tapestry weaver and a leather craftsman, who may be contacted by inquiring at Dunk Island.

MISSION BEACH (pop. 640) east of Bruce Highway 1640 km from Brisbane (turn off northbound at Tully, southbound at El Arish).
TRANSPORT: train Brisbane-Tully most days (34½ hrs); coach daily (28 hrs); none beyond Tully, 28 km away.

DUNK ISLAND 8 km south-east of Clump Point, Mission Beach.
TRANSPORT: flights Townsville-Dunk daily, Cairns-Dunk most days; frequent daily launch Clump Point-Dunk.

CLUMP POINT												
	Jan	Feb	Mar	Apr	May	Jun	Jul	Aug	Sep	Oct	Nov	Dec
Rainfall mm	503	587	608	330	219	149	99	78	72	79	128	185
Rain days	16	18	19	17	15	12	11	9	8	7	8	11
Sunshine hrs	Summer 6 +			Autumn 6 +			Winter 7 +			Spring 9 +		

Narragon Beach
Wylie Creek
Clump Point
to El Arish and
Bruce Highway ● **Mission Beach**

Mission
Beach

to Tully and
Bruce Highway

Brammo Bay
△ Mount Kootaloo
Arthur s●   Dunk Island
DUNK ISLAND
NATIONAL PARK

● **South Mission
Beach**

Tam-O'Shanter Point

0   2km

Timana (Thorpe) Island

Bedarra (Richards)
Island

Orchards and market gardens spread towards Mission Beach and Clump Point (below)

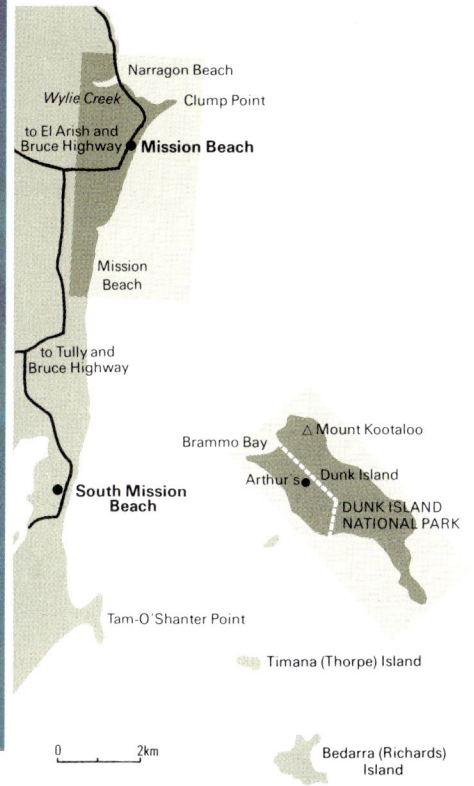

Kurrimine Beach and Bingil Bay

Kurrimine Beach offers visitors a rare opportunity to examine extensive coral formations without having to take a boat trip. At low tide, King Reef is within wading distance of the town beach, allowing a fascinating walk among coral growths and rock pools reaching 5 km out into the ocean. On a calm day, when the peace of the reef is broken only by mewing gulls and scuttling crabs, it is hard to picture this as the 19th-century graveyard of ships whose masters chanced the time-saving inshore channel.

One King Reef shipwreck, in 1878, has muddled amateur historians ever since. Survivors of the schooner *Riser* struggled ashore just north of where the town is now. They were killed by Ab-

origines, and the spot became known as Murdering Point. Six years earlier, in a more celebrated shipwreck involving 75 people, the brig *Maria* had been lost in the Palm Islands, off Ingham. Its captain and some of the crew escaped in a whaleboat and reached Tam-O'Shanter Point, south of Mission Beach. They, too, were slaughtered. When settlers came to the district in the 1880s they confused the two incidents and the two points. So the wide tidal inlet south of Kurrimine Beach is called, for no good reason, Maria Creek.

A shady park in front of the Kurrimine Beach shopping centre leads to a long stretch of honey-coloured sand. By the caravan park to the north, a 40-metre boat ramp gives access to sheltered

waters between Murdering Point and the reef, and to abundant fishing grounds off the Barnard Islands. But tractors stand by, because the tide leaves the ramp high and dry for most of the day.

South of the town, a sand track leads to Maria Creek, the banks of which are enveloped in mangroves and crackling with shellfish and crabs. Down a further track between coconut palms, the beach continues as a long spit extending to the creek mouth. Maria Creek National Park, south and west of the inlet, is a small, undeveloped reserve of swamp vegetation merging into open eucalypt forest. Camping is not permitted in the park. Garners Beach, backed by densely forested hills, enclosed by its own little

The map labels: MARIA CREEK NATIONAL PARK, Maria Creek, Murdering Point, Kurrimine, King Reef, Kurrimine Beach, Garners Beach, Bingil Bay, Bingil Bay, CLUMP POINT NATIONAL PARK, 0, 2km

reef and spared any through traffic, has a peaceful camping ground. The beach is dotted with the green fruit of big touriga (Calophyllum) trees. Once they were harvested for their seeds, which yielded a fragrant resin used as an ointment or in soap manufacture. South from Garners Beach, over a ridge with a good view of Bingil Bay, a pitted clay track leads to a shady picnic spot equipped with a stone barbecue.

On the scrubby slopes around Bingil Bay settlement, which has its own little beach, can be found tea plants cultivated by the pioneering Cuttens family. Seeds from these plants were among the stock used in 1960 to found the successful Nerada plantation, inland from Innisfail. South of the settlement, there are picnic facilities in Clump Point National Park but camping is not permitted.

King Reef's coral platform reaches almost to Kurrimine Beach; south of the Maria Creek mouth, Garners Beach is even more tightly reef-bound.

KURRIMINE BEACH (pop. 705) east of Bruce Highway 1650 km from Brisbane (turn off at Silkwood).
TRANSPORT: none beyond Silkwood, 12 km away; train Brisbane-Silkwood most days (35 hrs); coach Brisbane-Silkwood daily (28½ hrs).

BINGIL BAY east of Bruce Highway 1652 km from Brisbane (turn off at Tully or El Arish).
TRANSPORT: none beyond El Arish, 15 km away; train Brisbane-El Arish most days (35 hrs); coach Brisbane-El Arish daily (28½ hrs).

The coconut makes a comeback

HOLIDAYMAKERS like their beaches and resort islands to look 'typically' tropical—and the Queensland coconut industry is happy to oblige. Tourism has revived a century-old business of nursing seedlings from nuts and planting out palms such as those at Kurrimine, neatly spaced along the waterfront. First the trees were cultivated for oil, mainly to make soap. Now the purpose is decoration.

Cocos nucifera, the nut-bearing palm, is so widespread between South-East Asia and South America that no one is sure where it originated. It grows naturally on tropical Australian coasts and islands but its occurrence is haphazard: it is not indigenous. In pre-European times, some nuts were probably brought in canoes from islands to the north. More came by accident—they still do—as flotsam from the Pacific Islands.

Settlers interested in palm-oil production found the self-seeded Queensland trees stunted and low-yielding. In the 1870s they started planting nuts from Thailand, Malaysia or Singapore, supposing these to be of superior varieties. In fact they were just the same—the only difference was that Australia's palms had never been thinned out or weeded.

Plantations spread on coastal land from Mackay north. Most were in the rainy Innisfail district, although the biggest individual planting was only 10 km from the tip of Cape York. Oil yields were as high as any in the world. But the local industry met increasingly tough competition from New Guinea and the Pacific.

Planting tapered off in the 1920s, and with the manpower shortage of World War II most of Queensland's plantations were abandoned. Many palms were torn out later and sugar-cane was planted in their place. What coconut production remained in the 1950s went into pig and poultry feed. But before the decade was out *Cocos nucifera* found a new, photogenic role, fringing resort beaches and shading motels.

Innisfail and Mourilyan Harbour

Innisfail's sugar-cane plantations border the Johnstone River, which drains the most rain-soaked region in Australia

New paint on all Innisfail's public buildings in the 1970s gave a fresh face to dark walls stained by mildew. The town receives an average annual rainfall of 3641 mm—and 7772 mm fell in 1977. Figures like that explain the local saying: 'We don't measure in inches, we measure in yards.' Houses have a double allocation of guttering downpipes, and the streets are built over a maze of stormwater drains to channel the water quickly away from the town.

The sugar-cane plantation of Innisfail's first settler, Henry Fitzgerald, flourished on this high rainfall and on the cheap labour of the first wave of non-British workers to sweep into the area. Fitzgerald's cane-cutters were recruited from the New Hebrides (Vanuatu) or Solomon Islands, often in dubious circumstances. After the Palmer River goldfields failed, in the 1890s, Chinese miners drifted down from Cooktown to work as storekeepers and banana growers. Then Japanese and Spaniards also tried working in the canefields. Before World War I, Italians took on the backbreaking work of planting and cutting cane. They stayed in the district, rose to become plantation owners themselves and brought out their relatives. By 1924 non-British workers outnumbered British by four to one on the Johnstone River fields. Mourilyan was called 'Little Italy'. The Italian community had its own Camorra, a Neapolitan Mafia-style organisation known locally as the Black Hand. The leaders used arson, bombing and shooting to reinforce their extortion demands. But in 1934 an out-of-favour gang member, punished by having his ears sliced off, shot his attacker dead in the main street of Innisfail. That brought the society's activities out into the open and gave police a chance to tackle the ringleaders, several of whom were later deported.

East of Mourilyan, the modern harbour for Johnstone River sugar-handling is situated at the mouth of the Moresby River. Commercial fishing trawlers lie alongside the wooden beams connecting the jetty piles, while 30 metres above them a carriageway conveys raw sugar from the

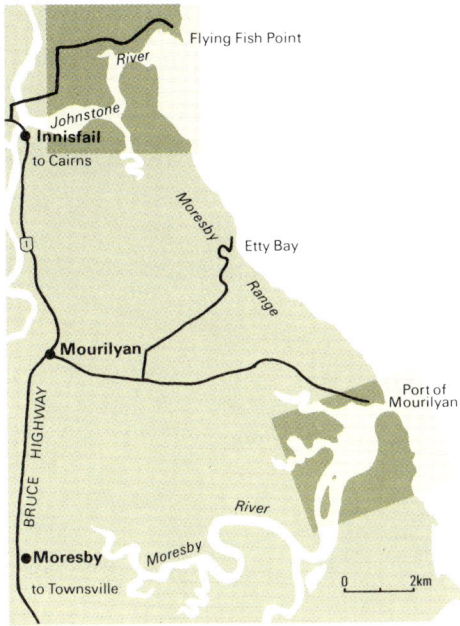

bulk storage terminal to waiting ships. The Australian Sugar Industry Museum in Mourilyan traces the growth and development of sugar production with displays of old machinery, short films and technical exhibits illustrating the process from growing to milling. The museum is open daily 09.00-16.30.

Amateur boating enthusiasts will find facilities at the mouths of both the Johnstone and Moresby Rivers. At Flying Fish Point a concrete ramp runs into the Johnstone beside the encrusted piles of an old jetty. Upstream the river is navigable to a sheltered mooring and a concentration of boating facilities at Innisfail. Etty Bay, 7 km east of Mourilyan, is regarded as the safest swimming beach in the Innisfail region. At weekends in summer, lifesaving club members drag the bay for box jellyfish. A caravan park on the beach provides for campers, while day visitors have picnic grounds and lavatories nearby. The bay is surrounded by national park land in the coast-hugging Moresby Range. But camping is not allowed in the park and there are no developed walking tracks.

INNISFAIL (pop. 7934) on Bruce Highway 1669 km from Brisbane.

TRANSPORT: train Brisbane-Innisfail most days (35½ hrs); coach daily (29 hrs).

SURF CLUB PATROL: at Etty Bay September-April, Saturday 14.30-17.00, Sunday and public holidays 09.00-17.00.

INNISFAIL												
	Jan	Feb	Mar	Apr	May	Jun	Jul	Aug	Sep	Oct	Nov	Dec
Maximum C°	30	30	29	28	26	24	24	25	26	28	29	30
Minimum C°	23	23	22	21	19	17	15	16	17	19	21	22
Rainfall mm	529	606	706	473	305	191	128	114	92	82	153	265
Humidity %	73	74	75	74	74	72	67	67	66	65	68	69
Rain days	16	17	19	18	16	12	11	10	8	7	9	12
Sunshine hrs	Summer 6 +			Autumn 6 +			Winter 7 +			Spring 9 +		

Sugar from the Johnstone River district goes by narrow-gauge railway to Mourilyan Harbour, isolated at the mouth of the Moresby River

Nature's shrinking storehouse

COASTAL plains from Ingham and Innis-fail to Cairns, and on north to Mossman, are seas of sugar cane. Picture all of this as dark, trackless tropical rainforest. For that is what it was, not so long ago. Some of the timber was useful and so the devastation began. Then vast tracks of forest were cleared for sugar cane, cultivated from West Indian stock, which became a main-stay of the Far North's economy—until world prices collapsed in the 1980s. Now it is appropriate to ponder the cost of the ecological sacrifice.

Tour the Atherton Tableland, among its tobacco plantations and cattle pastures. Picture these, too, as close-packed tangles of tall trees and vines, dripping with orchids and ferns. Remnants can be found, of course, around a scattering of volcanic features and in steep gorges that were too difficult to farm. Less accessible heights of the coastal ranges retain their covering. But the rest is gone.

North Queensland's rainforests, or what is left of them, were a lucky occurrence on a largely arid continent. Lofty ranges run exceptionally close to the seaboard, at just the right angle to catch moisture-laden southeasterly 'Trade Winds' off the Pacific. Australia's highest rainfalls are precipi-tated on volcanic basalt soils of unusual fertility, in temperatures that promote year-round growth.

The diversity is bewildering. More than 100 different tree species can be found in just a hectare of forest. Rarely does one kind seem predominant. In any case the massive, buttressed trunks are so similar and the foliage disappears into such a closely interwoven canopy that species are hard to tell apart.

Tropical rainforests are the busiest havens of wildlife to be found on land. From the topmost blossoms to the rotting leaf litter that carpets the ground, they support many of the world's rarest birds, mammals, insects and amphibians. And in the gloom grow herbs and mosses and fungi whose properties are little known. If their genetic material is lost to science, their potential can never be tapped. Then human survival, too, could be at risk.

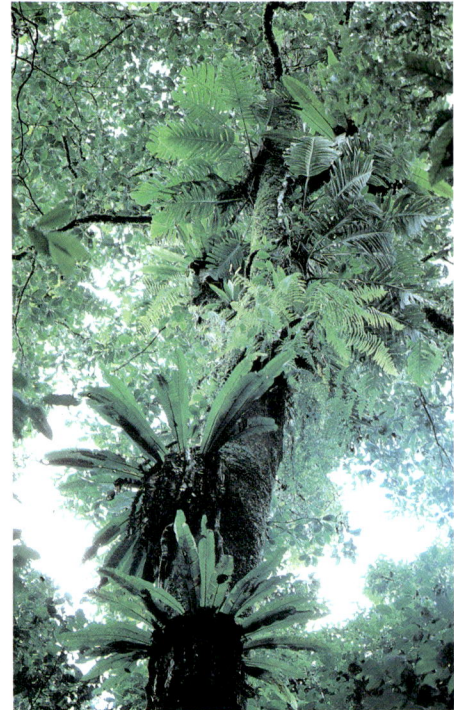

Birdsnest ferns by the Palmerston Highway

Rainforests of Cape Tribulation National Park, where road building has aroused bitter controversy

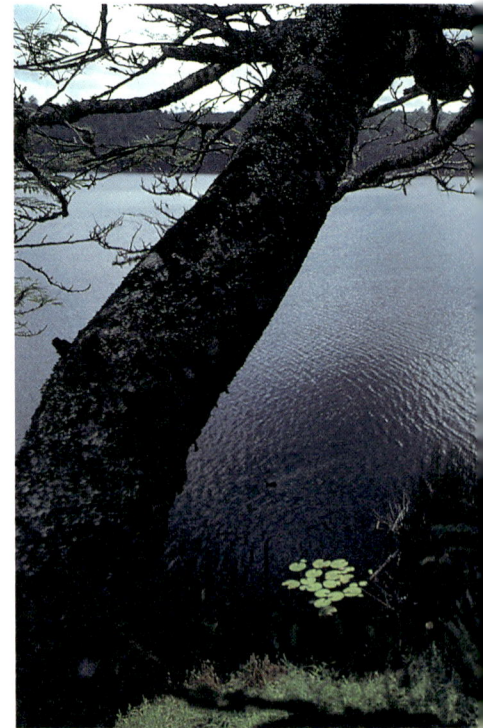

The volcanic Lake Barrine is surrounded by rainfore

The Boulders, Bellender Ker Range

Near Thornton Beach, Cape Tribulation

Macrozamia cycads in a rainforest clearing

Cairns

Any spring evening, spectators throng Marlin Jetty to see what luck the Cairns game fishing fleet has had. On rare occasions, cruisers fly blue and white flags to signal that they are bringing catches to be weighed. If so, onlookers can be sure the fish will be big ones—perhaps Pacific black marlin of 500 kg or more. Marlin are prized for their fighting qualities, but they are poor eating. So only those of remarkable size are brought in for weighing. Others are tagged for research purposes, photographed to provide the fisherman with a souvenir, and then released.

Since the late 1960s, when the feeding grounds of giant marlin were located 40-60 km off Cairns, the port has claimed pre-eminence for this type of fishing. Sailfish, tuna, barracouta and sharks are also abundant. In the heavy-tackle season, from September to December, wealthy enthusiasts fly in from many parts of the world. The emergence of this expensive sport, favoured by some celebrated entertainers, has added a gloss to a city which has been dedicated to pleasing visitors for more than 50 years.

Cairns was established in 1876 to serve miners swarming onto the Hodgkinson River goldfield, far inland over the Great Dividing Range. When an easier track was discovered between the

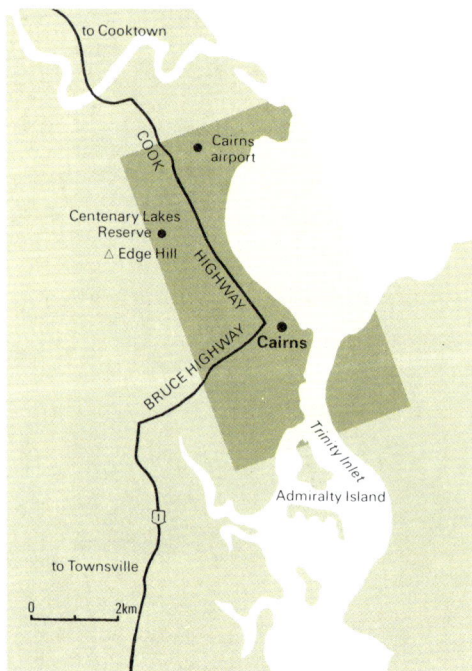

Hodgkinson and Port Douglas, Cairns quickly lost that trade. Instead it found a more secure future as the railhead and port for cane sugar from the surrounding lowlands, and for the rich agricultural production of the Atherton Tablelands. In the 1920s, in spite of its disadvantages—remoteness, an oppressively hot and humid climate in summer and autumn, a proneness to cyclones, and a lack of good beaches—it began to develop as a leading tourist centre. As a base for varied activity and scenic enjoyment, Cairns is still hard to beat.

Competing destinations clamour for the visitor's attention. There are day trips galore: by boat to Green Island or Michaelmas Cay; by train to the Barron Falls and Kuranda; by car or coach through the cool rainforest and dairying country of the Tablelands, or up the coast past a string of sandy swimming beaches to Mossman and beyond. Safari camping tours in four-wheel-drive coaches range from the Gulf of Carpentaria to Cape York. Fishing launch operators cater for all tastes and budgets—not just for the big-game enthusiasts. And Cairns airport is the centre of a busy network of light aircraft routes north and west, as well as to the resort islands of the Great Barrier Reef.

In the city itself, horse-drawn wagons take tourists through broad streets lined with palms and figs and divided by vivid flower beds. Hand-

some buildings from last century are preserved among new hotels, motels, restaurants and shops. A two-hour inland tour by paddlewheel steamer passes through the bustling port in Trinity Inlet and makes a circuit around Admiralty Island, nosing into creeks crowded by dense vegetation and alive with waterfowl—and sometimes crocodiles, according to the tour promoters.

The bulk sugar terminal, opposite the city end of Admiralty Island, is among Queensland's biggest. Inspection tours are offered at 15.30 on weekdays in the harvest season, from mid-June to the end of November. Also open for free inspection, 09.30-11.00 and 13.00-14.00 on weekdays, is the Royal Flying Doctor Service and

School of the Air radio base at Edge Hill. Nearby, the Botanical Gardens display 10 000 trees and plants from all tropical zones of the world. There are playground and picnic areas here and in the neighbouring Centenary Lakes reserve. An easy walking trail climbs to the west, giving excellent views of the city and its busy airport, the cane country and the Coral Sea coast.

CAIRNS (pop. 48 531) on Bruce Highway 1757 km from Brisbane.
TRANSPORT: train Brisbane-Cairns most days (37½ hrs); coach daily (30 hrs); Brisbane and interstate flights daily.

Game-fishing launches, luxury yachts and Barrier Reef tourist craft cluster in Trinity Inlet, still the focal point of the rapidly expanding city of Cairns

CAIRNS												
	Jan	Feb	Mar	Apr	May	Jun	Jul	Aug	Sep	Oct	Nov	Dec
Maximum C°	32	31	30	29	27	26	25	27	28	29	31	31
Minimum C°	24	24	23	22	20	18	17	18	19	21	22	23
Rainfall mm	399	441	464	177	91	51	30	26	36	35	84	167
Humidity %	62	65	65	63	62	59	56	54	52	53	57	59
Rain days	20	20	21	20	14	12	9	7	10	6	9	13
Sunshine hrs	Summer 6 +			Autumn 6 +			Winter 7 +			Spring 9 +		

Green Island, growing out of debris washed from its surrounding platform of coral, is being pushed gradually north-westward by prevailing currents

Green Island

Six metres below high-water level at the edge of Green Island's coral reef, a teeming array of tropical fish enjoy a unique view: they peer through thick plate glass at a procession of tourists approaching 200 000 a year. Notices remind the visitors that it is they who are in a tank—the fish have the run of an untamed ocean.

Of the thousands of islands and separate reef structures that make up the Great Barrier chain,

Green Island is one of the few genuine coral cays, and the only easily accessible one. All the major resort islands except Heron, nearly 1000 km south, are protuberances of the continental shelf with fringing reefs of coral. But Green Island grew from coral alone. Its tree-clad 'land'—still not much more than 1 metre above sea level—is the accumulation of rubble and sediments from thousands of years of wave erosion of its platform

reef. The debris was given fertility by salts from the sea, allowing the germination of seeds and spores blown by the wind or carried by birds.

Small private boats can share the island's ferry wharf, but access is cramped. Trippers from Cairns find it easy to cross by launch, motor-catamaran or hydrofoil. All services leave from Wharf Street, and all allow four or five hours on the island. That is time enough to walk its short

How the law protects the Great Barrier Reef

MATTHEW FLINDERS, searching for safe shipping passages off North Queensland in 1802, coined the term 'Great Barrier Reef'. His wording was misleading. The jumble of islands and coral structures he observed is not one reef, or one series of reefs. Nor do the outer reefs form a true barrier turning the coastal waters into an immense lagoon—although they do divert currents and intercept the ocean swell in many places.

Flinders' term stuck, however, and is now applied to an area of about 200 000 sq km—most of which is open water. The reef region is generally regarded as starting in the north at Bramble Cay, latitude 9° 09'S, and ending 24° 38'S at Breaksea Spit, off Fraser Island. Its width is that of the continental shelf, varying from 24 km at Cape Melville, north of Cooktown, to more than 200 km east of Mackay. This vast area includes hundreds of islands that are outcrops of continental shelf rock, although most have acquired fringing reefs of coral. Among these islands and beyond them emerge countless separate formations of coral. Their position and growth, in an apparently haphazard scattering of patches and ribbons, horseshoes and circles, is the response of coral polyps to currents, winds and wave action (see Coral Reefs, page 26).

Many of the outer formations and some close to the coast have never been exactly charted or investigated. In any case they are living, changing structures—growing below the waterline, eroding above it, and often producing shifting banks of coral sediments. Sometimes the debris of wave-eroded coral collects consistently enough for vegetation to take root, and a coral cay is formed. Two cays, Green Island and Heron Island, are well known as resorts. But their sandy superstructure is not entirely secure: Heron is subject to serious erosion and Green is creeping sideways off its coral base.

Collectively, the coral formations of the Great Barrier Reef region make up the most extensive structural system ever built by living creatures. The region has the world's biggest and most diverse assemblage of corals and associated marine life. But their continued existence relies on a delicate natural balance. It can be upset easily by human intrusion—however well intended—and could be irreparably wrecked by large-scale industrial activity and water pollution on the continental shelf.

Many islands and cays have long been declared national parks or wildlife sanctuaries, so that they can be protected by control of activities above the water-

Wistari Reef, off Heron Island, is awash at mid-tide—a condition of continuing coral growth

line. Since 1976, the Great Barrier Reef Marine Park Authority has been empowered by the Australian Government to issue declarations providing similar protection below the low-water mark, anywhere in the region that it sees fit.

Declaration of a marine park enables the authority to introduce a zone management plan. Activities such as tourist operations, boating and fishing, scientific study and specimen collecting can continue, but certain particularly vulnerable or unspoiled areas are made off-limits. And mining or oil drilling are prohibited altogether.

The first area to be gazetted under federal law, in 1979, was the Capricornia section. It covers the Capricorn and Bunker groups at the southern extremity of the reef region, including Heron Island, but not the islands and seabed closer to the coast between Gladstone and Yeppoon.

The Cairns section, from Dunk Island north to Lizard Island, was gazetted in 1981 amid dissension between the Australian and Queensland Governments. Declarations of the remaining sections were completed in 1983, bringing all but one percent of the Great Barrier Reef under protection.

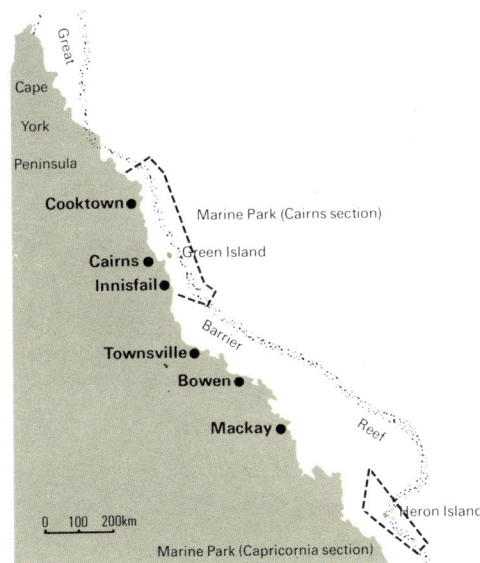

---

forest tracks or sandy beach, examine the reef surface at low tide, and have a swim and a picnic, without missing any of the prepared displays.

From the underwater observatory, viewers gain an insight into the complex balance of reef life. They see dozens of species of colourful fish along with anemones, clams and coral polyps—and sometimes marauding barracouta or mackerel. A huge black marlin which weighed 650 kg is mounted at the observatory entrance.

The diversity of the living reef can be further explored with hired snorkels, or more sedately in glass-bottom boats. A filmed dive off a reef edge is screened at the Castaway Theatre. Next door is the Marineland Melanesia, an aquarium with saltwater crocodiles, sharks and turtles, and reef

creatures including the poisonous stonefish and the destructive crown-of-thorns starfish.

Green Island was named not for its tall forest but for the chief astronomer on Cook's *Endeavour*. In the 1870s it was fought over by adventurers gathering *bêche-de-mer*, the sea-cucumbers prized by Oriental gourmets. Later an eccentric fisherman, George 'Yorkey' Lawson, settled alone on the island. He claimed it was haunted by the victims—black and white—of *bêche-de-mer* battles. After 1890 Lawson started promoting Green Island as a picnic place, and was made caretaker.

To combat problems of over-use the island was declared a national park in 1937—the year in which glass-bottom boats were introduced. The

surrounding reef was declared a marine park in 1974. Live coral, shells, fish, seagrass beds and even mangroves are protected: nothing may be taken from around the island. But tourist publicity has brought people in such numbers that damage has been inevitable, especially to the reef surface at intertidal level. Today the marks and sounds of man are inescapable. Green Island is no place for solitude. But its facilities are unsurpassed for convenient and thorough viewing of natural life on a coral reef.

GREEN ISLAND 30 km north-east of Cairns.
TRANSPORT: frequent daily boat services from Cairns (40-90 minutes).

Yorkeys Knob to Ellis Beach

Fishermen nosing their boats towards the hooked beach beside Yorkeys Point follow a long tradition—but not always a noble one. Many a traveller has had special reason to avoid the gaze of authorities at Cairns or Port Douglas. Yorkeys was a favourite of fugitives and smugglers last century, and well into the 1900s 'twang runners' rowed out to collect packets of opium thrown from the freighters. They sold the drug to elderly, hopelessly addicted Chinese left over from the Hodgkinson River gold-rush days.

The point, and later the hill and the town, acquired their names because the Yorkshire-born hermit of Green Island, George Lawson, would land his sacking-sailed boat at no other place. For nearly 30 years after 1886, he called regularly to sell fish and to tell tales of the apparitions he claimed to see on his island. Wild-eyed and unkempt, with a steel hook to replace a forearm he

lost while trying to stun fish with dynamite, 'One-Arm Yorkey' was an unforgettable sight.

Yorkeys Knob is noted for barramundi just after the wet season ends, and a boat ramp west of the point gives good access to the well-stocked waters of Trinity Bay. The sea here is muddy, with a steep slope and strong currents. Family groups favour the town beach, south of the Knob. Other clean waters and a beach shaded by casuarinas can be reached across a rickety footbridge from the caravan park north of the town. The Knob itself has a picnic ground and play area with pleasant views.

Trinity Beach, north of the steep green mound of Earl Hill, is a sheltered family playground for sailing, fishing and swimming. Short and compact, its esplanade is jammed with holiday units, motels, caravan parks and lodges. A sandy beach runs between rocky heads. The slopes behind are

blanketed by jungle-green forest. Clifton Beach, on around Taylor Point, is coarse-grained like Trinity, but bigger, flatter and less busy.

At Palm Beach the backshore is grassed, and shaded by a mass of drooping casuarinas. A camping ground and caravan park extend back towards Taylor Point. Immediately west of the beach road, massive paperbarks and spreading coconut palms shade the area around the Cairns Surf Lifesaving Club. The township of Palm Cove is well designed with smart, airy houses, neatly trimmed lawns, brilliant bougainvillea and frangipani, mango trees and palms. The Australian Bird Park, on the Cook Highway near

Beaches north of Yorkeys Knob, free of mudflats and mangroves, offer the best ocean swimming near Cairns—but mountain streams just inland are more refreshing, and safer in summer

Palm Cove, with more than 400 species of native birds in 2.25 hectares of tropical vegetation, and the Crocodile Park next door operate jointly as Wild World, open 09.00-17.00 every day.

Ellis Beach, north past Buchan Point and Double Island, surprises the traveller with its little cluster of constructions: motel, restaurant, caravan park, stone jetty and lifesaving club-house. There is no settlement at all—steep hills hemming the coast make it impossible. The facilities were installed in association with a proposed resort development on Double Island. When it was abandoned they were disposed of to separate interests. The beach has filled, making the jetty unusable by boats. A reef reaches out to the rocky stub of Haycock Island. The northern part of the beach has an away-from-it-all charm, enhanced by the frequency of streams in gullies cutting the hills. Sunbathers can cool off in clear, fresh water as a change from the often enervating heat of the tropical sea.

YORKEYS KNOB (pop. 1916) east of Cook Highway 1775 km from Brisbane, 18 km north of Cairns (turn off 2 km south of Smithfield).
TRANSPORT: bus Cairns-Yorkeys Knob daily except Sunday.

TRINITY BEACH (pop. 857) east of Cook Highway 1776 km from Brisbane, 19 km north of Cairns (turn off 3.5 km north of Smithfield).
TRANSPORT: bus Cairns-Trinity Beach daily except Sunday.

PALM COVE east of Cook Highway 1782 km from Brisbane, 25 km north of Cairns.
TRANSPORT: bus Cairns-Palm Cove daily except Sunday.
SURF CLUB PATROLS: at Palm Cove October-May, Saturday 14.30-16.30, Sunday 09.00-16.30; at Ellis Beach October-April, Saturday 14.00-16.30, Sunday 09.00-16.30.

Port Douglas and Mossman

The Mossman River meanders through mangrove flats to a disused port at the mouth; Mossman's sugar output now goes by rail to Port Douglas

Scenic touring and reef cruising have brought Port Douglas back to life, almost a century after it was doomed. The revival is demonstrated by new wharves, queues of luxury buses and launches, modern motels, and smart restaurants praised for their seafood. When game fishermen celebrate too enthusiastically, there are even echoes of the uproarious days when this town had 12 000 gold-fevered people—a boomtime that lasted just eight years.

Murder first put Port Douglas on the map. In 1877 a Chinese storekeeper was killed on the newly opened Hodgkinson River goldfields, 80 km inland. Christie Palmerston, the bushman

son of an opera singer, was accused of the crime and fled for the coast. The only known way out was over a punishing track to Cairns, which had just been founded to serve the diggings. But Palmerston blazed an easier trail to Island Point. A settlement sprang up as soon as the news got out. The fugitive was pardoned, and collected a £200 reward for finding the new route. By 1880 business houses, banks and government offices were moving from Cairns to Port Douglas. It seemed destined to take over from Cooktown as the leading city of the far north. All it needed was a railway to penetrate the rich hinterland. But tin was discovered on the Atherton Tablelands,

influencing the government in 1885 to give Cairns the railway, and later a sugar-loading terminal. Port Douglas declined almost as quickly as it had grown. It was already a virtual ghost town in 1911, when cyclonic winds and floods in two successive months destroyed or made uninhabitable most of its buildings.

Now modern houses and shops occupy much of Island Point, and further land is being reclaimed from mangrove swamps beside Dicksons Inlet. Other expansion is taking place to the south, with access to Port Douglas Beach and its 6 km sweep of clean, firm sand. Tour buses throng Princess Wharf, and a ramp upstream is capable of launching four boats at a time. Cabin cruisers and yachts jostle at the jetties and moorings. One cruise company, successful with tours to the coral cays of the Low Isles, has introduced a high-speed catamaran that offers a day trip to the distant outer reef. After an 80-minute journey out, passengers spend about three hours in the unspoiled Opal Reef area.

Mossman, northernmost of the sugar-growing centres, has been a stubborn survivor. Around a lawn triangle and squat stone war memorial are buildings as much as a century old. Down near the Mossman River mouth, on the Cooyar Beach road, is an inlet anchorage still marked on some maps as Port of Mossman. A ramp 200 metres in from the sea dips into a channel alongside mangrove mudflats. The river, filmy and opaque, is not navigable upstream, but a channel through a sand bar at the entrance gives access to the sea.

South of the mouth, Cooyar Beach is an enormous sand flat: even at mid-tide, there is a walk of nearly 400 metres to reach waters deep enough for swimming. Behind the beach is a grove of palms with occasional red-leafed java fig trees. Newell Beach, north of the river mouth, is a long strip of coarse sand with a steeper sea bed slope and better swimming.

Cool, shady relief from the steamy coast can be found in Mossman Gorge, 8 km west of the town. This is the southern end of the 56 450-hectare rainforest wilderness of Daintree River National Park, and the only part of it readily accessible to the general public. There are picnic facilities and a swimming pool, and the adventurous can climb deeper into the park along the boulder-strewn riverbed. The wilder regions of the park can be seen on a scenic drive north from Mossman to Daintree, skirting the Dagmar Range. Cairns coach tour operators, who run trips all the way to Cape Tribulation in dry weather, hint that crocodiles are to be seen basking by the Daintree River.

PORT DOUGLAS (pop. 675) east of Cook Highway 1822 km from Brisbane, 67 km north of Cairns (turn off 14 km south of Mossman).
TRANSPORT: bus Cairns-Port Douglas weekdays.

MOSSMAN (pop. 1611) on Cook Highway 1830 km from Brisbane, 73 km north of Cairns.
TRANSPORT: bus Cairns-Mossman weekdays.

PORT DOUGLAS	Jan	Feb	Mar	Apr	May	Jun	Jul	Aug	Sep	Oct	Nov	Dec
Maximum C°	31	31	31	30	28	26	25	26	28	29	31	31
Minimum C°	23	23	22	21	20	17	17	18	18	20	22	23
Rainfall mm	392	411	422	193	68	50	25	24	32	44	99	202
Humidity %	68	73	72	69	71	70	68	66	61	62	62	67
Rain days	17	17	17	14	11	8	6	6	6	7	9	12
Sunshine hrs	Summer 6 +			Autumn 6 +			Winter 7 +			Spring 9 +		

Dicksons Inlet shelters the cruise boats and fishing launches that have brought Port Douglas new prosperity

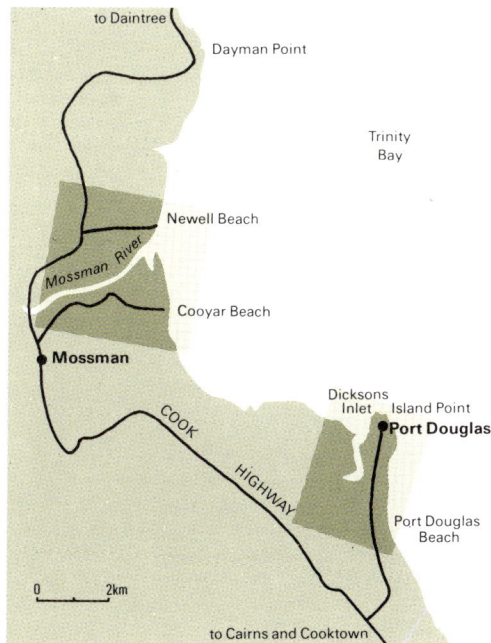

Cooktown

Cooktown owes much more than its name to the navigator James Cook. But for the bicentenary in 1970 of his exploration, and the Queen's interest in seeing the site of his longest stay ashore in Australia, the settlement could have faded into total obscurity by now. One more cyclone and it might have been abandoned. Instead the attractive presentation of historical relics, spurred by the royal visit, has led to a commercial revival based on tourism. That in turn has re-stored Cooktown as a centre serving agriculture and mining on Cape York Peninsula.

A stone cairn in the Endeavour River, opposite the police station, marks the spot where Cook beached his holed barque after grounding on a reef more than 40 km to the south-east. On the riverbank his crew set up a blacksmith's forge, carpenter's benches, livestock pens and a butchery. It took seven weeks to repair the *Endeavour*. In this time the river was explored for 30 km up-stream, and Cook's party made their only signifi-cant contact with Aborigines. Joseph Banks and other botanists collected 186 new plant species. The first dingo was sighted and the first 'kanga-roo' shot. It probably was a big black wallaroo.

Later explorers and pioneer settlers noted the site's suitability for a port, but no use was made of it until the discovery in 1873 of a rich goldfield on the Palmer River, across the ranges towards the Gulf of Carpentaria. Even though public an-

Spreading south to avoid mangrove flats beside the Endeavour River, Cooktown is enjoying a real estate boom; population doubled between 1976 and 1982

nouncement of the bonanza was delayed, the first steamer-load of miners arrived from the south just one day after an official port survey party. In a few weeks 'Cook's Town' grew from nothing to an avenue of tents stretching 3 km inland. This became Charlotte Street, lined with bars, stores, brothels and banks.

In the 1880s Cooktown had 94 pubs and supported an urban and mining population of 30 000—more than half of them Chinese. Its people were wracked by malaria, typhoid and dysentery, but most of all by gold fever. In 20 years the Palmer yielded more than 1 million ounces (over 28 tonnes). But· exhaustion of the field coincided with the worst years of the 1890s depression, accelerating an exodus from Cooktown. When a cyclone in 1907 caused severe damage, it hardly seemed to matter. Fear of a Japanese invasion brought a further withdrawal of population in 1942, and another cyclone in 1949 destroyed derelict buildings. Few could see a future for the town after that.

In 1969, however, the tiny community rallied to fight the demolition of St Mary's Convent. Built in 1889, it had been the district's only senior school for girls. But it was commandeered for military use during World War II and then abandoned. Support to save the old granite and brick building came from people and companies throughout Australia. The National Trust of Queensland and the Roman Catholic diocese of Cairns worked out a scheme to restore it as the James Cook Historical Museum, and the state government contributed half the cost. The museum is open 11.00-12.00 and 14.00-16.00 every day from April to October, and 10.00-13.00 daily except Friday in the off-season. It devotes a gallery to Cook but has other sections dealing with the activities of three races in the district—Aborigines, European miners and settlers, and Chinese. It contains a facsimile Chinese temple with relics from the original 'joss houses'.

Cooktown has two small national parks nearby. Endeavour River, on the north bank 5 km upstream, preserves the riverside dunes and vegetation much as Cook's exploring parties saw them. Mount Cook, on the town's southern outskirts, is a forested hump, 430 metres high, which dominated a scene painted by Cook's draughtsman, Sydney Parkinson—probably the first landscape painted in Australia. Neither park has public facilities or allows camping.

The cemetery at the western end of Cooktown also holds historical interest. Along with the local characters buried there, it contains the century-old grave of a pioneering martyr, Mrs Watson. She and her baby were left on Lizard Island with two servants while her husband was visiting the mainland. Aborigines attacked, killing one servant and wounding the other. Having no boat, Mrs Watson put to sea in a water tank with her baby and the injured man. They drifted for days before beaching on an island where all died from thirst.

Near a riverside playground in the town centre—with its warning sign, 'There are crocodiles in this river'—stands a cannon made in 1803. This is what the Queensland government sent to defend Cooktown in 1885, when all Australian settlers feared a Russian invasion. When volunteers tried it out it made an impressive noise, but the ball was lobbed only a few metres. Tourists from Sydney or Melbourne find the story comical—but people up from Cairns or Townsville mutter darkly about how the north always seemed to be expendable.

COOKTOWN (pop. 908) on Cooktown Developmental Road 2091 km from Brisbane, 334 km north of Cairns via Mossman and Mount Molloy. Dry weather only.
TRANSPORT: bus Cairns-Cooktown twice weekly in dry season (6-8 hrs); flights some days.

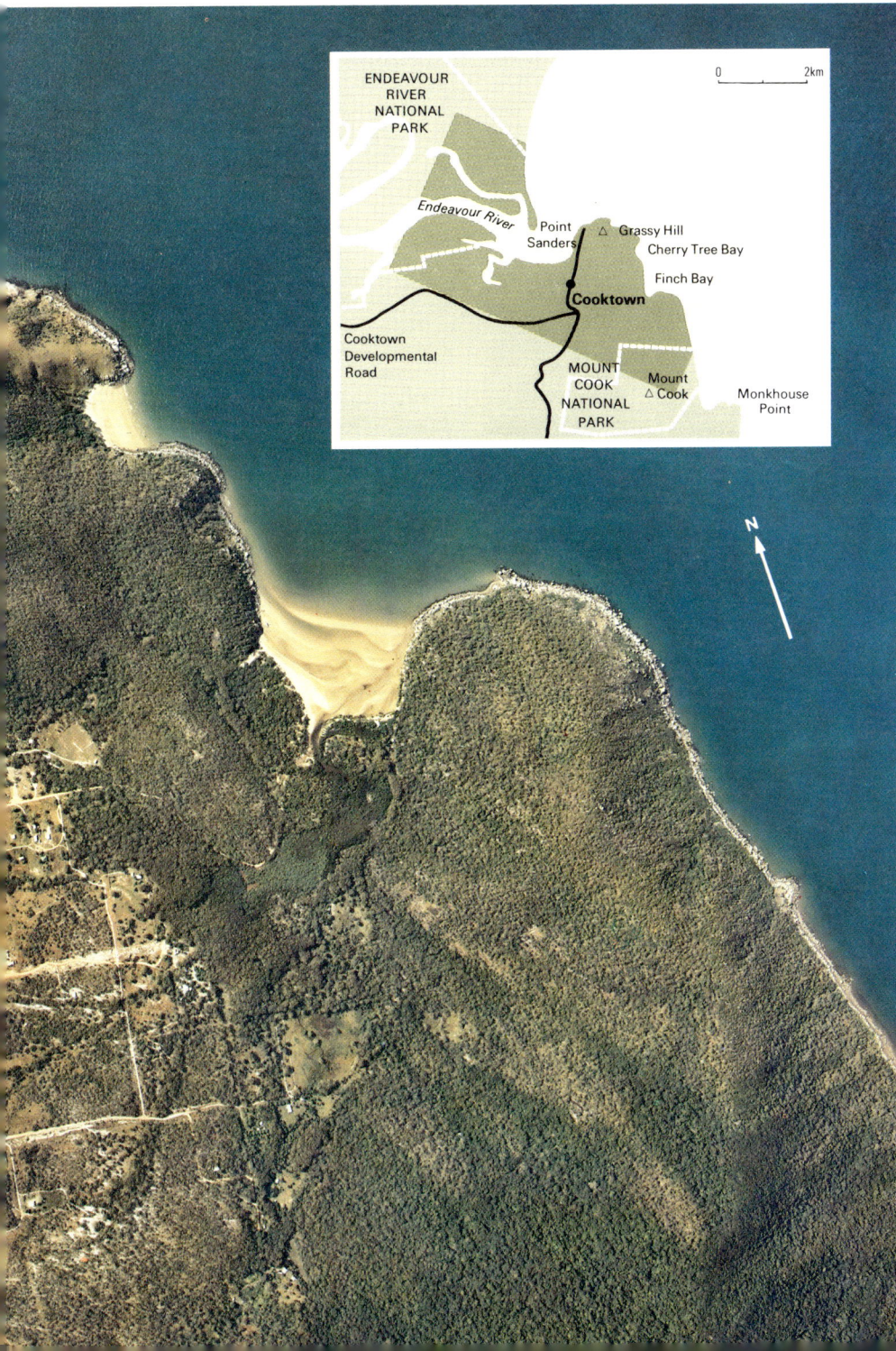

Map: Endeavour River National Park; Endeavour River; Point Sanders; Grassy Hill; Cherry Tree Bay; Finch Bay; Cooktown; Cooktown Developmental Road; Mount Cook National Park; Mount Cook; Monkhouse Point. 0 2km. N

COOKTOWN												
	Jan	Feb	Mar	Apr	May	Jun	Jul	Aug	Sep	Oct	Nov	Dec
Maximum C°	31	31	30	29	27	26	25	26	28	29	31	31
Minimum C°	24	24	24	23	22	20	19	20	21	23	24	24
Rainfall mm	369	368	391	209	75	52	27	30	16	23	64	160
Humidity %	71	72	74	71	70	70	67	66	63	63	64	67
Rain days	17	18	18	15	12	9	7	6	4	4	6	10
Sunshine hrs	Summer 6 +			Autumn 6 +			Winter 7 +			Spring 9 +		

Cape York Peninsula

At nightfall in the dry season, dozens of four-wheel-drive vehicles choke the approaches to the Jardine River crossing—advance camp for a final push to the top of Australia. Tents and cooking fires spread far along the banks as weary adventurers, four or five days up a demanding road from Cairns, rest before tackling the metre-deep river ford and the run to 'the Tip'.

The Jardine, starting in the last dwindling folds of the Great Dividing Range and flowing north and west to the rim of the Gulf of Carpen-

Roads to Cape York are hard on drivers and vehicles

taria, carries the greatest year-round water volume of any river in Queensland. With other rivers flowing east near Cape York, it creates a swamp barrier that was cursed by explorers and would-be settlers as the 'wet desert'—treacherous in the dry season and impassable in the wet. Even in the 1980s the Cape is cut off to surface travellers for at least half the year, from as early as November to as late as May. Drivers are unlikely to get as far as Cooktown after the first heavy rains close the Peninsula Developmental Road—better known to northerners as the Telegraph Line. But in the dry season, the creeks that have to be forded offer good campsites and cool relief from a hot and dusty journey.

Many visitors to Cape York go on bus tours operated by Cairns companies, with camping gear and food supplied. There are scheduled flights from Weipa or 'air safaris' from Cairns. Independent tourists need a fully equipped four-

Fording the Wenlock River, Cape York Peninsula

wheel-drive vehicle and should seek RACQ or police advice on road conditions. Because most of the route north of the Jardine is through Aboriginal reserve, they also need permission from the Northern Peninsula Reserves Community Council. It is best to apply in advance, by letter to the council chairman at Bamaga, Qld 4871, stating the proposed date and purpose of the trip, the names of travellers and the vehicle registration. Permits are sent by post with a list of reserve restrictions—for example, no firearms.

The first half of the route from Cooktown, to the old goldmining town of Coen, is a roller-coaster of high, forested ridges and river valleys. After Laura a detour is possible through Lakefield National Park, Queensland's biggest at 528 000 hectares. It embraces the Normandy, Laura and Kennedy Rivers, providing a habitat for scores of species of waterfowl as well as the rare golden-shouldered parrot. Bush driving experience is necessary to go right through the park, but a shorter and easier route from Musgrave clips the northern corner of it on the way to the palm savannahs and salt marshes fringing Princess Charlotte Bay.

About 300 km from the Cape, travellers have a choice of two other side trips: west to Weipa on the Gulf, or east over the Janet and Tozer Ranges to the wilderness of Iron Range National Park. Along with striking coastal scenery near Cape Weymouth, the park has evergreen rainforest including palms and pines seen otherwise only in Papua New Guinea. Insect-eating pitcher plants and sundews edge its marshes and creeks, and there are 50-odd orchid species.

North past the imposing 19th-century home-

The hopeless mission of Edmund Kennedy

CAPE YORK PENINSULA brought the downfall of Australia's worst-conceived exploratory expedition. The lives of a gifted leader, Edmund Kennedy, and nine companions were sacrificed to government ignorance. Alone, an Aboriginal tracker struggled to Cape York to tell of the tragedy. And all his ordeal proved was that the tropical coast, with its mangrove swamps and salt marshes, its sodden jungles and crowding ranges, offered no pathway north.

Kennedy, 29 when he was appointed to head the expedition in 1848, had no say in planning the journey, or even in where it was to be made. Colonial administrators in Sydney—advised by naval officers—ordered a landing at Rockingham Bay, north of Hinchinbrook Island. Kennedy was expected to reach the Cape by an eastern coastal route in four to five months.

Naval observations of the coast were unreliable. Mangrove swamps were often described as woodland. Mountain heights were underestimated and river courses misjudged. And the choice of a starting point could scarcely have been worse—Rockingham Bay's bogs and winding rivers allowed Kennedy's party no way north, or even west. They had to trek far to the south, and then inland over the Great Dividing Range. Most of the men were exhausted and ill before the slightest northward progress had been made. Nearly

four months passed before they saw the sea again, at Princess Charlotte Bay. They were only halfway to the Cape, but supplies were dangerously low and most of the packhorses were dead or lame. Kennedy had to reduce his party to make up time with the remaining fit horses. He stranded eight of his men—three of them dying—at Weymouth Bay, hoping to bring a ship to their rescue. Three more were left behind at Shelburne Bay. Kennedy pressed on with Jackey Jackey, a native of the Hunter Valley in NSW.

With two horses left, Kennedy came tantalisingly close to salvation. From the foot of Newcastle Bay he sighted Albany Island, where a supply ship had been ordered to wait. The island, close offshore, was only about 30 km north. Kennedy thought he and Jackey Jackey could reach it in a day by following the Escape River upstream. The navy claimed that this river flowed from the north. Instead it led the desperate pair south, into a slimy, pest-ridden sprawl of tidal swamp. The last of their food gone, Kennedy and Jackey Jackey combed a maze of crocodile-infested creeks in search of some way out of their trap.

Warriors of the Jadhaigana, an unusually aggressive tribe, stalked them. The weakened travellers had muskets and pistols, but incessant rain had dampened their gunpowder. After three days the natives attacked. The

horses bolted, wounded by spears, then Kennedy was skewered through the back and abdomen. Jackey Jackey was blinded by blood from a head wound and Kennedy was speared twice more, in the side and leg. The attackers withdrew and Jackey Jackey removed the spears from Kennedy's wounds. Then he went to retrieve their saddlebags. He returned to find that the warriors had set on Kennedy again—crushing his ankles to immobilise him while they stole clothing, weapons and equipment. The explorer died soon after.

Jackey Jackey buried Kennedy before the Jadhaigana attacked once more, and eluded them by wading up a creek. Then he began a long battle out of the swamps, heading west instead of north. He made less than 20 km in the first week, but after that he could swing north-east on easy grassland. Ten days after Kennedy's murder, the supply ship Ariel at Albany Island was alerted to the plight of the men left behind. Two were rescued at Weymouth Bay. The others were all dead. Jackey Jackey later led a search party back to the 'wet desert' of the Escape River, and found the tree in which he had hidden the expedition charts and journals. The tracker was acknowledged as a hero, and fêted by Sydney people. That seems to have been his undoing. Before long he, too, was dead—burnt in his own campfire after a drinking binge.

stead of Batavia Downs station there is easier country—scrubland with patches of open forest rich in birdlife. Within 100 km of the Cape the road skirts Jardine River National Park, but swamps and creeks restrict vehicle access. In sparsely vegetated country beyond the Jardine, the eye is caught by 'magnetic' termite mounds—elongated on a north-south axis—which the Cape has in common with the savannah grasslands south of Darwin. Soon after, approaching the township of Bamaga, a glittering vista opens of Endeavour Strait and the Torres Strait islands. 'The Tip' is less than 40 km on.

Bamaga, the northernmost settlement on the Australian mainland, was populated by Torres Strait Islanders in 1946 after freak tides spoiled water supplies on their native Saibai, close to the New Guinea coast. They have been joined by other islanders. An older community co-exists, amicably but separately, at Cowal Creek, 8 km down the coast. It was founded when three war-ring mainland tribes made peace and elected a joint government. They built permanent houses and planted gardens, to the surprise of white officials when the village was discovered in 1915.

Bamaga has a pleasant town centre with a grassy park. Its modern shops include a well-stocked supermarket. Visitors can camp at Red Island Point, just north. People taking the time and trouble to make friends with the locals can usually arrange a boat trip to good fishing grounds and pearl culture sites, or visits to the closer strait islands. Independent boating calls for the best possible charts, weather forecasts and seamanship: currents are fierce and the eastern side of the Cape is exposed to heavy winds and seas. Swimming is good in sheltered bays all around the Cape, but river mouths should be avoided—saltwater crocodiles often lurk there.

At Possession Island, just off the coast north of Bamaga, Captain Cook planted his second flag—the first was at Botany Bay—to complete Britain's claim to eastern Australia. The island is a national park, uninhabited and untouched apart from some traces of gold mining.

Opposite Possession, the coast road peters out in a single-vehicle track veering east to Air Queensland's Top of Australia Wilderness Lodge, comprising 24 units with room to accommodate upwards of 70 guests. The camp ground for casual visitors has a kiosk and ablutions facilities. A short walking track leads to the Cape itself—a boulder-strewn point facing the lighthouse on Eborac Island.

A fork from the coast road runs north-east to the ruins of Somerset, a garrison township founded in 1864 to protect shipping and conduct trade with the Malays. Planners hoped it would rival Singapore, but in 1877 the garrison was moved to Thursday Island for its superior harbour. Frank Jardine, a son of the first command-ant, stayed on to raise cattle and run a pearl shell business. Later he established Australia's biggest coconut plantation, of 15 000 palms. Some can still be seen, overgrown and bearing poorly, behind the homestead that was abandoned when Jardine's Samoan widow died in 1923, four years after his own death.

Rugged headlands march into Newcastle Bay on the rocky northern tip of Australia's east coast

BAMAGA (pop. 813) on Peninsula Developmental Road 2620 km from Brisbane, 863 km north of Cairns. Dry weather and 4WD only.
TRANSPORT: flights Cairns-Bamaga, Weipa-Bamaga some days.

▲ ⌂ ☺ ↪

Kennedy's expedition sketched by T. H. Huxley

Torres Strait and the Gulf

Queensland has governed Thursday Island since 1872, along with 70-odd other Torres Strait islands and islets sprinkled from Cape York all the way to the New Guinea coast. They represent the high points of a land bridge that brought the Aborigines to Australia at least 40 000 years ago. Sea levels were at their lowest during the peak of the last ice age, about 50 000 years ago, and the strait area probably remained dry for 40 000 years after that. Even now the average depth to the continental shelf is less than 20 metres. Torres Strait Islanders are ethnically different from mainland Aborigines. Their ancestors came to the region much later, after the strait was flooded, and brought a more advanced material culture. They are of mainly Polynesian stock in the eastern islands, and Melanesian in the west and south, with a substantial infusion of European and Asian blood around Thursday Island.

Soldiers and settlers moved from Somerset, Cape York, to Thursday Island in 1877. The island's harbour, Port Kennedy, was already the base for more than 100 Asian or European boats engaged in gathering sea-cucumbers, pearls, pearl shell and trochus shell. Thousands of natives were drawn into the trade, and they prospered at first. Tiny 'T.I.'—just 364 hectares—became the most populous island in the region, jammed with Torres Strait people and fortune-hunters of every nationality. Britons and Australians maintained a garrison and a coaling station.

By the 1920s most of the shell divers were Japanese. Operations were suspended when Japan entered World War II, and the divers were interned. After the war, clothing manufacturers used plastic instead of 'mother-of-pearl' for buttons, and shell was no longer wanted. Japanese investment, reviving in the 1950s, prompted a switch to pearl culture. That industry boomed briefly, employing hundreds of islanders, but a shell disease wrecked it in 1970 and a full recovery seems doubtful. Green turtle farming, introduced as a substitute, was abandoned in 1980. So the only industries of 'T.I.' and the other strait islands are fishing, crayfishing and prawning, in the face of competition from the high-technology operations of big mainland companies.

Because fresh water is scarce, only 17 of the Australian-governed islands are inhabited. All but three of them are reserved for natives. The non-reserve territories apart from Thursday Island are Friday Island, equally small, and Prince of Wales Island—the biggest in the whole group at 18 000 hectares. Friday Island is favoured for its fine beaches, and some well-to-do Thursday Island people maintain weekend cottages there. Prince of Wales, though it lacks good anchorages and a reliable water supply, also has weekenders and even some permanent homes. But it remains largely undeveloped because of its steep and rugged terrain.

Thursday Island is similarly hilly. That is why the airport is on neighbouring Horn Island, where US and RAAF aircraft were based during World War II. A launch brings visitors across to 'T.I.' to be greeted, surprisingly, by a dozen or more taxis. The island is a mere 2.4 km long and half as wide, but it has a network of bitumen roads. There are even hire cars, and a motel as well as four hotels. Visitors find plenty of opportunities for relaxed boating and fishing, and all water sports. Guided trips to nearby islands and cays can easily be arranged.

People who enjoy the offbeat and remote get their money's worth. Newcomers find the racial and cultural mix of 'T.I.' interesting. This is no tropical paradise, however. It has long been a haven for adventurers whose ways do not suit polite society. Tourists are confronted by public boozing and brawling when luggers and trawlers are in port. And they cannot ignore the economic dejection of the native islanders. Since the early

Quetta cathedral on Thursday Island

1970s more and more Torres Strait people have become dependent on unemployment benefits or social welfare allowances. Children are being trained in technical or commercial skills, but they will have to go to the mainland to use them. Thousands of men are already on the mainland, working or seeking work.

In the Gulf of Carpentaria, manganese mining has brought work and a bonanza in royalties for the people of Groote Eylandt. To the east, migrant Torres Strait Islanders and some mainland Aborigines find employment in bauxite mining at Weipa. Australia's aluminium industry was born here in the shelter of Duyfken Point—the first feature of the continent to be mapped by Europeans. Willem Jansz, exploring the New Guinea coast in 1606 for spices and gold, missed his way and sailed as far south as Cape Keer-weer (Dutch for Turn-again). He and later navigators pronounced the Gulf's muddy shores and flat, sparsely vegetated hinterlands worthless. The unusual redness of the low cliffs around Albatross Bay was noted by Matthew Flinders in 1803, but its cause was not grasped until the 20th century.

Aluminium is the third most common element in the earth's crust. But bauxite—aluminium hydroxide—is the only ore in which the metal is sufficiently concentrated to be commercially extracted, and it is relatively rare. Bauxite formation relies on regular short seasons of heavy rain to leach mineral particles from the soil, and prolonged dry seasons of extreme heat to draw up the moisture and evaporate it, leaving a deposit of metallic compounds. Most dissolve with the return of the wet season but bauxite, like iron, is insoluble. Year by year the ore accumulates. Round lumps about the size of grapes are found at Weipa, scattered in a band of loose clays 3-10 metres thick and under about 2 metres of topsoil. Their presence on the western side of Cape York Peninsula was suggested in 1902 and proved in 1947, but the concentrations did not seem pay-

Weipa is the only settlement of any size on the isolated western coast of Cape York Peninsula

Mudflats and mangroves line the mouth of the Limmen Bight River where it enters the Gulf of Carpentaria

the only towns, and they are more than 30 km from the seashore. The fishing village of Karumba, however, occupies a rare wedge of firm ground at the mouth of the Norman River. It was founded as the outport for Normanton beef but that is now trucked south. Karumba survives to serve prawning and fishing fleets—its receiving depot ships on to Cairns for processing—and fosters a small tourist industry. Most visitors are fishing enthusiasts who fly in, but main roads are driveable in the dry season.

THURSDAY ISLAND (pop. 2290) 40 km north-west of Cape York.
TRANSPORT: flights from Cairns or Weipa some days.

WEIPA (pop. 2436) west of Peninsula Developmental Road 2477 km from Brisbane, 720 km from Cairns (turn off 74 km north of Coen). Dry weather and 4WD only.
TRANSPORT: flights Cairns-Weipa daily.

KARUMBA (pop. 670) west of Gulf Developmental Road 2542 km from Brisbane via Cairns (turn off at Normanton).
TRANSPORT: flights Cairns-Karumba most days.

THURSDAY ISLAND												
	Jan	Feb	Mar	Apr	May	Jun	Jul	Aug	Sep	Oct	Nov	Dec
Maximum C°	30	29	30	30	29	28	27	28	29	30	31	31
Minimum C°	25	25	25	25	24	23	22	23	23	24	25	25
Rainfall mm	400	342	343	210	46	27	10	8	3	10	35	218
Humidity %	78	80	80	73	72	69	66	65	65	65	65	71
Rain days	20	22	23	17	11	12	8	5	5	3	5	14
Sunshine hrs	Summer 5 +			Autumn 6 +			Winter 7 +			Spring 9 +		

able. Only in 1955 were the Weipa deposits found to be the biggest and richest then known.

The clay layer is scooped from open-cut mines along the Embley River, and the bauxite is washed from it and crushed near a specialised ore-loading port. Since 1962 more than 125 million tonnes have been shipped out. Meanwhile Weipa town, well north of the dusty and noisy industrial operations, has come of age. Tall trees grow in grassy parks, laid out on fillings of ore-washing slurry. Lawns and gardens surround neat houses of pinkish-grey brick, baked from waste clay. Community recreation facilities match big-city standards. Weipa remains a Comalco town but welcomes visitors, most of whom call during air tours from Cairns. Inspections of the bauxite preparation and loading facilities can be arranged. Boating and fishing opportunities are good, and for most of the year swimmers have the cool waters of Lake Patricia—once a 300-hectare mining excavation.

The foot of the Gulf is a hostile zone of tidal flats, laced by rivers whose waters spread in deltas in the wet season. During north-westerly gales high tides can pile up on already-flooded land with disastrous consequences: 20 000 cattle were swept into the sea in 1939. The cattle-raising centres of Normanton and Burketown are

Captain Bligh's calendar

NO ONE is sure how Thursday Island was named—but William Bligh of the *Bounty* had a hand in it. After the mid-Pacific mutiny against him in 1789, Bligh and 18 companions sailed west in the ship's open 7-metre launch. They set a course for Cape York and Timor, because they had no way of knowing whether the First Fleet had succeeded in founding a New South Wales colony. One month later, after a stormy voyage of 5000 km, Bligh's party reached the far northern coast of Queensland.

Bligh gave the name Sunday Island to his second landing place, off Cape Grenville. Three days later, entering the Arafura Sea through Prince of Wales Channel, he ran close to what he called Wednesday Island. He roughly marked neighbouring islands, without naming them on his original chart. On later maps the names of Thursday and Friday Islands appeared, along with the Tuesday Islets. This may have been Bligh's own idea, or that of another navigator following the style he had set. Oddly, Australia has no Saturday or Monday Islands.

A dense cloud of large fruit bats darkens the sky over a swamp on the western fringe

Subject index

Place index

All towns and geographical features mentioned in *Guide to the coast of Queensland* are listed below. Page numbers in bold type indicate a major entry dealing with the place concerned